# GREAT-NESS DOESN'T CARE

# GREAT-NESS DOESN'T CARE

## HOW YOU BECOME THE GREATEST VERSION OF YOU

**JASON DUNN**

ELITE ULTRA-ENDURANCE ATHLETE

A Major Street book

An imprint of Moore Street Media
50/99 Moore Street
Leichhardt NSW 2040
Australia

majorstreet.com.au

Follow us! Majorstreetpublishing
Tag #majorstreetpublishing to show us your pics

ISBN: 978-1-923186-51-4

Published in 2026 by Major Street Publishing


Design and typesetting by Sara Lindberg, Moore Street Media



Printed and bound in China

10 9 8 7 6 5 4 3 2 1

# CONTENTS

SS GREAT
ATNESS
SS GREAT
ATNESS
SS GREAT
ATNESS
SS GREAT
ATNESS

# FOREWORD

There are books that inform you. There are books that inspire you. And then there are books that quietly confront you – books that don't merely ask you to think differently, but demand that you live differently.

*Greatness Doesn't Care* is that kind of book.

Jason Dunn has written a blueprint that is both simple and unsettling: simple because it's clear, structured and actionable; unsettling because it removes the hiding places we all tend to keep nearby – excuses, delays, 'someday' language, and the comforting lie that greatness belongs to someone else. From the earliest pages, Jason makes the argument that greatness doesn't care about your demographics, your history, your setbacks, or your current circumstance. It cares about whether you will rise – again and again – until your life matches your potential.

I'm writing this foreword not as a distant observer, but as someone who has spent a great deal of time with Jason, worked alongside him on various projects, and watched him operate under pressure, in uncertainty, and in moments when it would have been easier to choose comfort over conviction. I believe Jason Dunn is a phenomenal leader and a phenomenal person – because I've seen his leadership up close, and I've seen the kind of character that doesn't need an audience to do the right thing.

And that's why this book matters.

Because Jason doesn't merely share principles – he lives them.

In *Greatness Doesn't Care*, Jason introduces a sequence of steps – an ordered pathway of virtues and practices – that form the architecture of a great life: Greatness → Purpose → Courage → Mindset → Planning → Discipline → Presence → Belief → Sacrifice → Stillness → Movement → Resilience → Gratitude → Nutrition → Vulnerability.

That list is not presented as motivational décor. It's presented as a daily standard – something to practise, refine and embody. Jason's objective is clear: to demonstrate how anyone can follow these steps to reach their own version of greatness, 'step by step'.

But what makes this framework different is not the intelligence of the structure, though it is well designed. What makes it different is the credibility of the messenger.

Jason writes about greatness through the stories of people many of us admire – Martin Luther King Jr., Nelson Mandela, Burt Munro, Diana Nyad and the ancient Stoics – showing how radically different lives still reveal a shared pattern: purpose pursued with courage, discipline and integrity.

Yet the book doesn't stay at the level of admiration. It challenges you to translate admiration into action.

That's where Jason's voice carries unusual weight.

Because he is not writing from theory alone – he is writing from transformation.

In these pages, you'll see how purpose and courage are not presented as abstract concepts, but as lived realities. Jason describes courage as action in the face of adversity – effort fueled by belief and anchored in purpose, often requiring not one bold move, but 'many, perhaps even thousands, of interventions' over time.

That is not just a definition. It is a life philosophy. And it's one I've witnessed Jason practise consistently.

When Jason says purpose is an 'anti-fear weapon', he is not speaking poetically. He's speaking practically.

When he speaks about courage as choosing the more difficult path – the path that demands discretionary effort – he is describing a pattern he has lived, not a slogan he has borrowed.

One of the most compelling undercurrents in this manuscript is that greatness is rarely created through a single dramatic moment. It is created through the accumulation of decisions – often small, often private, often uncelebrated – where you choose the harder right over the easier wrong. Jason captures this powerfully through what he describes as a 'sliding door' moment: a choice that might look trivial to an outsider, but becomes monumental because it changes the trajectory of the person making it.

That idea – the quiet significance of choosing the harder path – is one of the most important leadership lessons in the entire book.

And Jason Dunn is the kind of leader who understands that.

Not because he read it somewhere.

Because he has lived it.

As you turn these pages, you'll notice something else: Jason doesn't present greatness as ego. He presents it as alignment. Greatness, in his view, is not about applause, image, or outperforming others. It's about becoming whole – your actions catching up to your values, your habits catching up to your purpose, your identity catching up to your calling. That's why the steps in this book are not just 'performance principles'. They are character principles.

They require honesty.

They require humility.

They require vulnerability.

And perhaps most importantly, they require courage – the kind of courage that not only withstands fear, but looks it in the face and walks forwards anyway.

That is why I say, without hesitation: in *Greatness Doesn't Care*, Jason doesn't just share facts – he lives these facts. He lives with a great deal of courage. And he is willing to share that purpose-driven courage with others, not as a performance, but as an invitation. If you read this book with an open heart, you will feel that invitation clearly.

This is not a book that ends when you close it.

It follows you.

It challenges you in the quiet moments – when the motivation fades, and the real work begins. It asks you the kinds of questions that separate wishing from becoming. It asks you to stop waiting for the perfect time and start taking responsibility for the direction of your life.

And then it leaves you with a conclusion that is both empowering and unavoidable: the final chapter of this journey is not written by the author – it is written by you.

So as you begin, I encourage you to read this book in two ways:

Read it for understanding – for the concepts, the stories, the steps, the clarity.

Read it for transformation – for the decisions you need to make, the habits you need to build, and the version of yourself you've been delaying.

Because Jason's central message is as direct as it is hopeful: greatness doesn't care about who you've been. It cares about who you're willing to become.

And if you let it, this book will help you become.

***Dr Trunnis Goggins II***

# INTRODUCTION

***'THE TWO MOST IMPORTANT DAYS IN YOUR LIFE ARE THE DAY YOU ARE BORN AND THE DAY YOU FIND OUT WHY.' – MARK TWAIN***

Greatness isn't reserved for the privileged or the perfect. It doesn't care where you come from, your age, what you look like, how much you have, your gender, your religion, or what you've been through. What it does ask of you is this: find your purpose – and chase it with everything you've got.

For Martin Luther King Jr., Nelson Mandela, Burt Munro, Diana Nyad and the ancient Stoics, greatness didn't care one iota about any of these demographics – except for their purpose and their indestructible passion to follow it, regardless of the personal cost. And neither did it care who I had been, or who I was, until I finally unshackled myself from my neurological captors and found my true purpose.

King stood unarmed against hatred and met it with love. Mandela lost his freedom but never his dignity. Munro chased a dream into his old age, defying physics and expectation. Nyad swam through darkness, jellyfish and fear until her goal became reality. The Stoics – including Marcus Aurelius, Seneca and Epictetus – taught that strength begins in the mind, and that we master life by mastering ourselves.

Each of these remarkable humans followed their own pathways to greatness, defying the odds and overcoming insurmountable adversity to achieve incomprehensible feats that changed the world and our perceptions of what is possible. For the terms of their life, they relentlessly practised, then mastered, each of the 14 steps to greatness, daily:

Greatness → Purpose → Courage → Mindset → Planning → Discipline → Presence → Belief → Sacrifice → Stillness → Movement → Resilience → Gratitude → Nutrition → Vulnerability.

Despite their dramatic differences, their pathways personify mastery of all 14 crucial steps. Unbeknownst to me at the time, my own path of self-discovery also followed these steps as I pursued mine. In writing *Greatness Doesn't Care*, my objective is to demonstrate how anyone can follow these essential steps to achieve their own version of greatness – whatever that might be – step by step.

Their stories are different, yet their message is the same: Greatness doesn't care who you are, where you start, or how many times you fall. It only cares that you rise.

One decision, one step, then another, exercising human agency, and before you know it, you've run and walked 250 million steps and cycled three times around the planet's circumference over 25 years – oh, and swum the equivalent of 80 times across the English Channel. Well, in a nutshell, that's my story. It is a story about transformation: from addiction in its many guises, wrong choices in favour of instant gratification, and stifled potential and excuses to overcoming extreme adversity, finding purpose and ardently working towards mastering the next 13 steps to foster an *UNLIMITED* mindset, which enabled me to go after my own version of greatness with everything I possessed.

# THE QUESTION THAT WOULDN'T GO AWAY

There comes a moment in every person's life when the noise falls away, and the question arises: *Is this all I'm meant to be?* For me, that moment arrived again and again and again.

For years, that question haunted me. I mistook comfort for peace, achievement for fulfilment and motion for meaning. I moved fast but not deep, mistaking activity for purpose, collecting moments of pride that quickly turned to quiet regret. But the voice inside – that persistent whisper that began when I was a boy with a dream – refused to die. It grew louder with each compromise, with each poor choice, with every day spent living beneath what I knew I could be.

That voice wasn't asking for recognition, although for decades I acted as though it craved just that. It was asking for the truth, for the courage to stop pretending I was satisfied. When I finally began to listen, I learned that greatness doesn't care about excuses. It doesn't wait for the right conditions, resources, or time. It demands only one thing – that you show up.

That's what I came to understand on the long roads, under the weight of training, during the nights when exhaustion met clarity. I realised that greatness doesn't belong to the chosen; it belongs to the committed. It rewards effort, integrity and consistency. It has no favourites; it simply responds to those who refuse to quit.

My motivation for chasing my own version of greatness changed dramatically over the course of decades. Eventually, it metamorphosed into the need to find peace within myself, to banish my consuming regret and ultimately to find happiness, which is the premise that underpins *Greatness Doesn't Care* – happiness and meaning through greatness. After all, isn't happiness and meaning what we all chase?

In many respects, I believed that I had found my greatness and, to some degree, happiness. The wisdom I've acquired through continual learning, self-development, self-acceptance and vulnerability has opened up whole new worlds in recent years that I never could have conceived of. My journey has taught me that greatness is an infinite quest for self-discovery that knows no boundaries and therefore no limits.

Misguidedly, when my quest for greatness began over 50 years ago, it was shaped by my upbringing, as my ego became the predominant driver of my desire. Twenty-five years later, having constantly chipped away at this flaw, I had managed to temper my ego, but there was still more work to do: I needed to learn how to banish it and replace it with existential and altruistic motivations. Over the last five years, I am delighted to share that I have finally achieved previously unparalleled progress and peace.

## SEASONS

You may have already listened to or read my first book, *UNLIMITED: The Art of Being Limitless*, in which I share excerpts from the two distinctive lives – or seasons of life, if you will – I have been blessed with so far, along with early glimpses of a third life that is evolving into my seventh decade on this earth. Each stage of my life has been shaped and enabled by everything I experienced before completing my first book at the age of 60. Essentially, *UNLIMITED* is a memoir that spans my first two lives and shares my life-changing experiences, which account for 90 per cent of the book. Reflecting, though, *UNLIMITED* was my novice attempt at conveying how anyone can find their greatness, regardless of where they find themselves in life right now.

In writing this book, my objective is to build on that memoir by showcasing how the steps I followed to discover my greatness replicate those taken by a select group of remarkable humans who have prevailed over seemingly insurmountable odds. These are steps that anyone can take to achieve their own greatness. Each chapter will reveal the essence and meaning of that step, its importance and how anyone can practise and master it to achieve greatness. To showcase each step, I have curated examples and philosophies from thought leaders and highly acclaimed individuals, along with insights from brilliant books that bring each step to life, which have helped shape my growth and my own experiences and continue to inspire me to this day.

My third life season, ushered in through the writing of *UNLIMITED*, inspired me to research and explore further what it truly takes to find greatness, and the steps anyone can follow to discover their own, regardless of their life to date. This exploration is underpinned by insights from people far more remarkable than I am, and driven by a relentless curiosity to uncover the common threads between my own growth and that of those who have left a lasting mark on history.

My intention in creating a replicable framework for greatness is simple: to help people identify where they are stuck or stalled, and to give them the confidence to step onto their own Greatness Bus at whatever stop they find themselves waiting. I hope that others might experience a life as rewarding and effusive as the one I have been fortunate to live. I believe I have finally achieved what I set out to do with *UNLIMITED* by writing *Greatness Doesn't Care*. Whether I truly have, only time will tell.

My first life season was punctuated by mistakes, choices to take the easier road and my willingness to succumb to addictions, excuses and diversions that I believed would deliver me happiness and self-actualisation – but never did. I call it my autumn.

To conceal my shortcomings, I exaggerated my identity to the point that I often felt like an impostor in my own mind, living with a limited mindset that stifled my true potential. I hated – a word I would soon banish from my thoughts and vocabulary, along with a handful of other toxic words – that imposter so much that, over time, my regret constantly and relentlessly gathered momentum to the point that profound change represented my only option for salvation. It was either that or open the floodgates and descend into a potentially irreversible state of depression as my remaining time on this earth diminished.

They say that 'time is a healer', and it can be with deliberate, focused effort towards self-development, peace, gratitude and self-healing. But time, if allowed to pass without significant action and purpose, will fester wounds to the point that they will become psychologically, physically and emotionally septic and paralysing.

Drowning in regret and suffering through undiagnosed depression, I will feel forever blessed that my second season – spring – began at age 35 and propelled me down an entirely different path. This transformation came without the need for any medical intervention – other than the 35 hospitalisations that I endured to save my life and my health.

Now, as I enter my seventh decade, a third life season is unfolding, revealing new and uncharted horizons that continue to accelerate my development. Blessedly, season three – my summer – continues to offer limitless possibilities for growth and happiness. Consequently, new versions of greatness, adaptations I could never have conceived of, continue to reveal themselves in my sixties.

This effusive state has continued to build momentum as new layers of capability are unearthed, turning once seemingly impossible feats into reality and banishing imposter identities from the forefront of my mind, displaced by newfound potential and possibility. From observing the changes in my own life and others' across my corporate career, sporting adventures, and current work, I have learnt that empowerment is self-perpetuating and can become *UNLIMITED* when embraced and nurtured.

For many, this seismic life shift is so transformational that it can lead them anywhere they can conceive of. For me, it clarified a purpose: dedicating my time to help others find their greatness. While *Greatness Doesn't Ca*re is lightly peppered with examples from my life that I believe will benefit others, my focus is to draw on the achievements of other inspiring people whose accomplishments make mine seem minor. My clear intent is to provide you with a blueprint and roadmap to greatness, enabling you to identify your first or next step towards achieving it.

I do not for a moment consider my views or journey to be exclusive, nor do I believe they will be right for everyone. They were right for me decades ago, and they remain so today, across many life seasons. Everything I have learned continues to expand my thinking and my capability, and to help me walk more effectively in the shoes of others – growing exponentially through their insights, experiences and wisdom.

## YOUR GREATNESS BUS

Although everyone's life roadmap is unique, the sequencing and construction of personal development is similar for most people. Like climbing a flight of stairs step by step, with each new skill, technique, practice, value, or virtue learned, implemented and rigorously practised takes you higher. Think of this roadmap as a bus route, along which the Greatness Bus travels, with many bus stops, each representing a value, skill, or capability that will accelerate your pathway to greatness and fulfilment.

Next, identify the skill, value, or capability you need to focus on to accelerate or begin your development towards greatness. And remember, you can hop on that Greatness Bus at any stop. Once you are on the move and heading towards your next destination, you can work on honing and then mastering that step as you surge towards greatness. For example, if you are already clear on your purpose and what it means to you, but you have yet to find the courage to take the next step, then courage is the stop that you are waiting at and where you should commit your focus. Or perhaps you have nailed your purpose and found the courage to get going, but have not yet defined your goal or created a clear High-Performance Plan that guides you and measures your progress towards your goal or goals. In this instance, planning is the stop where you need to hop onto your Greatness Bus.

While this is not an exact science, the steps are generally sequential, particularly the initial handful. Your bus, though, may need to revisit previously visited stops at different times due to setbacks or changes in the environment around you. Positively, revisiting a newly implemented skill becomes more intuitive as you gain greater capability. In other words, it won't feel like a game of snakes and ladders where you must start all over again from square one.

Often, I have found it necessary to revisit one or more previous steps, sometimes many times on any given day, and even thousands of times over the course of a decade or longer. Evolution, you see, is infinite both in the world around us and within ourselves when we choose to foster the path of self-development for as long as we feel inspired to do so. That, for me, is the essence of an *UNLIMITED* mind and a limitless life of greatness!

As you read or listen to each chapter, I hope you find yourself aligning with each bus stop that best identifies your current position. Getting on the bus will be your starting point and first, or next, step to greatness.

## GREATNESS HAS NO LIMIT

Unabated, my evolution continues every day, gathering momentum as my seventh decade rolls on. Although none of us can control time, we can control how we value it – and what we do and achieve with the time we are given. Blessedly, I came to understand that every day is a gift, and I committed to never wasting one. This became my daily litmus test and my personal challenge: never waste a day. This is the daily measure of meaning and progress that evokes quiet, positive reflection and introspection during and at the conclusion of each of my days. This is accountability!

Each evening, I ask myself a simple but confronting question to evaluate my day: 'Did you treasure this day, and did you give it your best shot?'

This self-accountability is non-negotiable. To reinforce it – and to prompt action rather than regret – I also ask myself earlier in the day: 'How will you feel about what you achieved today when you sit down tonight and reflect?'

Throughout this book, we'll explore the principles, skills, virtues and many other neurological practices that I believe will kick-start or advance your pathway to greatness, as they have mine.

One step is all it takes to get going. Often, that step is a determined decision to change – to refuse the easier road in that moment, the one most likely to deliver you to a destination you already know, or worse, return you to a place you have already been.

If you are content choosing the easier road, then the well-worn path may be right for you. You are most likely a satisfied and fulfilled person – and there is much to be admired in that. If that is the case, then I tip my hat to you, and you may have already read as far as you need to.

It's more likely, though, if you have chosen to read this book, that you are curious about what more might be possible for you. You may harbour some discontent with your current situation or identity. Or you may already be on your path to greatness and simply want to accelerate or go further.

The exciting aspect is that once you get started, this process will continually reveal new horizons that you have not previously conceived of. As your capability grows and your new mindset is infused with belief, you will begin to manifest limitless oceans of possibility.

It would be reasonable to say that I've endured more than my fair share of failure, brutal accidents, serious illness, and personal adversity. Setting aside the more minor knocks and scrapes, the tally is still confronting: two skull fractures; 16 fractures to my jaw; eight teeth shattered; three fractured vertebrae; 10 broken ribs; two leg fractures; a broken nose; knee surgery; ankle surgery; a severe haematoma; two primary hernias; the loss of six toenails; three bouts of pneumonia; severe ulcerative colitis; tuberculosis; multiple serious facial injuries; extensive skin loss; a toxic spider bite; multiple toxic ant bites; and kidney stones for good measure.

And in case you're wondering, less than 40 per cent of that damage can be blamed on my ultra-endurance adventures. The rest came from life itself.

There have been times when I have fought for my life, my dignity and my sanity, both in sport and in my personal and professional life. However, the struggle and hardship, epic failures and, on occasion, humiliation have served to inspire my determination to make them count for something meaningful. I refused to be a victim of life's random cruelty, my own mistakes and my failures. So, I welded my purpose onto my mind and my heart, and I refused to quit. Above all else, redemption fuelled me. Daily, I envisioned my redemption to the point that I could see and feel the euphoria I was destined for as I crossed each finishing line, or whatever endeavour was before me, and consequently banished those demons. And in those moments of redemption, I would be reborn. Nothing would stop me. Nothing!

Through that process, I came to understand what this book is about. It's not about greatness as the world defines it – wealth, recognition, achievement. It's about greatness as truth: the fullness of who you can become when you refuse to live a half-life.

Each chapter explores one principle in that pursuit – purpose, courage, discipline, belief, stillness, resilience, and more – not as abstractions, but as lived realities. They are the coordinates of a life that matters, a life that resonates beyond the moment.

I wrote this book not as a manual but as a mirror – for myself, and for anyone who has ever felt that quiet pull towards more.

Because greatness doesn't care if you're ready; it doesn't care about your fears, your failures, or your past.

It only cares that you begin.

# CHAPTER 1
# GREATNESS

**'GREATNESS IS NOT MEASURED BY WHAT A MAN OR WOMAN ACCOMPLISHES, BUT BY THE OPPOSITION THEY HAVE OVERCOME TO REACH THEIR GOALS.' – DOROTHY HEIGHT**

How do you define greatness? What inspires and drives humans to pursue their own dreams? Is there a clear pathway to greatness that anyone can replicate? What drives some humans to dedicate their entire lives to the pursuit of greatness? Is it the outcome or the quest that is the most meaningful and rewarding element of greatness? And what will it take for you to achieve your greatness?

These are a sample of the key questions that have frequently obsessed me over the years and, more recently, driven my research. I will seek to answer these questions throughout this chapter to provide essential context as you study each of the 14 steps to greatness.

Greatness varies significantly depending on who you are, how you measure it and whose standards you are using. The definition shifts depending on whether you are judging your own greatness, measuring yourself against others, assessing someone else's achievements, or responding to comparisons imposed from the outside.

In context, greatness should be defined as an accomplishment, or a series of accomplishments, that is profoundly meaningful to the person who has sacrificed, struggled and persevered to be the best they can be in pursuit of their purpose.

For some, it may mean prevailing over others, whether the competitor is an individual, a group, or a company. There are many instances where this definition is legitimate and where comparison is relevant. But the reality is that among the estimated 8.239 billion people on the planet (as of 10 August 2025), only one person can be the best in the world at any given endeavour. Only one person can win the gold medal at the world championships each year, or receive the Nobel Peace Prize, for example. By definition, everyone else – 8.239 billion people minus one – will not.

As an avid – perhaps obsessed – sports fan and athletics enthusiast, I often wonder how many people remember who the bronze medallist was in each event, or how they perceived their achievement. Not many, I presume, despite that individual having reached the extraordinary height of achieving third place among the 8.239 billion people on this planet. I wholeheartedly believe, though, that anyone who shows up every day and gives it their all is a champion.

For most people, the reality of being the best at anything is highly remote, if not nigh impossible. For example, a 40-year-old person who has never run, or at least not since the days of the school playground, is unlikely to win one of the major world marathons, even if they start running today and dedicate the rest of their life to this purpose. However, for that individual, greatness may come in the form of completing a marathon, a half-marathon, or a 10-kilometre run, regardless of the time. To that person, finishing is their greatness.

## COMPARISON IS A THIEF

These days, I regularly share posts in Facebook fitness communities – yes, I know, call me old – where I try to inspire, guide and support people to find their purpose, improve their fitness and nutrition, get started, accelerate their performance, plan effectively, build confidence and transform their mindset. I love this work. It aligns perfectly with what I see as my third life purpose: to help others move towards their own greatness.

Reading the stories people share – their struggles, small wins and quiet confessions – and the comments that follow, one theme shouts above the rest: comparison. Too many people measure their worth against someone else's performance or highlight reel. Over time, I've noticed two clear forms of comparison emerge. One is framed as 'positive', driven largely by ego and a need to feel superior. The other is more insidious, quietly convincing people to downplay or dismiss their own progress.

Comparison truly is the killer of belief, the thief of joy and, ultimately, the executioner of greatness. If you take nothing else from this chapter, let it be this: do not compare yourself or your progress to anyone else. Never diminish your efforts or achievements, publicly or privately, no matter how small they may seem in the moment. This is not about arrogance; it is about honesty. Acknowledge where you started, recognise how far you've come and celebrate your trajectory relative to your own past, not someone else's present. When you choose to frame your life this way, you lay a rock-solid foundation for everything that follows and open the door to possibilities you cannot yet see.

These are some of the key psychological factors we will unpack together. I believe that personal greatness is most fulfilling when it is driven by purpose rather than comparison, or any other external metric, and that it should only ever be measured against your current circumstances and evolving capabilities. Over the course of decades, observing my own behaviour and that of countless others, I've seen how often we become trapped by our own minds: stalled, stuck, or just starting, yet already shackled. Among these 'neurological captors', fear rules as king, guarding the locked gates behind which the path to greatness lies. In the next two chapters, we'll give fear the full attention it deserves.

Regardless of who is watching or judging, your own version of everyday greatness is defined by the struggle and adversity you endure and overcome. This is why I am convinced that, for most people, greatness cannot – and should not – be measured through comparison with others. The most meaningful form of greatness emerges from the pursuit of personal growth and mastery, fuelled by deeper drivers: altruism, existential questions and the longing for a life of purpose.

So why is purpose so powerful? At its most extreme, purpose can carry a person through mortal danger and seemingly insurmountable odds. History is overflowing with men and women whose deep sense of purpose propelled them to an extraordinary level of greatness that evokes awe, even if we can never fully comprehend the courage or sacrifice involved.

But the form of greatness I am most passionate about is the everyday version. It is quieter, closer and available to all of us. It lives in ordinary lives and simple decisions. It is something any of us can cultivate by practising, developing and integrating a sequence of skills, capabilities, values and virtues. My intention in this book is to show you that identity is not fixed. It can be reshaped step by step until you reach a point where you are no longer constrained by who you once believed yourself to be. You can effectively become *UNLIMITED* once you begin to live in alignment with your purpose.

Human greatness is not found in titles, possessions, or applause – it lives in the quiet spaces between intention and action. It is the capacity to rise beyond circumstance, meet adversity with grace and serve a purpose larger than oneself. Greatness is not inherited or bestowed; it is built, moment by moment, choice by choice, through courage, compassion and relentless persistence.

True greatness is humble. It does not announce itself or seek recognition. It reveals itself in the way one treats others when no one is watching, in the consistency of effort long after the excitement fades and in the refusal to let comfort become a cage. It is a harmony of strength and vulnerability, ambition and gratitude, stillness and movement.

It is seen in the teacher who believes in a struggling student, the activist who continues despite countless setbacks and the parent who quietly sacrifices for a better tomorrow. This dreamer endures years of failure before a single glimpse of success. Greatness does not belong to the extraordinary few. It is available to anyone willing to live with conviction, discipline and love.

To be great is not to stand above others, but to stand firmly within one's purpose. It is to embody one's values so entirely that the world is changed, however subtly, by one's presence. Greatness is not measured by what we achieve, but by what we awaken in ourselves and in those who cross our path.

## NO SILVER SPOON

The world often tells us that greatness is reserved for the chosen few, the gifted, the privileged, the lucky. However, history, if read honestly, tells a different story. The men and women we now call great were rarely destined for it. They were ordinary people who, when faced with extraordinary circumstances, chose not to shrink. They chose to rise!

Throughout my life, I have drawn inspiration, knowledge and wisdom from an ever-growing list of remarkable people in history. Among this pre-eminent cohort, there is a small, diverse group that has been the most influential and who each personify greatness: Martin Luther King Jr., Nelson Mandela, Burt Munro, Diana Nyad and the ancient Stoics. Throughout this book, I will briefly share and demonstrate how each of them practised and mastered the 14 steps to greatness.

Martin Luther King Jr. first inspired me at the age of 12 to spend weeks drawing his image so it could adorn my bedroom wall. He is often remembered for his dream – that lyrical, soaring vision of equality – but his greatness wasn't in his rhetoric. It was in his endurance. It was in the quiet nights before speeches, when fatigue clawed at him, when fear became a constant companion, and when the burden of expectation threatened to crush him.

He faced opposition not only from those who hated him but from those who doubted him. He was jailed, threatened and betrayed. Yet through it all, he remained rooted in conviction. He believed that love was stronger than hate, that justice was inevitable if enough people refused to turn away.

He once said, 'If you can't fly, then run. If you can't run, then walk. If you can't walk, then crawl. But whatever you do, keep moving.' That single sentence captures the essence of greatness: motion against resistance. It's not about speed; it's about refusal.

Nelson Mandela lived by that same principle. His greatness was carved over 27 years behind bars – years that could have bred bitterness but instead produced wisdom. In a space designed to strip away humanity, he discovered his own more deeply.

Mandela's greatness was not a triumphant emergence, but a transformation. He entered prison a fighter; he left a reconciler. He had every reason to hate, and yet he chose forgiveness. That choice – simple, impossible, profound – reshaped an entire nation.

His greatness wasn't in his politics; it was in his patience. He understood that anger burns fast, but integrity endures – that absolute power is not in domination, but in restraint. When he walked free, his spirit was already victorious, because he had mastered himself.

That, I think, is where greatness truly lives – not in what we conquer, but in what we overcome within.

Burt Munro's story echoes that same truth, though it played out in a different theatre. Long before he became a motorcycle racing legend of the Bonneville Salt Flats, he was just a man in a shed, working on an aging Indian motorcycle in a small town on the southern edge of the world.

There was nothing glamorous about his pursuit. His hands were scarred, his tools were crude, his resources scarce. He worked not for recognition but for the quiet satisfaction of perfecting something that mattered only to him. For decades, he filed, forged and tinkered, rebuilding his machine piece by piece, teaching himself through trial and error. People laughed. They told him he was too old, his dream too small, his goal too far. But greatness doesn't care about ridicule. It doesn't ask for permission. It just keeps working.

When Munro finally reached Bonneville and broke world records with a machine built by his own hands, it wasn't a miracle. It was the visible result of invisible years. His greatness was not the record itself, but the devotion that made it possible. Remarkably, the record he set in 1967 in the under 1000cc Streamliner Modified Fuel category still stands today!

Diana Nyad's greatness came decades later, born of the same stubborn resolve. She failed four times to swim from Cuba to Florida. Four times the ocean rejected her, throwing up storms, stings, exhaustion and hallucinations. But on the fifth attempt, at age 64, she succeeded.

Yes, you read that correctly: 64!

When she finally staggered onto the shore 53 hours later, her voice cracked with salt and triumph. 'Never, ever give up,' she said. 'You're never too old to chase your dreams.'

That wasn't a slogan. It was scripture, written in endurance and pain. Her greatness lay not in the distance she swam, but in the faith that compelled her to enter the water again, despite failure having already written her story four times over.

The Stoics – those quiet architects of character – understood this same law of life. For them, greatness had nothing to do with glory. It was measured in self-command. Roman emperor Marcus Aurelius wrote, 'Waste no more time arguing what a good man should be. Be one.'

To the Stoics, greatness meant mastery of the self, living according to virtue and acting rightly regardless of recognition. Seneca, a Roman Stoic philosopher, wrote that hardship reveals character; Epictetus, once enslaved and later a teacher of Stoicism, taught that true freedom lies in the control of one's own mind.

Their wisdom survives because it was lived, not theorised. They didn't seek ease; they sought alignment. They believed that greatness isn't the absence of difficulty, but harmony within it.

## EMBRACE THE STRUGGLE

If something is easy to achieve, can it truly be called an achievement? Would it fill you with pride or stir a lasting sense of accomplishment? For most of us – and certainly for me – the answer is no. Ease rarely ignites the soul. It is the difficult, the daunting and the seemingly impossible that awaken our deepest drive, as they did for me. Growth is born not in comfort but in challenge. Pride is not found in reward, but in the struggle that precedes it.

Greatness is not defined solely by outcomes, but by what it takes to achieve them. It is measured in courage, resilience, sacrifice, risk, planning and discipline: the unseen virtues that forge strength from adversity. Greatness is never given. It is earned, built and paid for through persistence.

Throughout my career in financial services, I've witnessed a scenario that perfectly illustrates this truth – a contrast that exposes the vast gulf between when greatness is earned and when it merely appears to be. It concerns the pursuit of wealth, a goal often positioned at the top of life's ambitions, and one that, in its best form, reflects many of the same virtues that define true greatness.

Consider two paths to the same outcome: wealth earned through years of hard work, and wealth acquired instantly through chance – say, a lottery win. Both lead to financial success, yet they differ profoundly in their meanings, emotions and sustainability.

Earned wealth is built slowly and deliberately, shaped by character along the way. It is the result of sacrifice, discipline and endurance. Each decision, each setback, each risk taken becomes a thread in the tapestry of achievement. The result carries the weight of the journey – a pride that fortune's whim can never replicate.

By contrast, the sudden acquisition of wealth often lacks foundation, which I have experienced firsthand many times. Studies suggest that within a year of a significant lottery win, a third of winners are worse off than before, and within a few years, nearly 70 per cent lose everything they gained. Without the personal transformation that accompanies effort, wealth becomes fragile, easily lost, misunderstood, or misused.

Emotionally, the difference is just as stark. The euphoria of instant gratification is intense but fleeting. Many winners face pressure from family, friends and opportunists; they trade their peace for paranoia and guilt. With no history of discipline or understanding to anchor them, they are unprepared for the weight of abundance.

By contrast, those who earn their success through endurance and sacrifice develop an unshakable appreciation for it. They understand not only how to create value, but how to sustain it. Their wealth, whether material or spiritual, carries purpose because it reflects growth, wisdom and the countless invisible moments of perseverance that shaped it.

True greatness, then, lies not in what we possess but in who we become in the process of earning it. Struggle gives meaning to success; adversity gives weight to achievement. A life without challenge may be comfortable, but it will never be fulfilling. Greatness is not the comfort of possession; it is the pride of perseverance. It is the quiet knowing that what you have, you've built, and how you've lived matters infinitely more than what you've gained.

Often, when faced with a choice, our instinct is to avoid struggle and opt instead for a more pleasant activity, route, or pathway. Comfort has quietly become the modern-day equivalent of Nirvana. This tendency is particularly evident when risk is involved or when the more demanding option requires sustained effort. Over time, the habituation to the evasion of struggle dulls ambition. The desire to be better than before slowly fades, until even the idea of an intentional life flickers and goes out, like a candle in a strong wind.

Yet struggle is not an anomaly in life; it is a certainty. More than that, it is also essential – alongside its cousin, failure – if one is to achieve any meaningful version of greatness. This evokes a fascinating mental equation: a life without struggle and failure equals a life with little prospect of greatness. Furthermore, a life devoid of struggle towards purpose is one inadequately filled with short-term gratification.

At this point, a familiar question tends to arise. What about parenting or caregiving? Isn't that a meaningful life? Isn't that purpose enough? It certainly is. But it is also one of the clearest examples of how meaning and struggle are inseparable. Parenting brings adversity, uncertainty and sacrifice in abundance, along with the opportunity to discover a deeply personal form of greatness. Parenting begins with purpose, and it demands courage, planning, discipline, resilience, gratitude, hope and countless acts of endurance along the way.

Struggle and failure, then, are not merely inevitable; they are essential to achieving greatness. Imagine for a moment that you could learn to accept struggle and failure as the crucial stepping stones to greatness. Furthermore, what if you could learn to embrace struggle to the point where, when adversity occurs, you can immediately flip it on its head and instinctively welcome it?

It has been my great fortune to develop this mindset when the going gets tough. When it feels like all hope is lost, practising this technique can transform your mindset and boost your resilience, which I will examine in detail in Chapter 4: Mindset.

I have come to believe that we must first experience negative thoughts, experiences and situations to appreciate the positive aspects of life. How can you feel and appreciate happiness if you have not experienced sadness and loss? In other words, struggle is a necessity that can be harnessed to reset your mind to think and feel positively in any confronting situation. Yes, you can rewire your mind with consistent practice.

My favourite example of this powerful practice comes from running up hills. Anyone who has done it knows how challenging it is. Running uphill amplifies various types of stress, both physical and mental, far more than running on level ground, and it almost always triggers the same internal response: *this is so hard.*

I can say this with absolute confidence, having run up and down hills more than most humans for a very long time. In fact, at the very core of my training for IRONMAN events and then ultramarathons were gruelling hill repeat sessions. A typical training week included at least one six-hour hill-rep session, and sometimes more: hours spent running up and down the same stretch of road, again and again, accumulating kilometre after kilometre of ascent and descent.

Over those hours – on legs already worn thin from heavy weekly mileage – my mind would reliably turn against me: *Why are you doing this? Why don't you just stop and go home? It would be so much easier*. When the weather turned cold or the heavens were dropping a month's worth of rain at once, the discomfort and beguiling thoughts ratcheted up significantly. I'm sure you can picture it.

We all experience these inner voices that we must negotiate, fight and wrestle with, to battle and prevail over. The alternative, though, is to concede defeat and give in to them, because it is *hard* after all. So, the choice is simple – stop or keep going, a decision that your inner voice may ask you to make many times over the course of six hours. It's simple, though – if you stop, you lose, but if you go on, you win. Stop – lose. Continue – win.

Having faced that exact choice more times than I can begin to reconcile, I learnt how to fight back. How to turn the struggle against itself. How to mute that beguiling voice. Well, at least until the voice gathers strength again, which it will.

The first technique I employed to strengthen and callous my mind was to eliminate the toxic word 'hard' from my vocabulary, both in challenging moments and in everyday life. Acknowledging that something is hard instantly drains your positivity and resilience, validating the need to take a break. So, rebuke it. Banish it and replace it with a positive thought or affirmation. This is the process I have followed since 1990, along with removing 'disappointment', 'hate' and 'can't'.

The affirmation I used that became my mantra was: 'To be truly successful in life, you must first do what you don't want to do, when you don't want to do it – until you do.'

When frequently practised, the need to recite any affirmation verbatim gradually dissipates, replaced by an instant cognitive association that this struggle being experienced is precisely what is required to be truly successful. Struggle, success. Struggle, success.

Another technique that worked equally well in countering the negative inner voice was to smile. Yep, that's all – smile. Smile as broadly as you can. Smiling is a powerful tool, as it triggers the release of serotonin, a neurotransmitter that plays a crucial role in mood regulation and overall wellbeing. When you smile, it triggers a cascade of chemical reactions in your brain, including the release of serotonin, dopamine and endorphins. These 'feel-good' neurotransmitters contribute to positive emotions, stress reduction and even pain relief.

Be aware, though, if you practise this while running up hills, you may attract the attention of passers-by. I've experienced many strange looks that I can only assume are the result of someone thinking that I have a screw loose. Okay, that aside, this is a remarkably effective technique that I have pulled out of my resilience toolkit thousands of times, instantly evaporating negativity and discomfort, at least long enough to lift my mind out of the hole it's buried in.

Be prepared, though – the voice will return. It might come back 10 minutes later, or 30. One never knows how long it will take for it to return, but it will, until you either finish what you set out to do or quit. While racing IRONMAN triathlons and ultramarathons, though, as the hours tick by, that voice seems to return every few minutes, which can amount to hundreds of times over the course of a race spanning 12 hours or longer.

The credit for this highly effective technique goes to Eliud Kipchoge – aka 'The Goat' – one of the greatest athletes of all time, and the most successful marathon runner of all time. Often, towards the end of a competitive marathon, when the pain and discomfort are at their peak, Kipchoge will suddenly, out of the blue, smile. While watching coverage of several major global marathons, I've noticed that commentators debate whether Kipchoge's smile or grimace is the cause. Still, the consensus is that he is smiling to counter the extreme, debilitating discomfort he is experiencing. Whatever the reason, it worked a treat for me.

## WHY GREATNESS?

Not everyone defines or seeks greatness in the same way. For some, it can mean fame and power. For others, it signifies quiet mastery, deep relationships and changing one's life for the better, or it can be as significant as seeking reform or social justice on a societal or global scale.

The allure of greatness began calling me at a very young age, and to find and achieve greatness soon became a lifelong quest. From where this innate desire emanated, I can't quite pinpoint, nor have I been able to define it so definitively, but it began on my 11th birthday, when I was given a hardback copy of *The Guinness Book of World Records*. From that day on, my desire to find greatness burned brightly.

That desire, though, even from the tender age of 11, was driven by a mixture of internal and external validation, underpinned by ego, and it persisted as the predominant driver for more than 40 years. Consequently, my ego became the main influencer of my identity. With time and wisdom, I grew to despise the identity that it had shaped. I learned that no matter what self-talk you adopt, your flaws still exist, hidden beneath the façade you present to others. With this wisdom, I discovered that you can only outrun yourself for so long until reality catches up and corners you. And if it doesn't track you down, you will most likely exist in a lonelier world because others around you will gradually drift away, and your growth as a person, on every level, will stall.

As the years have passed, my inclination to outrun that reckoning has diminished, drawing me to confront and make peace with my flaws and mistakes, and commit to becoming the best person I can be. Most pursuits are fuelled by a variety of deeply rooted psychological, social and existential reasons, such as a desire for meaning and purpose, need for recognition and validation, pursuit of mastery and growth, aspiration towards cultural and societal influence, fear of obscurity or death, and calling to altruism and service, which I have summarised in the following table:

| CATEGORY | EXPLANATION |
|---|---|
| **DESIRE FOR MEANING AND PURPOSE** | **Existential drive:** Many people strive for greatness to feel that their lives have meaning beyond mere survival or routine. |
| | **Legacy:** Greatness is often linked with leaving a lasting impact - something that outlives the individual and gives their life a narrative arc. |
| **NEED FOR RECOGNITION AND VALIDATION** | **Social approval:** Humans are social beings and often seek affirmation from others. Greatness brings admiration, respect and a sense of status. |
| | **Self-worth:** Achieving greatness can affirm one's value and competence, bolstering self-esteem. |
| **PURSUIT OF MASTERY AND GROWTH** | **Challenge and achievement:** The drive to push boundaries and overcome challenges is inherently satisfying and can lead to personal excellence. |
| | **Intrinsic motivation:** Some individuals are driven by internal passion for a craft, field, or cause - greatness is a by-product of sustained effort and commitment. |
| **ASPIRATION TOWARDS CULTURAL AND SOCIETAL INFLUENCE** | **Role models and narratives:** Cultures glorify heroes, leaders, innovators and artists, shaping what people aspire to. |
| | **Economic and systemic rewards:** Societies often reward greatness with wealth, influence, or opportunities, making it a rational pursuit. |
| **FEAR OF OBSCURITY OR DEATH** | **Mortality:** Seeking greatness can be a response to the fear of death - if one achieves something monumental, they 'live on' in memory, history, or culture. |
| | **Avoiding insignificance:** Greatness may be a means of escaping the fear of being forgotten or living an unremarkable life. |

| CATEGORY | EXPLANATION |
|---|---|
| CALLING TO ALTRUISM OR SERVICE | **Desire to help others:** For some, greatness is not about personal glory but about making a meaningful contribution to the world. |
| | **Moral or spiritual calling:** Many pursue greatness to fulfil what they see as a divine, ethical, or philosophical mission. |

For me, the form of greatness I admire the most is that which grows out of a purpose to help others – whether that purpose serves a single person or millions. Close behind is when it's achieved through a personal or collective quest to become the best one can be in a chosen endeavour or field.

Throughout this book, I'll share my own metamorphosis, beginning with early childhood through to the present day. Along the way, I'll describe the seismic shift from external to internal validation and from instant to earned gratification. This shift has undoubtedly shaped me into a better person and expanded my capabilities far beyond the limits I once believed existed. I will also explore how each new level of capability reveals another horizon that seemed out of reach or even out of view. This was not an overnight epiphany; it has taken close to 50 years to emerge.

My intention is to focus on examples and insights that show how purpose, growth and service can reshape a life. At the centre of all of this sits purpose – your life purpose – which will shift, evolve and change over time.

Throughout history, and in the lives of countless everyday, unsung heroes, greatness has often been achieved through a clear sense of purpose: a guiding mission or calling that shapes decisions, sustains sacrifice and makes perseverance possible. In the next chapter, we will delve deeper into the remarkable power of purpose.

As we progress through each chapter, my goal is to help you understand how each step on the pathway contributes to greatness, and to identify which step, or steps, you should focus on next to start, accelerate, or resurrect your pathway towards greatness.

This is the point at which you hop on the Greatness Bus. You may already have established what greatness means to you. If not, I hope this first chapter has evoked reflection and contemplation on the different perspectives and motivators that underpin your search for greatness. To be clear, I believe that your purpose will define your greatness, so please do not be discouraged at this point if you haven't already worked out your greatness, as that will materialise once you have discovered your purpose.

I've come to believe that greatness isn't born in comfort. It's found in friction, in the resistance that forces growth, in the struggle that strips away everything false until only purpose remains.

When I look back at my own path, I see the same truth unfolding in quieter ways. I've failed more than I've succeeded. I've trained until my body broke, dreamed until hope thinned, pushed through moments when belief was a whisper. But each time, something more substantial emerged – a deeper knowing that greatness doesn't reward talent; it rewards persistence.

It's not about being the best. It's about being better than who you were yesterday, than the voice that says you can't, than the fear that begs you to stop.

Greatness doesn't care about how fast you get there or how loudly you arrive. It cares only that you keep going.

It doesn't care about applause, but it will echo in your silence. It doesn't care about legacy, but it will leave one anyway. It doesn't care about your comfort – only your commitment.

And when you give yourself entirely to that pursuit, you discover something liberating: Greatness doesn't belong to the extraordinary. It belongs to those who show up when it's hardest to.

The truth is that greatness doesn't care who you are. It only cares that you rise.

# *REFLECTION, ACTION AND GROWTH*

## DEFINE YOUR VERSION OF GREATNESS

**Reflection:** If you stripped away titles, applause and comparison, what would *your* version of greatness look like in your everyday life?

**Action:** Write a one-sentence personal definition of greatness, then list three ways your current life already reflects small pieces of that definition.

## NOTICE WHERE COMPARISON CREEPS IN

**Reflection:** In which situations do you most often compare yourself to others (work, appearance, fitness, parenting, finances)? How does that comparison distort the way you see your own progress?

**Action:** Choose one area and write a 'before and after' reframing:

Before: 'I'm behind because…'

After: 'Relative to where I started, I've grown by…'.

Commit to practising this reframing every time comparison shows up this week.

## EMBRACE THE STRUGGLE

**Reflection:** Think of a time when you endured real struggle or failure. Looking back honestly, how did that experience shape your character, discipline, or resilience?

**Action**: Identify one current challenge you're facing. Write down one sentence you will say to yourself when it feels toughest (e.g. 'This is the price of my greatness.'). Next, write one small action you will take *today* to move through, not around, that struggle.

## USE PURPOSE AS YOUR ENGINE

**Reflection:** When have you felt most alive, most 'you', or most aligned – when the effort was hard but meaningful? What does that moment suggest about your emerging purpose?

**Action**: Choose one concrete step you will take in the next seven days (a conversation, a commitment, a practice, a plan) that moves you closer to living in alignment with that purpose. Write it down, including a specific day and time.

# CHAPTER 2
# PURPOSE

***'IT'S NOT ENOUGH TO HAVE LIVED. WE SHOULD BE DETERMINED TO LIVE FOR SOMETHING.'*** *– WINSTON CHURCHILL*

Purpose is the beginning of everything. It is the spark that turns movement into momentum, struggle into sacrifice and time into meaning. Without it, even success feels hollow. With it, even failure becomes a source of fuel.

Purpose is not something you always find in a single moment of clarity. It reveals itself slowly, through experience, reflection and courage. It's shaped by what breaks your heart, what lifts your spirit and what refuses to leave your thoughts when the world grows quiet.

For years, I misunderstood purpose. I thought it was a destination – a single, shining goal that, once reached, would answer everything. But purpose isn't fixed. It evolves as we do. It's less a map and more a compass, guiding us towards what matters most, even when the path ahead is uncertain.

Inside every person who achieves greatness, whether their achievements are recognised and admired by millions or only by themselves and a handful of close friends and family, lies a purpose or purposes that burn brightly and bring true meaning to their life. Purpose is their constant companion, flooding their thoughts daily, focusing and inspiring them for the day ahead. And when the chips are down, when they reach their lowest points, when hope seems to have faded away, their purpose beats deep within. In those moments, they find courage. They see salvation, and they find the strength to rise from events that have brought them to their knees, pursuing their purpose with relentless determination. I wholeheartedly believe this because when the random events of life brought me to my knees, and when I was in the depths of my lowest moments, my purpose shone brightly and resurrected me.

## THE COMPASS OF A MEANINGFUL LIFE

Martin Luther King Jr. found his purpose in the face of injustice. It wasn't handed to him; it was born out of witnessing pain he could no longer ignore. He could have chosen safety, silence, or self-interest, but he decided on service instead. His purpose was rooted not in ambition, but in empathy and in the deep conviction that the world could, and must, be better.

That conviction gave shape to his courage. Purpose does that. It gives suffering meaning, discipline, direction, and endurance in faith. Without it, courage becomes chaos and effort becomes noise. With it, everything aligns.

King once said, 'If a man has not discovered something that he will die for, he isn't fit to live.' Harsh words, perhaps, but honest ones. Purpose demands commitment. It asks you to orient your entire life around what matters, and to sacrifice what doesn't.

Nelson Mandela lived that truth in a way few ever will. His purpose was freedom – not just his own, but that of his people. It guided every decision he made, from joining the resistance to enduring 27 years behind bars. He could have walked away many times, compromised, softened, yielded. But purpose, once awakened, doesn't let you rest. It keeps calling.

Even in confinement, Mandela's purpose kept him alive. Each day in prison was a continuation of his mission, not a pause. He educated his fellow inmates, studied his captors, and planned for a future he couldn't yet see. Purpose gave him patience. It transformed time itself – turning what could have been wasted years into preparation.

When he finally emerged, his purpose hadn't dimmed; it had deepened. He no longer sought victory over his oppressors, but unity with them. That is the evolution of true purpose – from self to service, from ambition to compassion.

Burt Munro's purpose was simpler in form but no less powerful. He wasn't driven by politics or revolution. His purpose was creation – the act of building something beautiful through effort. It might seem small compared to the grand causes of King or Mandela, but purpose isn't measured by scale. It's measured by sincerity.

Munro's devotion to his machine – to refining, testing, failing and beginning again – was sacred. It gave his days meaning and his years direction. Purpose made his life larger than its circumstances. It connected him to the universal truth that all great things are built, not born.

That same truth guided Diana Nyad across the open sea. Her purpose was endurance, expressed through the human spirit in movement. She wasn't just swimming towards a destination; she was swimming towards meaning.

After her fourth failed attempt, she could have surrendered. She was older, exhausted, and scarred, both physically and emotionally. But her purpose wouldn't let her stop. It called her back to the water, whispering the same quiet challenge that purpose always gives: 'Not yet'. Purpose doesn't protect you from pain; it redeems it. It gives you something worth suffering for.

When Nyad finally reached the Florida shore, she wasn't celebrating the distance she'd covered, but the alignment she'd achieved – the unity between her will, her effort and her purpose. That's the essence of greatness: to live in alignment with what you were meant to do, no matter the cost.

The Stoics understood this long before we did. They believed that purpose was not a luxury, but a moral duty – the reason we exist at all. Marcus Aurelius wrote: 'The soul becomes dyed with the colour of its thoughts.' He meant that what you think about and what you devote yourself to shape who you become.

Epictetus, born a slave, found purpose in teaching freedom through philosophy. He had no wealth, no title, no power, yet he lived with more direction than emperors. Seneca wrote that the tragedy of life isn't that it ends too soon, but that we waste so much of it on things that don't matter.

To the Stoics, purpose was what connected man to nature, self to virtue, action to meaning. It was the antidote to chaos, the calm centre of a turbulent world.

I've come to see it that way, too. Purpose doesn't eliminate difficulty. It just makes it worth it. The miles, the training, the exhaustion. They're bearable when they're aligned with meaning. When I train now, it's not just for races or records; it's for my overall wellbeing. It's for what those efforts represent – the pursuit of potential, the commitment to growth and the refusal to waste this brief, miraculous life.

Purpose simplifies everything. It cuts through distraction, excuses and doubt. It reminds you why you began and why you must continue. When you lose sight of purpose, life becomes heavier. When you rediscover it, even the hardest days carry light.

Martin's purpose was justice. Nelson's was unity. Burt's was a creation. Diana's was endurance. The Stoics were virtuous. And mine – and perhaps yours too – is to live fully, honestly and courageously while giving everything I have to the work of becoming.

## WHY 'WHY?'

The first question I ask anyone seeking help or coaching is: 'What is your purpose?' Invariably, that question evokes an expression of considerable thought, or a blank look as if to say, 'Help me out here'. Mostly, though, if a response is forthcoming, it will be in the form of a goal, which instantly aligns with an old identity of mine.

Occasionally, a goal will appropriately represent a greater purpose. Goals are admirable, but they mainly do not reflect the true meaning. This is why 90 per cent of people who make New Year's resolutions fail to achieve their goals.

From there, we proceed to draw out the underlying reasons and emotions that, either consciously or unconsciously, form the nucleus of their goal. It is not my modus operandi to judge anyone's goal, nor is it to encourage another person to dream bigger. Instead, my objective is to elevate a goal to a meaningful purpose. This requires an individual to define precisely what achieving that goal will mean and how it will feel. Let's park that thought for a moment and revisit it later in this chapter.

The power of purpose in your daily life will drive you infinitely further than you would have gone without one, enabling you to overcome the most extreme adversity. It will increase your longevity, improve your vitality and energy, enhance your mental wellbeing and foster happiness, among other life-changing benefits. Throughout this chapter, we will explore the power of purpose by examining the lives of a handful of truly remarkable individuals, the role purpose played for the Stoics, how it has shaped and transformed my own life, and how you can discover and define your own purpose – if you have not already found it.

## WHY WE NEED MEANING

Purpose and the search for meaning have fascinated me for almost three decades. One of my favourite reads in recent years on the importance and philosophy of purpose – one that also shaped my thinking and desire to understand mine and how it has defined others – is Viktor E. Frankl's seminal book *Man's Search for Mean*ing. Frankl's book is both a memoir and a philosophical exploration of human existence, drawn from his experiences as a Holocaust survivor and his work as a psychiatrist. The book is split into two parts: the first is a harrowing but reflective account of his time in Nazi concentration camps, and the second introduces his psychological theory known as logotherapy. Here is a summary of my key learnings of Frankl's core principles.

At the heart of Frankl's philosophy is the idea that the primary human drive is not pleasure, as Freud suggested, or power, as Adler suggested, but meaning. Through his lived experiences, Frankl explains how people can endure unimaginable suffering when they believe it has a meaningful purpose. Furthermore, meaning is unique to everyone and can be discovered, not invented; even in the worst circumstances, such as a concentration camp, life can still have purpose. Finding that purpose is vital to psychological survival. The significance of his principle of discovering purpose is paramount.

## FREEDOM OF CHOICE AND ATTITUDE

One of Frankl's most profound insights is that even when everything else is taken from a person, one freedom remains: the freedom to choose one's attitude. This idea, more than any other, reshaped how I think about adversity and became the catalyst for changing my mental direction in moments of crisis.

Frankl illustrates this principle through the prisoners who, despite having no control over their environment or fate, could still decide how to respond. This insight became the cornerstone of Frankl's belief in human agency, even in the face of extreme suffering. Furthermore, suffering becomes bearable – even noble – when it is faced with dignity and a sense of purpose.

His core philosophy resonates deeply with me. It has equipped me with the tools and mindset to overcome the adversity that has tested me countless times, thereby measuring my worthiness of greatness. I've experienced some extremely dark and challenging times, during which I felt I had entered a seemingly infinite dark tunnel, with no end or light in sight. Perhaps the best example happened many years ago, when I was suddenly and unexpectedly plunged into a situation, through no fault of my own, that drove me to the edge, both emotionally and financially, and threatened to destroy my life.

Admittedly, it took frequent daily practice and focus to choose not to become a victim, and I achieved my first impossible long-term goal later that year, despite all the odds against me. Although my story pales in significance when compared to Frankl and the millions of persecuted humans he refers to, the process and core principle are the same.

## FINDING MEANING IN THREE MAIN WAYS

Frankl explains that meaning in life can be discovered in three principal ways:

1. **Through work or accomplishment.** Creating something of value, such as a book, a business, or a piece of art, or accomplishing a goal, gives life purpose. Similarly, contributing to society or one's field creates a sense of responsibility and identity.
2. **Through love and relationships.** Love allows one to see the essential traits of another person, not just in romantic love, but also through compassion, friendship and connection, which lend value to life. Frankl frequently referenced his love for his wife as a sustaining source of hope in the concentration camp.
3. **Through suffering.** When suffering is unavoidable, the attitude towards it can be a source of meaning. Choosing to suffer with dignity transforms pain into purpose. However, Frankl does not glorify suffering; he insists that it should not be sought but can be meaningful when unavoidable.

Sometimes I draw the parallel between the physical and mental suffering that I, and millions of other people, subject ourselves to in the pursuit of our goals in ultrarunning, IRONMAN and a diverse range of sporting endeavours. Over the course of relentlessly training for more than 18,000 hours over a period of 23 years, I have come to learn that experiencing pain is essential for a variety of reasons. Pain symbolises struggle. The greater the battle, the greater the pain and the greater the consequent reward when you persevere.

Channelling emotional pain into physical pain was a cathartic experience that drove me to find places within myself where I chose to exchange my emotional and psychological pain with physical pain, and therefore purpose. Consequently, I came to expect that I needed to be exposed to life's pain, storing and harnessing it to inspire and motivate myself not to quit when the physical pain became all-consuming. This felt like the ultimate search for meaning and purpose in suffering – make it count!

Interestingly, the most common question I am asked by people who cannot comprehend what I subjected myself to is why I choose to seek out and endure relentless physical discomfort and pain for up to 25 hours per week, then push myself to endure the extreme pain and discomfort that is inevitable when contemplating 24 hours in unimaginably brutal environments. The answer I often give is tailored to my purpose, as it seems the only response that they can come close to comprehending. While there is an element of truth in my explanation, there is a more profound truth – that it is the pain and suffering that brings meaning to my purpose, to my struggle and to any feat that necessitates this measure of suffering.

This, I know, is what so many other athletes seek out and embrace. I can imagine, though, how that explanation would be received. Few would understand. Perhaps this was most eloquently explained by John Collins, co-founder of the legendary Hawai'i IRONMAN. When asked why athletes take on the herculean challenge, he said, 'The difference between those who get it and those who don't is those who have, get it, and those who have not, don't.'

In other words, the drivers and the experience are so life-changing and profound that you cannot possibly convey 'why' and what this means to anyone who has not completed an IRONMAN or a similar endurance event.

## EXISTENTIAL VACUUM

Frankl observed that in modern society, many people experience a feeling of emptiness or 'existential vacuum', often due to a lack of meaning or purpose, especially in a post-religious, materialist world. He also observed that people may fill the void with pleasure (hedonism), power, or distraction – but these do not truly satisfy the need for meaning. This condition can lead to depression, aggression, or addiction.

Throughout my life, I have fallen into the grip of an existential vacuum – one shaped and sharpened by my own imperfections and amplified by decades spent in the financial services industry. Even while I was part of that world, I sensed the undercurrents of its culture surrounding me. Yet only after leaving it behind did I gain the distance to see it clearly. What once felt familiar now appears starkly polarised, a landscape transformed by time and perspective.

## LOGOTHERAPY: HEALING THROUGH MEANING

Frankl's therapeutic method, logotherapy, is built around helping patients find meaning in their lives, rather than focusing on their inner conflicts. 'Logos' is Greek for 'meaning', so logotherapy is meaning-centred psychotherapy. It differs from psychoanalysis by focusing less on the past and more on the future and one's responsibility to find purpose. In this context, the therapist's job is to help the patient become aware of their unique possibilities for meaning.

## RESPONSIBILITY AND MORAL INTEGRITY

Frankl believed that meaning implies responsibility to oneself, others, or a greater cause. He suggested that freedom must be paired with responsibility, even proposing a 'Statue of Responsibility' on the US West Coast to balance the Statue of Liberty. Ethical choices, especially in times of crisis, define our humanity. In the face of suffering, loss and dehumanisation, Viktor Frankl discovered that meaning is the source of resilience and the most profound human need. *Man's Search for Meaning* is ultimately a call to live intentionally, find purpose even in hardship and recognise the freedom we always retain to choose our attitude.

## BLUE ZONES

Like many others, I suspect, my awareness and curiosity about the 'Blue Zones' and the impact of purpose on wellness and longevity were piqued by *Live to 100: Secrets of the Blue Zones*, the top-rated Netflix series that aired in 2023. The concept of Blue Zones refers to regions of the world where people live significantly longer and healthier lives than the average person.

The term was popularised by National Geographic explorer and author Dan Buettner, who identified five areas where people frequently live to 100 years or more: Okinawa, Japan; Sardinia, Italy; the Nicoya Peninsula, Costa Rica; Ikaria, Greece; and Loma Linda, USA (a Seventh-day Adventist community).

### PURPOSE AND LONGEVITY

A striking commonality across all Blue Zones is that people live with a strong sense of purpose. This purpose contributes significantly to their overall wellbeing and longevity.

In Okinawa, the concept of 'ikigai' (生き甲斐) refers to 'a reason for being' – a motivating force that gives people a sense of purpose and direction. Older Okinawans often describe ikigai in personal, practical terms, such as caring for grandchildren, gardening, or maintaining friendships. This sense of meaning is strongly correlated with lower stress levels, improved mental health and a longer life.

Nicoyans refer to their purpose as 'plan de vida', or 'life plan'. It represents a deep-rooted sense of responsibility and engagement in life, often continuing well into old age. Elders often live with extended family and remain actively engaged in community life, which reinforces a sense of purpose and belonging.

In the Mediterranean regions of Ikaria, Greece, and Sardinia, Italy, purpose often stems from intergenerational family bonds, spiritual life and agricultural or community work. Elders are respected, involved in family decision-making and continue to engage in meaningful work or social roles, like helping with grandchildren or participating in religious and cultural traditions.

Loma Linda's Seventh-day Adventist community in California views life as a divine gift and lives with a clear sense of purpose. That purpose is grounded in faith, service and a health-conscious lifestyle.

## HOW PURPOSE INFLUENCES LONGEVITY

Scientific research supports the idea that having a strong sense of purpose can reduce stress and cortisol levels, strengthen immune function, improve cardiovascular health, lead to healthier lifestyle choices and promote better resilience and mental health.

In Blue Zones, purpose is not an abstract concept but a daily, lived experience – whether through caring for others, contributing to the community, or spiritual fulfilment. This embedded sense of meaning plays a critical role in promoting long, healthy lives, not just through psychological resilience, but also through behaviours and relationships that foster longevity. The power of purpose – a clear sense of meaning and direction in life – has a profound impact on wellness and longevity. More than just a motivational concept, purpose influences not only physical health and mental wellbeing, but also our lifespan.

### PSYCHOLOGICAL BENEFITS OF PURPOSE

Having a sense of purpose gives people a reason to get up in the morning, especially during life's complex or uncertain moments. Purpose also creates resilience against stress and acts as a buffer against anxiety and depression by offering a broader context in which setbacks are seen as part of a meaningful journey. People with purpose are more optimistic and report higher levels of happiness, contentment and life satisfaction. This leads to improved focus and motivation, as the sense of direction helps prioritise healthy habits and long-term goals.

### PHYSICAL HEALTH AND LONGEVITY

Purpose isn't a luxury – it has real biological benefits. People with a purpose tend to have lower cortisol levels, the body's primary stress hormone, which is associated with reduced inflammation and enhanced immune function. Studies also show that individuals with high purpose are less likely to suffer from heart attacks and strokes, with better all-around cardiovascular health. Furthermore, purposeful living promotes physical activity, better diet choices and regular health screenings.

A 2019 landmark study published in *JAMA Network Open* found that a strong sense of life purpose was associated with a significantly lower risk of all-cause mortality, suggesting that purposeful living may promote longer life. A 2014 study published in *Psychological Science* found that individuals with a strong sense of purpose had a 15 per cent lower mortality risk over a 14-year period compared to those without. Even after accounting for factors such as age, gender and emotional wellbeing, purpose remained a key contributor.

Overall, the behavioural influence of purpose encourages healthier choices. People who live with a clear sense of purpose are more likely to remain physically active, exercise regularly, sleep better and more consistently and choose more nutritious foods. They tend to view their body as an essential asset in service of their mission, rather than something to be depleted or neglected. Together, these behaviours support physical, emotional and psychological wellbeing and are associated with greater longevity. In this way, purpose not only adds more life to days, but more days to our lives.

Another significant impact and benefit of purpose is that it unites people and communities. This unity fosters activities such as volunteering, caregiving, mentoring, or participating in a religious or spiritual community. In turn, each of these serves a distinct purpose. These roles foster stronger social networks, which are independently associated with longer life and greater wellbeing. In Blue Zones and among long-lived populations, purpose is not something one 'finds' once and for all – it's woven into daily routines.

Purpose fuels wellness by aligning daily actions with meaningful goals. It makes people more likely to take care of themselves, stay engaged with life and persevere through adversity. In many ways, living with purpose is like having an internal compass that keeps health, connection and longevity on course.

## THE ONE THAT GOT AWAY AND THE ONE THAT CHANGED EVERYTHING

At the tender age of 12, my purpose was crystal clear: to become a professional football player in the English First Division. This was my first real purpose. There was hardly a day over the next four years that I didn't think about my purpose and what I needed to do to fulfil it.

I can't quite pinpoint when I became an Arsenal fan, but I've been a diehard fan ever since. From the age of 13, I would travel on my own by train to watch my beloved Gunners play at Highbury, London. Come rain or shine, I would stand shoulder to shoulder with the thousands of devoted Gunners fans in Highbury's North Bank, despite the often-intimidating act of catching the train to and from the stadium. Back in those days, this was a dangerous excursion.

An accomplished player from an early age, I found myself playing three to five competitive games a week by the age of 13. These games were played across school representation at Monk's Walk and Welwyn Pegasus on Sundays, as well as at the dual county representative level for schoolboy teams and for the Sunday League National Association.

Playing as the number nine centre forward, I absolutely loved playing football, and there was nothing in this world that I loved more than scoring goals. I dreamed of scoring goals – literally. Fortunately, I was destined to score goals.

At the age of 14, my new team, Panshanger Yellows, made a significant announcement: we were embarking on a tour to the USA. This was quite a considerable development some 46 years ago, when travel wasn't as accessible or affordable as it is today. The prospect of playing against teams in the USA, especially during a time when soccer was rapidly gaining popularity and was the fastest-growing sport in the USA, filled me with excitement. To top things off, we were going to watch my hero, Pelé, who, back then, was the world's greatest football player.

By then, my parents had separated, and it was decided that my mum would travel with me. The adventure that followed turned out to be the most fantastic time of my life to that point. Our days were filled with matches, interspersed with trips to enormous shopping malls that were unlike anything we had in the UK. We fully immersed ourselves in American culture, relishing burgers, mall trips, going to the movies, and even seeing *Grease* within a day of its world premiere. However, the pinnacle of the experience for me was watching my idol, Pelé. What an unforgettable night that was.

When I returned, my passion for football and my desire to play in the top flight remained at the forefront of my mind, and my love of the game was as strong as ever. But the time had come to knuckle down and focus on my studies, which I threw myself into, just as I did with everything that I set my sights on. Football wasn't my only sporting pursuit; I also did cricket, cross-country running and athletics, representing my school and district teams. Despite pushing myself to the point of vomiting as I ran towards the conclusion of the county cross-country championships, I secured a commendable seventh place. This is where my passion for running took root.

As I approached 15 years of age, distractions became too tempting, as they often do, and I didn't possess the character to resist. Girls and boozy nights out at local pubs became appealing pastimes, even during some school lunch breaks. Smoking entered the picture around this time as well, which, accompanied by the consumption of alcohol, didn't align with my sporting dreams. Nonetheless, destiny handed me my big chance at the age of 15.

After a state football cup final representing my school – a match we narrowly won – we received a call at home from the head scout at Southend Football Club, then competing in England's Second Division, offering me an apprenticeship with the club.

My delight was palpable, made even more effusive by the fact that their head scout had told them I was more talented than Danny Greaves, the son of one of England's greatest ever footballers and a true national hero. For days, I practically levitated, bragging to all my mates and anyone else who would listen. Until, that is, the reality of the burden of having to travel for many hours each day by train to get to their south coast home, while attempting to study for my O levels, sank in. Elation soon turned sour, and the growing knot in the pit of my stomach gradually shaped my destiny, giving me little choice but to follow my head and not my heart. I couldn't quit school for a perilous shot at my dream.

And so, my dream died. For a few years, it sat dormant like an old, discarded pair of shoes – scuffed, dirty and out of fashion – at the back of my wardrobe as I distracted myself with other, less meaningful aspirations. Moving to the other side of the world at age 17 to pursue a new life in Australia partially filled the void left by letting that dream go. Then, shortly after arriving, I almost died.

I knew something in my life had to change radically. I could feel it in my bones. I needed purpose – something that would shake my world to its core – but I had no idea where to look or how to begin. To this day, I still can't say with certainty whether I found my purpose or whether it found me. Perhaps it doesn't matter. What matters is that I was searching for meaning with every fibre of my being – and eventually, I found it.

These days, when I mentor or coach others – often informally, or pro bono – about life, career, health, or fitness, it's usually because I've crossed paths with someone who seems to be searching too. Sometimes, they sense that I might be able to help them. I've often thought their motivation arises from a deep human longing to be heard. Many people go through life without feeling truly listened to, and so when they encounter someone genuinely curious about their story, they open up.

It's not uncommon for strangers to share their innermost thoughts with me – hopes, fears, dreams and regrets. My partner, Lisa, often laughs when she asks over dinner, 'So, who did you meet today? Whose life did you change the course of this time?' It is a privilege I never take for granted.

Time and again, I meet people who are struggling with direction, clarity, or confidence in making decisions that truly matter. Some share their goals enthusiastically. Yet no matter the conversation, my first question is always the same: What is their 'why'?

Sometimes I'll go straight to the heart of it and ask, 'What is your purpose?' – a question that almost always evokes silence and deep reflection. When an answer finally comes, it's often framed as a goal, not a purpose. And while goals are a great starting point, they lack the emotional gravity that gives life real meaning.

Let me share a real-life example.

A good friend once referred a young man – let's call him David – to me. David wanted help preparing for an IRONMAN triathlon. We met for coffee, and as we talked, I listened carefully, probing gently beneath the surface. On paper, David was a high achiever – a decorated state-level cricketer, ambitious and disciplined. To the outside world, he seemed unstoppable.

But as we peeled back the layers, a different story emerged. David was stuck. Each time he reached a short-term goal, he would hit a wall – a deep, unmotivated lull that stalled his progress. It became clear he was chasing achievements not for himself, but for the approval of others. At the root of it all was his desire to earn his father's admiration, a man who had accomplished extraordinary feats in his lifetime.

When I asked David what his purpose was, he froze. After a long pause, he shrugged and admitted quietly, 'I really don't know.'

Before we wrapped up, I asked him to reflect on a few questions and do some personal homework. Together, we unpacked his craving for external validation – how his identity had become a performance for others rather than an honest expression of who he truly was. He began to realise that his unease extended beyond sports. It affected his friendships, his sense of connection and his self-worth.

When I shared my observations, David sat back, eyes wide with a kind of awakening. Then he smiled faintly and said, 'You know what, Jason – you're absolutely right. Wow. So… what do I do now?'

At our next meeting over coffee, David immediately and proudly produced the piece of work he had completed, which mapped out many admirable goals across the key tenets of his life, which I recognised. Over the course of our conversation, I helped David bring his purpose to life, elevating the many goals he had recorded into a meaningful reality, which revealed a beaming smile. From there,

David went away and refined his goals into a purpose that now guides and inspires him daily.

## GOALS DO NOT EQUAL PURPOSE

While goals are undoubtedly meaningful and essential, they are rarely the same thing, unless one discovers and lives both daily. The story I have just shared is a pertinent example of how goals and purpose are related, but different. Perhaps the best example I can share concerns my life-changing purpose versus my first impossible goal, which both materialised at about the same time. No doubt, my first impossible goal was the genesis of my life-changing purpose.

My first impossible goal – and by far the biggest I had ever set – was to qualify for the legendary IRONMAN World Championship in Hawai'i. At 35, I preferred the lounge to exercise, smoked a packet of cigarettes a day, couldn't swim, feared drowning and could barely ride a bicycle. By any rational measure, qualifying for Hawai'i epitomised an impossible goal.

Yet as I watched that iconic race on television, something in me shifted. My life took a dramatic turn, and nothing – and I mean nothing – would ever be the same. That, I could not have imagined. That's what happens when you choose courage. When you chase purpose, everything changes.

That moment lit the spark. But the fuel behind it was deeper: a desperate longing for purpose I hadn't felt since my teenage years in the UK. What began as a goal quickly revealed itself as something more fundamental. I needed to prove to myself that I could achieve something beyond my comprehension – not to impress others, but to restore belief in myself. Intuitively, I knew this was the path to my own greatness.

Before long, that purpose evolved. It became a quest to discover how far I could push myself – psychologically and physically – and, in doing so, to banish regret and find peace within myself. The distinction became clear: the goal was finite, but the purpose would endure, transcending setbacks, failure and doubt. At the time, I had no idea how many of those I would face and overcome.

Purpose became my internal validation; the goal, my external one. Over the next two decades, I set and pursued numerous notable goals as I transitioned from IRONMAN triathlons to ultramarathon running, and then to trail ultramarathons. Among the most challenging were qualifying for the IRONMAN World Championship, becoming the Australian National 100-kilometre Running Champion, earning eligibility for the elite 100-kilometre World Championships, and qualifying for the Western States® 100-Mile Endurance Run – most of them after the age of 45.

Over the next 27 years, my purpose expanded well beyond sport. While the goals I set for myself across duathlons, IRONMAN races, road ultramarathons and trail ultramarathons continued to challenge my mental and physical limits, the same principle applied to my career. That journey culminated in a series of senior leadership and CEO roles focused on rescuing and revitalising businesses, protecting jobs and accrued benefits, nurturing people and helping others build stellar careers.

Yet at 62, I am not done. Each day, my purpose now centres on helping hundreds of thousands of people discover their own greatness through my writing. In the words of the legend David Goggins, I am 'Never done!'

While we have already explored purpose through the lens of herculean feats, a purposeful life can be equally rewarding when it inspires everyday greatness and meaning. Over the course of a lifetime, our roles inevitably change. For example, we may change our friendship groups, get married, have children, pursue a career, or perhaps retire. Typically, these are the primary life stages that consume most of our time, focus and energy, and by osmosis, they often become our identity. The risk is that when our identities are too strongly linked to any of these roles, it can leave us feeling lost or uneasy when things change, or even regretful, as we may have neglected other aspects of our lives, especially as we age.

Having a sense of purpose can help us rebalance and avoid reactive ups and downs. Purpose enables us to better cope with stress and bounce back from difficulties, or to be motivated to exert additional discretionary effort.

Purpose is linked with a stronger sense of identity and improved mental health. Having a sense of purpose is also associated with better physical health – for example, a lower risk of stroke, heart disease and Alzheimer's disease. Health benefits like these probably explain why people with purpose tend to age well and live longer.

These associations are thought to occur partly because having a sense of purpose increases healthy practices such as physical activity and social connections. This buffers against loneliness, which is known to affect physical health.

## LESS WILL GIVE YOU MORE

As my life has unfolded, I've come to recognise the vast chasm between what I once believed would bring happiness and meaning, and what truly has. That realisation has revealed a profound truth: less is indeed more.

In today's frenetic, digital world, saturated with information, advertising and the endless noise of social media, an artificial narrative surrounds us. We are told who to be, what to own and how each new form of instant gratification will somehow complete us. It is, at times, difficult not to be drawn into that alluring but hollow current. Most of us, it seems, crave *more* – more possessions, more recognition, more validation. By *more*, I mean the shiny symbols of status: the newest car, the luxury holiday, the designer brand, the outward proof of worth. These desires are not new; they stem from our timeless human need to feel seen, valued and enough.

Yet in modern times, social media has amplified this craving to an unprecedented extent, fuelling our innate longing for recognition. It's human nature to want to feel good about ourselves, and I do not judge this. Instead, I intend to offer a perspective that inspires reflection, introspection and, ultimately, growth towards genuine fulfilment and greatness.

I have not been immune to the pull of instant gratification and status. At times, I, too, have been swept into that whirlpool. But I am grateful that those moments have passed and left no lasting hold. For most of my life, I have avoided sharing personal information on social media, opting for privacy over exposure. The only platform I ever used was LinkedIn, which was purely out of necessity as a senior corporate leader. Until recently, I didn't even have an Instagram account, and I hadn't posted on Facebook since creating my profile a decade earlier.

That has since changed – dramatically. Aligning with my purpose to help others uncover their own greatness demanded that I step beyond my comfort zone and share my life openly. Doing so meant confronting fear yet again, ushering in a fresh chapter of growth, one I never expected to experience beyond the age of 60.

Throughout my career in financial services, I pursued what so many in that field strive for: financial freedom. I was aware of the mistakes people make when preparing for the future and was determined to avoid them. I set an ambitious standard for myself to achieve financial independence for my family and create lasting peace of mind. To me, wealth has always meant security and comfort, not status. I have never cared for the appearance of success, only for its substance.

Perhaps this clarity stems from decades immersed in finance, where I often found satisfaction in investment gains or in the relief of avoiding losses. Over time, however, I grew uneasy with the realisation that I was using those fleeting victories to fill deeper voids within myself. As I've grown older, my focus on money – at least the pursuit of it – has faded, replaced by things far more meaningful.

For decades, I chased accumulation as though it were the key to freedom. Yet, somewhere along the way, I realised the chase itself had lost meaning. In hindsight, I can see clearly that my purpose had begun to wane long before that realisation dawned. My bucket was full, but much of my life felt empty.

*The Molecule of More* by Daniel Z. Lieberman and Michael E. Long is an intriguing book that argues that dopamine – a chemical in the brain often associated with pleasure – is more about anticipation, motivation and desire than enjoyment itself. This fascinating book makes the case that dopamine is the biological force behind our endless striving, often at the expense of present contentment, a fate that I suffered for decades. What I love about this book is that it captures the essence of the shortcomings of a life driven by the absence of actual presence.

Here are some insights into how the book explains this dynamic:

| CONCEPT | WHAT'S HAPPENING | THE LIVED EFFECT | THE CORRECTIVE BALANCE |
|---|---|---|---|
| **DOPAMINE DRIVES DESIRE, NOT SATISFACTION** | Dopamine spikes in anticipation, not fulfilment. Once a goal is reached, levels drop. | Achievement feels underwhelming; satisfaction is fleeting. The chase resumes. | Shift focus from outcomes to experience and meaning in the present moment. |
| **TWO BRAIN SYSTEMS SHAPE WELLBEING** | The dopaminergic system is future-oriented and goal-driven; 'here-and-now' systems support contentment and connection. | Life becomes dominated by striving, planning and comparison, leaving little space for ease or enjoyment. | Deliberately activate presence-based systems through rest, relationships and embodied experience. |
| **PROGRESS CAN BECOME ADDICTIVE** | The brain treats advancement as a signal to keep seeking rather than to feel complete. | Restlessness, burnout and the feeling that 'enough' is always just out of reach. | Redefine success to include sufficiency, stability and enjoyment – not only growth. |
| **DOPAMINE IS NOT THE ENEMY** | Ambition, creativity and exploration all rely on healthy dopamine function. | Without balance, ambition crowds out peace and perspective. | Use dopamine intentionally to pursue purpose, not endless accumulation. |

| CONCEPT | WHAT'S HAPPENING | THE LIVED EFFECT | THE CORRECTIVE BALANCE |
|---|---|---|---|
| CONTENTMENT LIVES IN BEING PRESENT | Presence activates non-dopaminergic systems linked to safety, connection and wellbeing. | Deeper satisfaction, stronger relationships and greater emotional stability. | Practise mindfulness, gratitude, routine and embodied awareness. |

## FINDING YOUR PURPOSE

At this stage, it's essential to explore the concept of purpose, both the kind that arises intuitively and the kind that is consciously crafted and deeply defined. Many people live guided by unspoken, instinctive purposes that emerge naturally through different life stages, such as getting married, raising children, building financial stability, or pursuing career growth.

It's reasonable to assume that these stages carry with them familiar intentions such as:

- providing a good life for one's family and children
- raising children with the right values
- building wealth and ensuring financial security
- preparing for retirement
- losing weight and improving health.

Each of these can sound like a purpose, but in truth, they often function more as goals. This distinction matters because when purpose and objective blur together, their collective power diminishes. The key lies in understanding the difference between the two, then bringing that distinction to life through deliberate articulation.

My rule of thumb is simple: create a clear, emotive statement when defining purpose.

If you've already set a goal, work backwards to uncover the deeper reason behind it – the 'why' that gives it emotional weight and endurance. This transformation often determines whether you succeed or fall short.

Take one of the most common New Year's resolutions as an example: 'I want to lose weight.'

While admirable, this goal carries little emotional impact. Even when quantified – 'I want to lose five kilos' – it often remains uninspiring. It's no surprise, then, that nearly 90 per cent of New Year's resolutions fail within the first month, often due to poor planning, lack of discipline, or wavering courage. But at the heart of most failures lies something simpler: the absence of purpose.

Now, reimagine that same goal infused with meaning: 'My purpose this year is to lose weight and grow stronger by eating well and exercising regularly, so I can feel energised, look my best and live a vibrant, healthy life.' Or, 'My purpose this year is to rediscover physical and mental wellbeing so that I can become my best, healthiest, and most brilliant self.'

Notice the difference? These statements ignite emotion and commitment. Defined with meaning, they transform ordinary goals into powerful compasses – guiding you through challenge, temptation and doubt. When courage and discipline are required, purpose becomes the anchor that keeps you moving forwards. I know this truth intimately; I've drawn on my purpose thousands of times in business, life and every race and training block I've ever faced.

Over the course of my 35-year career in financial planning, I've seen how few people truly define their purpose. In thousands of client interviews about lifestyle, finances and the future, most spoke only of loose goals, not deep, intentional purposes.

Why? Because few appreciate the scale of the task at hand, or the level of thought it deserves. Many are too busy, too distracted, or unaware of what it takes to achieve true financial independence. The consequence is predictable: a lack of focus, poor time and resource allocation and, ultimately, unfulfilled potential.

Success, by contrast, begins with defining a purpose that inspires action.

When asked about retirement, most people say something like: 'We want to retire comfortably.'

It sounds reasonable, even responsible – but as a statement of life's most significant financial milestone, it lacks life, colour and conviction.

Now compare it to this: 'We want to live our golden years in comfort and freedom – to choose how we live and where we go without any financial worry.'

Same intention, yet a world apart in energy, vision and clarity. One drifts, the other drives. And that's the quiet, transformative power of a well-defined purpose.

## HACKS TO FIND YOUR PURPOSE

One beneficial practice is finding some time to journal. This allows you to organise your thoughts and can increase wellbeing. Writing down things that make you feel happiness, anger, or sadness can reveal topics that matter to you. For example, have you experienced something that felt unjust? Often, purposes are aligned with social justice, such as tackling poverty, increasing access to education, reducing obesity and challenging racism.

Identifying and listing your values can help you focus on your purpose and the actions you can take to support it. For example, suppose you've identified the climate crisis as something you feel strongly about, but your values tend towards avoiding social disruption. In that case, you are unlikely to get involved in a protest, regardless of how much you support the issue. You may instead focus on a different way of connecting with your purpose, such as recycling more or driving less.

Find your passion. What do you love to do? If you love dancing and want to tackle poverty, consider exploring ways to get involved in teaching dance to disadvantaged children. If you love reading, consider ways to apply it, such as reading to patients in a hospital or supporting children's reading in schools.

Get involved. Purpose is about something bigger and beyond the self. Is there a way to bring together the things that matter to you with a way to give back? Volunteering helps to create a sense of wellbeing and purpose, and can connect you with others.

Remember, purpose is not something we achieve at a certain point in time. It's a journey of discovery rather than a destination. To find your purpose, take the time to reconnect with yourself. I guarantee you that investing time in discovering your purpose will indeed change your life irrevocably. Your purpose will fill you with promise, hope and meaning. Most of all, it evokes a life of meaning and pride as you go in pursuit of your own greatness, whatever that might be or mean to you.

Purpose doesn't care about applause or approval. It doesn't need recognition. It only asks that you follow it with humility, persistence and faith. And when you do, you'll find that purpose gives back far more than it takes.

It provides direction to your days and dignity to your life.

It gives meaning to your movement, and movement to your meaning.

# *REFLECTION, ACTION AND GROWTH*

## LISTEN TO THE CALL WITHIN

**Reflection:** What experiences, memories, or injustices have stayed with you far longer than they should – the things you can't shake, the thoughts that surface when the world around you falls quiet? What might they be pointing you towards?

**Action:** Write down the three moments in your life that stirred the strongest emotion (pain, pride, injustice, inspiration). Circle the one that feels most unfinished – that's where you begin exploring your purpose.

## SEPARATE PURPOSE FROM GOALS

**Reflection:** Which of your current ambitions are truly yours and which are echoes of expectation, validation, habit, or fear? If no one were watching, applauding, or judging, what would you still feel compelled to pursue?

**Action:** Choose one current goal and rewrite it as an emotive purpose statement using this format: 'My purpose is to… so that I can…' Keep refining it until it moves you.

## DECIDE WHAT YOU'RE WILLING TO BEAR

**Reflection:** Meaningful purpose demands sacrifice. What discomfort, fear, or challenge are you genuinely willing to endure because the meaning behind it is worth more than the pain it asks of you?

**Action:** Identify one behaviour, habit, or distraction you need to let go of to move closer to your purpose. Commit to replacing it with a single aligned action this week.

## ENVISION THE LIFE YOU'D BE PROUD OF

**Reflection:** If you were looking back on your life at age 90, which actions, contributions, or transformations would make you feel proud that you lived with intention, courage and meaning?

**Action:** Write a one-paragraph 'future memory' describing the life you want to have lived. Highlight one sentence that feels most true and take one concrete step towards it today.

SS GREAT
ATNESS G
SS GREAT
ATNESS G
SS GREAT
ATNESS G
SS GREAT
ATNESS G

# CHAPTER 3
# COURAGE

***'COURAGE IS KNOWING WHAT NOT TO FEAR.'* – PLATO**

Courage breaks the gravitational pull of fear.

Fear keeps people exactly where they are – repeating the same choices, the same patterns, the same life. Courage doesn't remove fear; it simply refuses to let fear decide.

And the moment fear stops making your decisions, life opens in ways it never has before.

When you boil it down to its most basic level, courage is a decision that precedes an action, or actions, despite the perceived risk or risks. A risk, therefore, is a person's perception, which may be well-founded or exaggerated. Whether the risk is real or as serious as perceived, deciding and acting requires courage.

Courage, then, is action in the face of fear. In any confronting situation, the degree of courage required must be equal to or greater than the degree of fear. The intensity of fear felt will vary considerably for each person, based on their experience and the perceived or real degree of risk and consequences. There is also a counterbalance in terms of consequence that comes into play, relating to the result of not taking that risk.

This mental calculation can be refined through focus and practice and evaluated on a more logical basis. Research suggests humans make the majority of their decisions emotionally – often cited as around 70 per cent – which makes this approach particularly compelling. By deliberately increasing the logical component, we can counterbalance emotional bias and make more considered, balanced decisions. A similar philosophy has underpinned the Stoic way of life for thousands of years, which we will explore shortly.

When we think about courage, our minds instinctively default to extreme examples – moments that evoke awe, inspire us and instil a deep sense of admiration. Such extreme examples epitomise the virtue of courage. They include the courage required by an exhausted, wounded, hungry, mud-saturated young soldier when faced with climbing out of and over the edge of a trench during World War I while under heavy fire from a hostile enemy force, or the unidentified Chinese man, dubbed the 'Tank Man', who stood in front of a column of tanks in Tiananmen Square in Beijing on 5 June 1989. This act of defiance occurred after the Chinese government's military crackdown on pro-democracy protesters, and the image of the man facing the tanks became a powerful symbol of peaceful resistance.

Courage begins where comfort ends. It is the quiet defiance of fear – the willingness to stand, speak, or move when the easier choice is to retreat. Courage doesn't roar; it whispers, 'Try again'.

If greatness is built from many stones, courage is the foundation. Without it, purpose remains an idea, belief a theory and discipline a ritual. Courage gives them life. It is the act that transforms thought into motion and conviction into creation.

## MOVING FORWARDS IN THE PRESENCE OF FEAR

Martin Luther King Jr. understood that courage is not the absence of fear, but the mastery of it. Fear followed him everywhere, present in the threats scrawled across his mail, the late-night calls promising death, the awareness that any speech might be his last. Yet he walked forwards. He preached love in a world armed with hate.

Courage, for him, was moral rather than physical. It wasn't a matter of fighting back; it was the choice to stand still in the storm and answer violence with grace. That's the kind of bravery that changes the world – not the swing of a fist, but the stillness of a heart that refuses to hate.

His courage came not from arrogance but from faith – that truth, though fragile, would outlast lies. 'Faith,' he said, 'is taking the first step even when you don't see the whole staircase.' It is courage's twin – the quiet conviction that the step will hold.

Nelson Mandela's courage was shaped by years of fear. He once admitted that courage was not his natural state. 'I learned that courage was not the absence of fear,' he said, 'but the triumph over it.' The man who never knew freedom learned to create it within himself.

Courage, for Mandela, was endurance. It was about keeping his heart open after betrayal, maintaining his dignity when humiliated, and holding onto his faith in humanity after 27 years of chains. When he finally walked free, he didn't emerge hardened; he appeared whole. That is the ultimate act of courage: not merely to survive suffering, but to stay kind because of it.

I've come to understand that courage rarely feels like bravery in the moment. It feels like uncertainty. It feels like shaking hands, a quickened pulse and a step taken without guarantee. Courage is never comfortable; if it is comfortable, it's not courage yet.

During endurance races, courage often disguises itself as persistence. The body breaks first, then the mind, and what's left is a choice – to stop or to continue. Every occasion when I crossed a finish line was built on thousands of these moments: small, unseen acts of courage strung together until they form a path.

It's not about conquering fear but about carrying it. Courage doesn't erase doubt; it coexists with it. It says, 'I'm afraid, but I'll go anyway'. That's the moment when transformation happens, and the point at which we stop negotiating with limitations and begin living beyond them.

Burt Munro lived that moment every day. He had no resources, no recognition, only the stubborn audacity to believe his dream mattered. Every failure could have been final, but he met each one with quiet resolve. His courage wasn't loud; it was consistent. To keep working, year after year, when the world isn't watching – that's courage. To chase perfection in obscurity, to risk ridicule in pursuit of something invisible, is greatness taking shape in silence.

Diana Nyad's courage took a different form. It was elemental, raw, defiant. The ocean is not a forgiving opponent. It humbles everyone who enters it. During her swims, Nyad faced pain so consuming it bordered on delirium: hypothermia, jellyfish stings, hallucinations. Yet courage kept her moving – stroke by stroke, breath by breath.

Her courage was not reckless; it was rooted in preparation, in purpose. Each time she failed, she learned. Each time she was beaten, she adjusted to the situation, and her final crossing wasn't luck – it was the accumulation of a thousand small acts of courage, layered until they became inevitable. When she staggered onto the Florida shore, her message to the world was simple: 'Never, ever give up.' Behind those five words is the most valid form of courage. It is the refusal to let defeat define you.

The Stoics taught that courage was the first virtue because it makes all others possible. Without it, wisdom becomes mere theory, justice becomes mere sentiment, and discipline becomes mere routine. Courage, to them, was not only the willingness to face danger but the strength to face truth.

Seneca wrote that fortune tests the brave. Epictetus taught that adversity is not punishment but opportunity – 'the occasion for the exercise of virtue'. Marcus Aurelius, an emperor surrounded by chaos, reminded himself daily that fear was not the enemy; avoidance was.

Their courage was inward – the courage to think clearly amid confusion, to remain calm amid noise, to choose virtue over comfort. They believed that fear is inevitable, but servitude to fear is optional.

I've learned the same on the road, in the still hours before dawn when you lace up your shoes knowing pain awaits. Courage isn't the absence of dread before the first step; it's the faith that the step is still worth taking.

Every time I've tested myself, fear has been there, whispering doubts and reminding me of past failures. But there comes a point when you stop arguing with fear and start walking beside it. It becomes a companion, not an enemy. You stop waiting for it to disappear and learn to move forwards anyway. That's where life expands.

Courage doesn't change the difficulty of the path; it changes *you*. It builds a self that can withstand more, love more deeply, forgive more quickly, and act with greater truth.

King's courage changed laws. Mandela's softened hearts. Munro's courage redefined what was possible. Nyad's shattered the limits of age. The Stoics reshaped how humanity faces suffering.

## WHAT COURAGE REALLY FEELS LIKE

My appreciation of courageous and heroic acts of valour was magnified when I worked for Lord Michael Ashcroft. A British–Belizean billionaire businessman, philanthropist, author and political figure, Michael's extensive philanthropic endeavours were driven by his deep passion for and obsession with acts of courage from various conflicts, particularly World Wars I and II.

When I knew Michael, he had acquired more than 150 medals of valour, including double VC crosses, some of which were valued at more than $10 million. Notably, Michael has donated most of his collection to major museums, allowing everyone to understand and appreciate the many courageous individuals who risked their lives for peace.

Remarkably, Michael could remember the details of each story and recite any of them at the drop of a hat, such was his admiration for each of those courageous heroes. In 2015, Michael invited me to the gala opening night of the WWI Centenary Exhibition at the Melbourne Museum. It was a truly humbling experience and a great privilege that evening to immerse myself in the history, bravery and heroism of the ANZACs.

There were many moments that evening when I had to fight back tears as I read tribute after tribute to brave men and women. It was a night that will never fade from my memory.

That experience also stirred the same deep wave of emotion I had felt years earlier while visiting the memorial site and museum at Sandakan in Borneo. There, the story of the Sandakan Death Marches is told, where thousands of Australian prisoners of war were forced by Japanese guards to march hundreds of kilometres through dense jungle. Exhaustion, starvation, disease and dehydration claimed almost every life. It remains one of the highest casualty rates suffered by Australian forces in any conflict.

## FEAR CAN BE REPROGRAMMED

Acts like these clearly involve greater courage than, say, the courage required to walk onto a stage to deliver a public speech. Yet, despite these apparent differences in risk and consequences, for many people it may be just as daunting to climb over the edge of a trench to face enemy fire as it is to present to a group. However, the quantum of fear and the courage required to face it are commensurate with the individual's perception of it. So, in many respects, they are more similar than you would think.

Fortunately, this means that the degree of fear any person experiences, particularly when their perception exceeds reality, can be influenced through practice and action, gradually decreasing with each subsequent action. Persist with this practice, and you will eventually become the master of your fears, rather than them being the master of you.

Somewhere deep within us all, I believe courage – whether self-inspired or inspired by others – can be found and expressed. Courage starts with a single determination: to stand up, to face fear, and to dare to believe in a better life, better health, a better self, or a better world. Courage is a determination to reject the status quo, a belief in a higher purpose or positive solution to any set of destructive, harmful, or benign circumstances. It is a powerful, sometimes frightening, yet empowering stance that requires action in the face of adversity. Courage requires massive discretionary effort to transform your current circumstance, followed by many, perhaps even thousands, of interventions driven by a belief in and connection with your purpose. Innately, it is fuelled by a deep-seated desire for better – for ourselves, our family, our workplace, our community and our world.

Courage requires the bravery to stand up and be counted – to choose the more difficult path that demands discretionary effort, because greatness transcends insurmountable circumstances. Courage is all around us and always has been. It is what saves lives, changes the world and affirms what is most human in us. It is the virtue that I believe is most admired because it requires sacrifice to give shape to hope. In its purest and most selfless form, the stakes could not be higher. For countless people throughout history – and indeed today – the greatest act of courage is to choose to risk one's own life for a higher purpose, protecting or creating a better life for family, friends, or country.

Once you have discovered your purpose, which is clearly defined and understood, finding the courage is your next step towards greatness. But let's be clear before we move on that purpose is your ultimate anti-fear weapon. That said, cultivating your mindset will also be the next step that enables you to be brave enough.

## AWAKENING COURAGE: THE FIRST FLICKER

For the entirety of my adult life, until the age of 35, my courage was summoned countless times, and on occasion, it surfaced when needed. But there were also myriad moments when it remained dormant and hidden. On many occasions, I found myself uncertain about whether the task or situation required me to confront my fears, address potential failure, or make significant sacrifices and exert discretionary effort.

Rarely did I choose the most challenging road, and I resisted the idea of pushing my mental and physical limits. A pattern of poor choices shaped my life, each one reinforcing a growing sense of regret over the opportunities I had squandered. That regret hardened into shame, fuelled by my awareness and acceptance that I was not what I purported to be. In its most abhorrent form, over too many beers at a function, I would skilfully insert into conversation the claim that I could have been a professional football player in the UK. Sadly, 'I could have' became my catch cry. 'I would have' and 'I could have' became my story and legacy, and I had grown to hate both. Yes, *hate*, a word I later banished from my thoughts and vocabulary.

Finally, I discovered my true purpose – and with it, the courage I had been missing. Each day, I faced my deepest fears head-on and never backed down. Almost by chance, I was confronted by my darkest fear of all: drowning. I was forced to make a decision that I knew, deep down, I could no longer avoid if I wanted to escape a lifetime of underachievement relative to my latent capability.

I grew up in the UK, where swimming is taught in many schools as part of the sporting curriculum, but only at a rudimentary level – enough to reduce the risk of drowning, not to build confidence. My fear was so deep-seated that it often formed the nucleus of many nightmares, to the point that submerging my head underwater for just a few seconds was so frightening that it triggered instantaneous panic.

And yet, the challenge before me was to swim 300 metres in a tidal river at Noosa, surrounded by more than 100 other competitors fighting for space. I had just 10 weeks to overcome my fear of drowning, or at least manage it, by learning to swim 300 metres in the relative safety of a swimming pool. For days, I obsessed over summoning the courage to visit the pool. The fear was debilitating, causing my hands to sweat at the very thought. A few days later, I found the courage to go. It was one almost infinitesimal step, but my first real one towards my own everyday greatness.

That evening, I contemplated the enormity of the challenges that lay ahead. I concluded that I probably couldn't die on the bike – an assumption that would prove naïve as the years rolled by – but swimming among a dense group of athletes in a tidal ocean river felt far more dangerous. As I worked through how to avoid drowning, another fear surfaced: the humiliation of being rescued in front of hundreds of spectators. Ironically, that fear would later become a reality in another race on a world stage – a story for another chapter.

For the moment, I set aside the looming prospect of humiliation and confronted the reality before me: I had just 10 weeks to determine my fate and to avoid a potential death by drowning. To quell my deep-seated fear, I understood that I first needed to nurture belief in my ability to swim 300 metres without succumbing to panic or doubt. The path forwards was unmistakable: begin humbly, progress steadily over seven weeks and build the strength and confidence to conquer that distance.

As I prepared for my inaugural visit to the local pool, anxiety crept into every corner of my mind. My heart raced each time I imagined stepping into the pool complex – the mere thought of it sent waves of dread through me. When I parked my car outside the pool, I sat in silence, drawing deep breaths to calm my racing pulse. But fear had anchored me in place. I sat motionless, paralysed by indecision for 15 minutes. My palms were slick with sweat as I wrestled with the impulse to start the engine and drive away. I couldn't have known it then, but those minutes – fraught with hesitation and self-doubt – were among the most decisive of my life. Somewhere deep inside, I sensed that what hung in the balance was far greater than a swimming lesson. It was, in truth, a battle for my future self.

In that moment, I recognised a familiar adversary: the mocking inner voice that resurfaced whenever I confessed, often over a casual drink, that I *could have* achieved more, that I *should have* been someone greater but wasn't. That self-deceptive declaration, meant to impress others, had always been my defence mechanism. It was a way of asserting potential without ever having to prove it. Yet the truth was plain: I had ability, yes, but not the courage, not the heart, not the discipline to turn potential into achievement.

There, in that darkened car outside the swimming pool, those two forces – fear and regret – collided once more, waging their familiar war within me.

Later in life, I refined the ability to make crucial decisions in just four seconds when faced with the choice between the easier and more challenging paths, a principle I explain in more detail in the next chapter. Four seconds became a precious commodity that helped curb or nullify any inclination to procrastinate. Yet it also fine-tuned my capacity to follow my gut, which often proved accurate. With ample practice, this decision-making would become instinctive. But in that moment, I was still sitting in the damn car.

Without question, this was a quintessential 'sliding doors' moment. To an outside observer, my decision might have appeared trivial – hardly the stuff of transformation. Yet that very perception reveals a common blindness: the failure to recognise the quiet significance of choosing the easier path. In that instant, I understood with piercing clarity that surrendering to fear would deal a mortal blow to the fragile resolve I was building within myself. At the same time, I sensed that walking through the doors of that swimming centre would trigger a chain reaction. It would compel me to choose the more challenging road over the comfortable one repeatedly.

Fortunately, the voice advocating a permanent change couldn't be ignored. With a decisive turn of the ignition, I snatched my bag and strode towards the entrance. This was the moment – my opportunity to prove to myself that I could become so much more than I had been. The pool was packed, with many lanes occupied by squad swimmers gliding through the water with grace, while recreational swimmers crammed the remaining lanes and hustled for clear water. This was my worst nightmare!

I took a few deep breaths and slipped into the chilly water as a small gap opened between swimmers. I ducked under, pushed off and was away. Almost immediately, another swimmer's arm brushed my head, startling me to the surface. I gasped, then forced myself back again and kept going. The far wall felt impossibly distant. When my hand finally found the steel edge, I clung to it, gulping air and spitting out chlorinated water. Every stroke had been a struggle, but I had done it – 25 metres, head submerged. A quiet realisation cut through the fear: I could do this!

Confident swimmers streamed past, turning effortlessly, lap after lap. After a few minutes, I pushed off again. Even in that relatively brief span, there were moments when I teetered on the edge of becoming overwhelmed as the looming possibility of drowning caused panic to surge within me. Two laps became 50 metres. On the third, my heart pounded – adrenaline, fear and effort colliding. A swimmer clipped my foot, then grabbed it. I stood briefly, gasping, let them pass, then plunged back under to finish the final stretch.

I had done it – 100 metres. It was undeniable progress towards that magical 300-metre target. I went on to complete my training, and on that fateful day of the BRW Sprint Triathlon, I did indeed survive, although I had to flip onto my back mid-swim to regroup. After completing the swim in last place, I powered home to finish eighth out of 105 competitors. My life was changed forever! My new identity had begun to take life.

## HACKS TO FIND YOUR COURAGE

Finding courage – especially in the face of fear, uncertainty, or discomfort – can feel daunting. However, there are reliable, evidence-based strategies to develop it. Here are some of the most effective ways I have found over time.

### UNDERSTAND YOUR FEAR

Fear is complex. Broadly, it tends to fall into one of two categories: rational fear, which is protective and responds to a genuine threat (such as standing near the edge of a cliff with no barriers), and irrational fear, which arises without real danger (such as the fear of clowns, or coulrophobia). While both can feel equally intense, they are rooted in very different mechanisms and therefore require different approaches to management.

The first step is to slow down and clearly identify what you're *actually* afraid of, such as failure, rejection, or pain. Naming the fear gives it boundaries. From there, ask yourself: 'What is the worst that can realistically happen?' More often than not, the fear is exaggerated or irrational. When examined honestly, you can reframe the fear as a sign that you're on the edge of growth, not danger.

Creating perspective, particularly in the moment when fear or anxiety strikes, can be achieved by taking a step back and placing the concern or fear into perspective.

To illustrate this, I want to share an exercise from a development day I attended 30 years ago. Early in the session, the facilitator asked us to imagine a series of wildlife scenarios. We were then instructed to align a current issue in our own lives with the scenarios that best matched its *true* level of threat.

## Which scenario best reflects your issue?

1. You are floating in the open ocean after your boat has sunk, 50 kilometres from shore you are treading water as multiple large shark fins circle you.
2. You have been accidentally left behind on safari, near a cluster of climbable trees, while a pride of lions circles nearby.
3. You trip while walking along the banks of the Amazon river and fall into waters populated by piranhas.
4. You are walking along a bush track and encounter a venomous snake curled on the path a few metres ahead.
5. You are spring cleaning and uncover a nest of redback spiders.
6. You are walking past a garden gate when an overprotective Jack Russell bolts out and tries to bite your ankle.
7. You are gardening and unearth a nest of green ants that immediately begin biting.
8. You are sitting around at an evening barbecue when mosquitoes start to bite.

The purpose of the exercise is not to dramatise fear, but to calibrate it. By matching your issue to one of these scenarios, you separate *actual* severity from *perceived* severity. The scale runs from scenario one – representing near-certain danger – through to scenario eight, a minor irritation that will pass quickly.

With practice, you will gradually master this technique, relax many concerns, and reduce damaging stress levels, allowing you to move more expediently towards solutions and a positive mindset daily.

## START WITH MICRO-COURAGE

Take small, manageable risks that stretch your comfort zone, such as speaking up in a meeting, asking a challenging question, or trying something new in front of others.

Early in my corporate career, I was acutely aware – as many of us are – that certain group scenarios can be daunting and often prompt people to avoid engagement. One of the most familiar examples is group training. When a facilitator asks for volunteers to come to the front of the room to role-play or demonstrate a newly learned skill, the response is often the same: eyes drop, bodies stiffen, and an unspoken plea fills the room – *please don't pick me*. That was me. I would shift in my seat, sweat forming under my arms as I avoided the facilitator's gaze at all costs. And when, as so often happens, no one volunteered, the facilitator would begin scanning the room to select participants. I dreaded that moment.

Then, one day out of the blue, I found the courage to volunteer. And guess what? My fear melted like butter in a microwave as I confidently bounded to the front of the room. My colleagues chuckled, perhaps nervously, relieved that they had been spared. Immediately, I heard that voice in my head say, 'What's the worst that can happen?'

The answer, of course, was simple. The worst didn't happen.

From that day on, I vowed to put my newfound courage into practice without hesitation. Over time, these acts of courage built confidence, making larger acts feel more accessible.

## VISUALISE THE BRAVE VERSION OF YOURSELF

Visualise yourself confronting the challenge with courage and imagine the pride and liberation that will follow.

I have relied on this technique hundreds of times over the years – whether standing before an audience of 500 accomplished clients who, on paper, had suffered significant losses during the Global Financial Crisis, or deep in the throes of an IRONMAN race, utterly spent, as that seductive inner voice urged me to quit, go home and escape the suffering. I can say with absolute conviction that this single practice has been instrumental in my journey towards greatness.

Of all the moments when I've applied it, one stands above the rest – the moment that transformed the impossible into reality. That defining breakthrough, which I recount in detail in my first book, *UNLIMITED*, occurred in 2003. For now, let me briefly share that cathartic moment of redemption.

Taupō, New Zealand, 2003, was my seventh IRONMAN race – and my third in Taupō. Exactly one year earlier, I had experienced my greatest self-imposed race failure. It was truly epic! In fact, it remains one of the most significant failures of my life, and one I felt great shame and deep regret over.

By 2002, my IRONMAN performances were improving. I set faster times, and the dream of qualifying for the IRONMAN World Championship in Hawaiʻi was edging closer to reality. Only a handful of years earlier, I had been unable to swim a single lap of a 25-metre pool. Now, momentum was building – and so was my confidence.

Too much confidence, as it turned out.

I went into the 2002 Taupō race wildly bullish about my prospects. Somewhere along the way, I allowed that voice in my head to rob me of my dreams by quitting at the 150-kilometre mark on a long stretch of false-flat road while riding into a gale of headwind on my bike. The truth was simple, even if it was uncomfortable: I had started too hard and blown my race. Ashamed, I made excuses to everyone, who, in turn, graciously accepted them. However, that consultation was short-lived. You can convince anyone but yourself of why you quit. Only you know the truth, and you can't escape that reckoning. So, my shame was deep.

I swore to myself that I would be back to avenge my epic failure, starting with a five-hour run early the next morning. As I ran along the lakeside and the eerily quiet rural roads around Taupō, my meditative state brought the clarity and resolve I desperately needed. I would be back for redemption!

So, there I was, 12 months later, facing the same 3.8-kilometre swim, 180.2-kilometre bike and 42.2-kilometre run, but this time bigger and bolder than ever. Having been consumed by revenge and redemption for the last 12 months, I foolishly made many of the same mistakes again. For over an hour, that voice began to whisper, then shout 'STOP!' repeatedly. Ironically, this unravelled exactly as it had the previous year, on the same stretch of road where I had left my dream. Close to throwing in the towel again, I knew that my dream would die for good if I quit again at this pivotal point. So, I summoned every mental trick I could from my toolkit.

For a good few minutes, I imagined two scenarios: the first projecting myself forwards to later that evening, when I would sit in the hotel room describing the perfectly feasible reasons why I had quit, replicating the same excuses that I had quoted exactly one year ago, knowing I would feel an even more profound shame than ever before. This scenario cut to the very core of my being.

Then I conjured the emotions I knew I would feel if I found the courage to go on and finish – regardless of the time or outcome – even though I would once again miss out on qualifying for the legendary IRONMAN World Championship. I imagined the person I would become by refusing to quit: the man I claimed to be, the identity I believed was truly mine. That vision was so powerful that I found the courage and strength to carry me forwards.

In that moment, the equation became simple: stop and lose; keep going and win!

Nowadays, when I recall that brilliant day, it brings tears to my eyes, allowing me to indulge in a quiet moment of private reflection. I recount the event in intimate detail in my book, *UNLIMITED*. However, on that day, I found the courage to run my fastest ever IRONMAN marathon and finally qualify for Hawai'i after many attempts and several near-misses. If I had to pick my favourite passage from *UNLIMITED*, it would be my recollection of the Hawai'i qualification ceremony the next day, at which I arrived oblivious to my qualification status.

Often, life presents moments that require us to summon and exercise courage. In these moments, we instinctively switch to fear mode, imagining a negative, harmful, or damaging outcome. Fight-or-flight moments often require an instant decision, even when we have some time on our side.

Imagine for a moment that you are at the exit door of a small plane with a parachute strapped to your back, waiting to jump. Feels terrifying, right? At this moment, your heart will most likely be racing, as your mind grapples with the potentially grave consequences of the action confronting you. Your body is now undergoing a powerful chemical and physiological response primarily designed for survival. The autonomic nervous system regulates this response, involving a cascade of hormonal and neurotransmitter activity.

Unaddressed, the long-term or repeated exposure to fearful situations can cause chronic or repeated fear responses, like in PTSD or anxiety disorders, which can dysregulate cortisol levels – either too high or too low over time. This can also lead to hippocampal atrophy (affecting memory), causing amygdala hyperactivity and a heightened fear response, and can alter prefrontal cortex functioning (impaired regulation of emotional reactions).

As you can see, a great deal is happening when we experience fear, so it is hardly surprising that, without serious intervention in the moment and on an ongoing basis, exercising courage will be challenging. It wasn't until I met my partner, Lisa, a few years ago, that I realised that I was suffering in such a way, manifesting as undiagnosed PTSD courtesy of the many high-impact accidents I had sustained over decades. Often, triggered by sudden noises around me, I flinch or physically jump, which, in hindsight, I now realise is because of the sheer volume of violent impacts from accidents that have had a profound psychological effect on me. This is hardly surprising as impact accidents are among the top causes of PTSD.

Among the most effective techniques I've regularly deployed to inspire courage is visual rehearsal. Done well, it builds confidence and reduces emotional resistance before action is required.

During long training phases – often 11 months of the year, culminating in just two significant races – fear regularly raised its ugly head. It most often appeared on Sunday mornings, as I prepared for

60- to 70-kilometre training runs on a hot summer's day or a cold, wet winter morning. While not a life-threatening situation for a conditioned athlete, these sessions were daunting. Running for six hours at a pace of 11 to 12 kilometres per hour guarantees pain, discomfort and long stretches of solitude. The fear was not of failure but of the suffering I knew lay ahead, hour after hour.

In response, I learned to visualise two outcomes.

The first option was completing the key weekly training session, which would be accompanied by the commensurate sense of accomplishment, as well as many hours of adrenaline from such a significant physical effort.

The second option was to take the day off and do something enjoyable, which would alleviate the pain and discomfort, but not the regret I would feel later that day as I reflected on my choice to take the easier route.

This highly effective visual rehearsal technique works for me every time because I know that choosing the easier pathway becomes an increasingly tempting option until it becomes my identity. But I will never allow myself to go back there again. The optimal impact, though, came when I deployed this tactic in a race scenario that I had trained for over 12 months, where the stakes were higher and the temptation to quit far louder.

When you use visual rehearsal, ask yourself: 'What would I do if I were already brave?'

## LEARN FROM ROLE MODELS

Perhaps you already have role models from whom you learn and draw valuable insights regarding courage. If not, you won't have to look far to find remarkable humans who have lived with and demonstrated courage. Frequently reading or listening to stories of courageous people and understanding how they faced fear and acted despite it will help you grasp their mindset, which you can use as a blueprint.

It is also essential to manage your physiology, as fear is a physical response, and so is courage. Practising breathing techniques, grounding, or mindfulness to calm your nervous system in the moment can be potent, as a calm body supports a courageous mind. Another helpful practice is to share your fear or challenge with someone you trust. Verbalising fear can reduce its power, and a new perspective often leads to clarity and courage.

As I mentioned earlier, defining your 'why' and discovering your purpose will make finding your courage much easier. You can also ask yourself, 'Why does this matter to me?' and 'What's at stake if I don't act?' A strong reason often creates a firm resolve.

Find a way to accept discomfort as an element of the process. Courage doesn't mean the absence of fear; it means acting alongside it. Don't wait for fear to disappear – it rarely does without deliberate action. What matters is not eliminating fear, but moving through it with courage, without becoming discouraged when some fear remains, even after you've acted bravely. Over time, your experience will temper your fear, and what once felt overwhelming becomes manageable.

You could also start a courage journal or add a specific courage activity to your existing journalling to track your brave actions, big or small. As with any journalling, this will enable you to reflect on what you have learned over time, validating how much you have grown, especially in times when you are really challenged. Think also of training your courage like a muscle. Like strength or discipline, courage improves with repetition. The more often you act despite fear, the easier it becomes.

## SEVEN-DAY STOIC COURAGE-BUILDING CHALLENGE

In the spirit of Stoic philosophy, I have included a challenge that I undertook many years ago, when I believed I had demonstrated my fair share of courage. I was surprised by how much I learned. The challenge trains you to develop inner strength, moral resilience and clarity under pressure. Each day includes a core Stoic principle, a practical exercise, one or more reflection questions and a quote from a Stoic philosopher.

## DAY 1: FACE DISCOMFORT VOLUNTARILY

**Principle:** Courage is built by facing what we fear, not avoiding it.

**Exercise:** Choose one minor, voluntary discomfort today:

- Take a cold shower.
- Eat a bland meal.
- Wear simple, unfashionable clothes.
- Skip a minor comfort (e.g. coffee, snacks).

**Reflection questions:** What did I feel when I removed comfort? Was I still able to act well?

**Stoic quote:** 'Is this the condition I feared?' – Seneca, *Moral Letters to Lucilius*

## DAY 2: SPEAK THE TRUTH RESPECTFULLY

**Principle:** Courage means speaking the truth, even when it's hard.

**Exercise:** Identify a situation in which you would typically remain silent to avoid discomfort (e.g. disagreement, criticism, or awkward feedback) and speak honestly with calmness and kindness.

**Reflection questions:** Was I afraid to speak? Why? How did I feel afterwards?

**Stoic quote:** 'If it is not right, do not do it. If it is not true, do not say it.' – Marcus Aurelius

## DAY 3: VISUALISE ADVERSITY (PREMEDITATIO MALORUM)

**Principle:** Courage includes mentally preparing for hardship.

**Exercise:** Spend 10 minutes imagining one difficult situation you fear (e.g. illness, failure, rejection). Visualise how a courageous Stoic would respond – with composure, virtue and dignity.

**Reflection questions:** What emotions came up? Can I still act with virtue in that scenario?

**Stoic quote:** 'He robs present ills of their power who has perceived their coming beforehand.' – Seneca

## DAY 4: ENDURE WITHOUT COMPLAINT

**Principle:** Courage is silent strength in adversity.

**Exercise:** When faced with frustration, pain, or discomfort today, refrain from complaining. Endure it quietly and mindfully. Let your character – not your words – show your strength.

**Reflection questions:** Did I complain today? Did silence make me stronger or weaker?

**Stoic quote:** 'Don't let your misfortune make you miserable, and don't make others suffer with you.' – Epictetus (paraphrased)

## DAY 5: DO THE RIGHT THING, NOT THE EASY THING

**Principle:** Moral courage means choosing virtue over ease.

**Exercise:** Look for a moment today when doing what's right is harder than doing what's easy (e.g. returning a favour, apologising, staying late to help). Choose the more challenging, better path.

**Reflection questions:** Did I choose ease or principle today? What did it cost me to do what's right?

**Stoic quote:** 'Difficulties show what men are.' – Epictetus

## DAY 6: ACCEPT WHAT YOU CANNOT CONTROL

**Principle:** Courage is living without fear of fate.

**Exercise:** Notice something today that frustrates or worries you but is outside your control (e.g. a delay, a rejection, someone else's anger). Accept it. Say: 'This is not up to me. I accept it with courage.'

**Reflection questions:** Did I waste energy resisting the uncontrollable? Could I have faced it better?

**Stoic quote:** 'Make the best use of what is in your power and take the rest as it happens.' – Epictetus

## DAY 7: REMEMBER DEATH (MEMENTO MORI)

**Principle:** Courage comes from living in full awareness of death.

**Exercise:** Take 10 to 15 minutes to reflect on your mortality. Write a short note or journal entry, imagining today is your last full day. What would you do differently? What matters most?

**Reflection question:** Am I living with courage, or just existing with fear and habit?

**Stoic quote:** 'You could leave life right now. Let that determine what you do and say and think.' – Marcus Aurelius

**Optional exercise – daily courage journal template:** At the end of each day, journal: What did I fear today, and how did I face it? What challenge strengthened my courage? How will I act with greater resolve tomorrow?

Later, I will share the enormous power of replacing the doubt, failure, apathy and negativity that may be created by circumstances you have little or no control over with optimism, stoicism and the motivation to channel adversity into hope, action and solutions. Remember, courage is the ability to overcome, or at least become the master of, your fears and not let the things in your life rob you of your potential and greatness.

Courage, then, is not a gift reserved for the chosen few. It is a muscle available to all of us, strengthened each time we refuse to surrender to the easier path. Sometimes it roars in the trenches, in courtrooms, in hospital wards and open oceans. More often, it appears in far quieter places: in parked cars outside swimming pools, in offices where a truth needs to be spoken, in living rooms where a dream is finally admitted out loud. Each moment you act despite fear, no matter how small it seems, you are voting for a different future self.

With practice, courage becomes less about dramatic heroism and more about daily alignment. It is choosing the hard conversation over silent resentment, the early alarm over another excuse, the risk of failure over the certainty of regret. It is saying yes when everything in you wants to stall, and no when the world demands your compliance at the cost of your integrity. Bit by bit, these decisions stitch together a new identity – one in which you no longer need to boast about what you 'could have' done, because you are quietly, consistently doing it.

You will never completely banish fear, and you don't need to. Fear is part of being human. What matters is whether you allow it to dictate the limits of your life. Purpose will steady your hand. Logic will temper the story your emotions try to tell. Habits and practices will help you act before doubt has time to negotiate you back into smallness. But in the end, it always comes down to a choice only you can make in those four seconds between impulse and retreat.

So, when the moment arrives – and it will – when your heart is racing, your palms are sweating and the old voice of regret whispers that it's safer to stay where you are, remember this: you have been here before, and you will be here again. Each time, you are being invited to decide who you are becoming – not what you *say* you value, not what you *promise* you'll do 'one day', but what you are *willing* to do *now*.

Courage, in the end, is not about conquest or bravado. It is about truth – about living a life that is congruent with who you know you could be. Fear will always knock; courage is the hand that opens the door and walks out anyway.

Greatness doesn't care how afraid you are. It cares only that when the moment comes, you choose to move.

## *REFLECTION, ACTION AND GROWTH*

### CHOOSE COURAGE OVER COMFORT

**Reflection:** Where in your life right now are you choosing comfort over courage?

**Action:** Identify the specific situation. Ask: What exactly am I afraid of? If I rank that fear honestly (on the 'shark to mosquito' scale), how serious is it really?

### LOOK 12 MONTHS AHEAD

**Reflection:** If you project forwards 12 months, what will you regret more: acting and failing, or staying safe and never trying?

**Action:** Based on that, what is one meaningful, uncomfortable step you can take this week that aligns with who you *say* you want to be?

### PRACTISE MICRO-COURAGE

**Reflection:** What is one 'micro-courage' act you can take in the next 24 hours?

**Action:** Write down what action you will take (e.g. a challenging conversation, volunteering to speak, making a decision you've been avoiding, or starting something you've been postponing) and when you will do it. Debrief in your journal afterwards.

### LET PURPOSE GUIDE COURAGE

**Purpose:** How clearly is your purpose guiding your courage, actions and decisions?

**Action:** Finish this sentence truthfully: 'This scares me, but it matters because…'

Choose one Stoic-style practice (e.g. visualising adversity, accepting what I can't control, silent endurance) to use next time fear shows up.

SS GREAT
ATNESS G
SS GREAT
ATNESS G
SS GREAT
ATNESS G
SS GREAT
ATNESS G

# CHAPTER 4
# MINDSET

***'IT IS NOT THE MOUNTAIN THAT WE CONQUER BUT OURSELVES.'* - SIR EDMUND HILLARY**

If you have any ambition of achieving greatness, then developing and nurturing your mindset must sit at the top of your list. Greatness, happiness and fulfilment critically depend on your mindset. Greatness begins and ends with your state of mind, which is why I regard this chapter as critical as any step.

Mindset is the soil from which every great life grows. It is the invisible architecture behind every act of endurance, courage and creation. Everything we become begins in thought, in the stories we tell ourselves about what is possible, who we are and what we deserve. If the body is the instrument of action, the mind is the conductor that decides what music will be played; it decides what limits will be honoured and what dreams will be pursued. Change the mind, and the entire composition of life changes with it.

Alongside purpose and courage, mindset is the most significant driver of greatness because it shapes how a person interprets challenges, failures and opportunities. Specifically, mindset defines how people respond to challenges and can be generally categorised as either a 'growth' mindset or a 'fixed' mindset. It also enables transforming failure into learning, drives consistency and resilience, shapes vision and purpose, and equips leaders to influence others through exemplary leadership.

The earliest and most influential traditions concerned with the development of the mind emerged between the 6th and 3rd centuries BCE. Among the earliest were the Eastern philosophies of Buddhism and Taoism, which emerged in the 6th century BCE, laying the groundwork for others to follow. Buddhism teaches that the mind is malleable and that suffering comes from untrained mental habits. Through mindfulness and effort, people can transform themselves. A core principle of Buddhism is that thoughts play a decisive role in shaping one's character and life experience: 'What you think, you become'. Taoism, however, encourages living in harmony with life and developing inner strength and balance through perspective and self-awareness.

These Eastern traditions were followed by ancient Greek philosophy in the 4th century BCE, particularly through the work of Socrates, Plato and Aristotle. While there were common elements of mind development, they each saw the world slightly differently. Socrates believed in the power of questioning and self-examination to develop the mind and character. In contrast, Plato emphasised that knowledge is not fixed and that people can learn and grow through reason and education. Aristotle taught that virtue is developed through habit and practice, not innate talent – a clear growth-oriented mindset. As historian Will Durant said in summarising some of Aristotle's teachings, 'We are what we repeatedly do. Excellence, then, is not an act, but a habit.'

The 3rd century BCE saw the early origins of Greek Stoicism, followed by the more famous and now popular Roman Stoicism, practised by key figures such as Epictetus, Seneca and Marcus Aurelius. The Stoics focused on developing a mindset rooted in self-mastery, rational thinking, resilience in the face of adversity and ongoing personal growth and improvement. They believed that people could train their minds to remain calm, wise and virtuous regardless of external events – very similar to a modern growth mindset.

## THE ARCHITECTURE OF INNER STRENGTH

Martin Luther King Jr. possessed one of the most powerful mindsets in history. His conviction was rooted in vision – not the kind that ignores hardship, but the type that sees beyond it. His mindset wasn't naïve optimism but disciplined belief.

He once said, 'We must accept finite disappointment, but never lose infinite hope.' That sentence is the blueprint for greatness and the acknowledgment of pain without surrender to it. His mindset allowed him to see injustice not as inevitable, but as an invitation. Every march, every sermon, every act of civil disobedience came from that inner architecture – a mind trained to see purpose where others saw futility.

Nelson Mandela's mindset was forged in confinement. In the beginning, he fought against his imprisonment, consumed by anger and frustration. But over time, he realised that the only freedom that truly mattered was internal.

He could not control his cell, his captors, or his fate, but he could control his thoughts. He could decide who he would become despite his circumstances. That decision changed everything. He once said, 'As I walked out the door towards the gate that would lead to my freedom, I knew that if I didn't leave my bitterness and hatred behind, I'd still be in prison.' That is the mindset made manifest, the recognition that liberation begins in the mind long before it happens in the world.

Burt Munro's mindset was one of relentless curiosity. He refused to see limitation as final. Each failure became data, each setback a lesson. His mind worked not against the laws of physics, but with them, bending them patiently until they served his vision. Where others saw impossibility, he saw opportunity. That's the power of mindset – it determines whether obstacles become walls or doors.

Munro's life was a meditation on possibility. He didn't dwell on what he lacked; he focused on what he could learn. He proved that mastery isn't about genius, but about mental persistence and the refusal to stop improving.

Diana Nyad's mindset was forged in salt and solitude. The ocean, vast and unforgiving, has a way of reflecting the mind's actual condition. Out there, stripped of comfort and control, she faced the rawest form of truth, which is the dialogue between endurance and doubt. She said, 'You can't swim across the ocean of life just by standing on the shore.' That was her mantra, her mental engine. Her mind didn't deny pain; it transcended it by accepting it.

Every stroke was a negotiation with discomfort, every hour a meditation on belief. When her body failed, her mind carried her. When her mind faltered, her purpose lifted her back. That's the paradox of mindset: it's both fragile and infinite. It can fracture in a moment, yet it can also hold the weight of entire worlds if aligned with meaning.

The Stoics understood this better than anyone. To them, mindset was not about positivity, but rather about perception – the ability to see things as they are, without distortion.

Epictetus taught that 'it's not what happens to you, but how you react to it that matters'. Marcus Aurelius reminded himself daily to 'be tolerant with others and strict with yourself'. Seneca wrote that fortune cannot harm the man who governs his mind.

They believed that suffering begins not with events but with our judgments about them. Change the judgment, and the suffering changes too. Their mindset was one of radical responsibility – an unflinching acceptance of control where it exists and surrender where it does not.

I've felt that truth most vividly in the long miles of training, the ones that break you down until your thoughts are the only company you have. In those moments, your mindset is exposed. There's nowhere to hide from it. If it's weak, it will turn against you. If it's disciplined, it will become your greatest ally. Over time, endurance becomes mental architecture. Every repetition strengthens belief. Every small victory builds resilience. Every failure, when faced with honesty, refines perspective.

Greatness doesn't care about talent, but it cares deeply about mindset. Talent can fade and opportunity can vanish, but the mind, if trained, tended and tested, will carry you further than anything else.

King used his mind to elevate justice. Mandela used his to forgive. Munro used his to innovate. Nyad used hers to transcend. The Stoics used theirs to endure.

## FIXED VERSUS GROWTH MINDSET

Although many thought leaders have contributed extensive insights and research on mindset development, the most widely recognised framework was developed by Dr Carol S. Dweck, an American psychologist and professor at Stanford University. Her work on 'fixed' and 'growth' mindsets was formally introduced in the early 2000s and popularised with the publication of her book *Mindset: The New Psychology of Success* in 2006.

Dweck had spent decades researching motivation, personality and human development before consolidating her findings into a simple, influential theory: that people's beliefs about their abilities shape their success in all areas of life. Her early research, conducted in the 1970s and 1980s, examined how children responded to failure. She observed that while some children rebounded from setbacks quickly, others were devastated by even small failures. These studies led her to discover the role of beliefs – especially how people view intelligence and ability.

As I learned early in life, the mind holds most of the cards in the game of life and of greatness. The reality is that you must develop and nurture your mind to find your best in life, or simply let the world around you dictate your life and become the victim of fear. For many and possibly most humans, mindset is the thief of both potential and greatness, as it was for me for decades. At the very heart of every human is fear, driven by a plethora of triggers that manifest in many ways depending on the degree of fear being felt or experienced. Fear affects us all at some stage in our lives, and our ability to take the necessary steps to keep moving or to start moving towards greatness. Consequently, we will focus much of our attention in this chapter on addressing fear.

# THE OBSTACLE IS THE WAY

Ryan Holiday is a multiple best-selling American author, marketer and media strategist whose work has played a significant role in bringing Stoic philosophy into contemporary culture. Writing at the intersection of personal development, philosophy and business, Holiday draws heavily on ancient Greek and Roman Stoicism – a philosophy focused on resilience, control and virtue. Across his body of work, *The Obstacle Is the Way* is, in my view, a must-read for anyone seeking greatness in their life. In this book, Holiday distils Stoic wisdom – particularly the teachings of Marcus Aurelius, Seneca and Epictetus – into a powerful, practical philosophy for modern life. The central idea is that obstacles are not merely barriers to progress; when approached with the right mindset, they become the path forwards. What follows are my favourite messages and philosophies from this book that have most shaped my thinking and practice.

## THE STOIC FRAMEWORK IN PRACTICE

### 1. Perception: How you see the obstacle

- You cannot control events, but you can control how you interpret them.
- Emotional reactions such as fear, frustration, or anger distort reality.
- Calm, objective perception restores clarity and choice.

As Epictetus observed: 'It's not things that upset us, but our judgments about things.'

When perception is corrected, obstacles stop appearing as threats and begin to reveal opportunity.

**2. Action: How you respond to resistance**

- Progress requires deliberate, disciplined action – not force or panic.
- Action is about doing what you can, with what you have, right now.
- If one approach fails, adapt and try another persistence compounds.

Holiday emphasises that momentum is built through small, consistent steps, taken despite uncertainty or discomfort.

**3. Will: How you endure what you cannot change**

- Some circumstances cannot be altered – only endured.
- Inner resilience is built through patience, humility, and acceptance.
- Amor fati – loving one's fate – transforms hardship into fuel.

Endurance reframes suffering as instruction rather than punishment.

Every obstacle carries a hidden advantage: a chance to learn, improve, or reveal strength. Holiday illustrates this through historical figures such as Ulysses S. Grant, Amelia Earhart, Thomas Edison and Steve Jobs – individuals whose defining breakthroughs were forged through resistance, not ease.

Failure, in this framework, is far from being final; it is a stepping stone if we choose to see it that way.

At its simplest, the philosophy can be distilled into these truths:

- Control what you can, ignore what you can't.
- See clearly, act rightly, endure willingly.
- Obstacles are not in the way; they are the way.
- Growth is inseparable from adversity; to wish away challenges is to wish away the very conditions that create greatness.

## YOU ARE WHAT YOU SAY: LANGUAGE AS DAILY STOIC PRACTICE

Negative words – whether thought or spoken – have a powerful impact on your mindset, shaping the way you perceive yourself, others and the world around you. Moreover, your thoughts and words will shape your identity, and, if left unchecked and allowed to dominate your mental state, they will kill any chance you have of greatness.

Negative language has predictable consequences, including:

- Reinforcing limiting beliefs, turning doubt into identity.
- Triggering emotional responses, increasing fear, anger, sadness and anxiety.
- Distorting perception, as the brain searches for evidence to confirm negative narratives.
- Draining motivation, encouraging avoidance and passivity.
- Straining relationships, influencing how others perceive and respond to us.
- Affecting physiology, elevating stress hormones and reducing mental clarity.

When you repeatedly say or think negative things, such as 'I'm not good enough' or 'This will never work', those thoughts harden into self-fulfilling beliefs that limit growth and success. Over time, this can create a default emotional state that's reactive and defensive, rather than calm and open.

Negative self-talk also exacts a physical cost. Persistent pessimism can drain energy, lower motivation and increase stress, often manifesting as fatigue, poor sleep, or mental fog. Spoken aloud, negativity can push others away, create conflict, or attract other negative mindsets – subtly shaping how people perceive you and how you connect with them.

## COUNTERPOINT: WORDS AS TOOLS

Just as negative words can harm, positive and mindful language can heal and strengthen. Choosing empowering words – even internally – can gradually reshape your mindset towards resilience, gratitude and possibility.

Around the same time that my life began forging new pathways, I became acutely aware of the power of language and its impact, not only on those around me but, perhaps even more significantly, on my own psychology and overall positivity. In essence, you are what you say, both to others and to yourself, and the words you use shape both your external image and your internal mindset.

To influence or transform your own mindset and capabilities, as well as how you present yourself via your demeanour to others, it's crucial to pay close attention to your choice of words and make the conscious decision to alter any negative language or self-talk – moving away from who you do not want to be and how you do not want others to see you.

From my own experience, there is absolutely no doubt that the words you speak to yourself both internally and externally, and the way you think, have a profound effect on your ability to grow and achieve, especially when it comes to accomplishing seemingly impossible feats. For example, if you think or say that something is hard, it will be hard.

At that time, I began to pay close attention to my interactions with others, particularly those I needed to influence in my professional career, and noticed recurring patterns in their vocabulary. As I delved deeper into the significance of their language and its connection to mindset, I became increasingly convinced that I could gauge a person's level of positivity and their willingness to change based on their choice of words.

Consequently, I concluded that most people never come close to realising their full potential, let alone achieving the seemingly impossible, because they restrict and limit their own minds. You cannot accomplish the extraordinary if your mind is constrained and hindered by negative conditioning from external influences. Many people spend their entire lives without achieving anywhere close to their full potential, simply because others and their surroundings have conditioned their minds to react negatively.

As you practise and nurture a positive mindset while adapting both your spoken and unspoken language, you'll become increasingly adept at recognising the mindsets of those around you. You may find, as

I have, that you can sense a person's mindset within just 30 seconds of meeting them. Once you've mastered your own language and thereby influenced your mindset, you'll easily identify those individuals whose abilities and potential will likely remain limited forever. These are the people who can drain your energy and positivity. If you lead a team, regardless of its size, just one person with a negative mindset can consume more of your time than everyone else combined.

These individuals are unlikely to reach their full potential. Nor will they be able to resolve problems or challenges efficiently. Instead, they tend to dwell on issues and may draw others into their negativity, perhaps seeking comfort in shared misery. As the saying goes: 'Misery loves company.' I've come to accept that it's my responsibility to reach out to such people to see if I can help. However, suppose those people choose not to respond positively to the prospect of breaking free and helping themselves. In that case, I quickly decide to move on and continue to surround myself with people who exhibit positivity, act with integrity, and embrace courage.

In 1999, I made a deliberate and conscious decision to transform my vocabulary – an act that would, in turn, reshape my entire mindset. Over the course of two weeks, I devoted myself to an intentional exercise: identifying words with predominantly negative connotations and removing them from both my spoken vocabulary and my unspoken thoughts. My goal was to uncover 10 words that no longer served me.

After much reflection, I was both surprised and encouraged to discover that I could identify only four. This, I realised, was a reassuring sign that my internal dialogue was already largely positive – there remained only a few lingering words that continued to limit me. Those four words were: 'disappointed', 'hate', 'can't' (particularly when directed at myself) and 'hard' (the most common word my mind conjured during training or racing).

Each of these words carried a weight that, consciously or not, shaped my inner world and outward actions. Here's why they had to go.

'Disappointed' is a profoundly emotive, judgmental and corrosive word – one that people use all too casually in everyday situations.

Many remain unaware of its toxic ripple effect, not only on their own attitude but also on those around them: family, friends and colleagues.

To say 'I'm disappointed' is to imply moral or personal superiority, to pass judgment that someone's actions or behaviour fall beneath your expectations or values. In this sense, the word is often used, consciously or not, to belittle, shame, or control.

Upon reflection, I realised how seldom this word was appropriate. Often, it was simply destructive. For that reason, I consciously and permanently removed it from both my vocabulary and my thoughts.

'Hate' is perhaps one of the most venomous words in the English language and a term that carries immense emotional and psychological toxicity. Yet it is used far too freely.

People frequently express hate towards trivial inconveniences: 'I hate the traffic', 'I hate Mondays', or 'I hate when the bus is late'. Each careless use allows negativity to infiltrate the mind and erode one's sense of peace and perspective.

When you truly listen, you'll notice how often this word is spoken, and how little it ever helps. I found that by erasing 'hate' from my vocabulary, I became calmer, lighter and far less reactive to the minor irritations of daily life.

The word 'can't' is not a limitation – it's a declaration of unwillingness. It doesn't mean you cannot; it means you *will* not. It reflects a choice to prioritise comfort over confronting challenges.

Whenever I heard myself say 'I can't', I began to question it. Was it truly impossible, or was it simply uncomfortable? I came to understand that can't is a self-imposed barrier, not a factual one. To remove it from my vocabulary was to reclaim my agency and replace resignation with possibility.

The phrase 'This is hard' is another silent saboteur. The moment we label something as hard, it becomes so. That single thought has the power to drain motivation, weaken resolve and invite retreat.

I learned that difficulty is subjective; it exists only in the mind. By refusing to describe tasks as hard, I removed the mental permission to quit. The task remained the same, but my relationship to it changed entirely.

Take a moment to reflect on your own vocabulary. What words, spoken or unspoken, might be quietly undermining your progress, confidence, or peace of mind? Which ones deserve to be retired from your speech and thoughts forever?

The words we choose shape the world we experience. Change your language, and you will change your life.

At this point, it would be beneficial to pause and consider words or phrases that might be worth eliminating from your vocabulary or speech.

## FEAR

Fear, whatever its derivation, is the most potent and prevalent killer of greatness. Fear can manifest itself in various forms, from paralysis and inaction to reduced creativity and low self-confidence, ultimately leading to conformity. If left unchecked or unfaced, fear will conquer, because fear is the greatest thief of greatness. Sir Edmund Hillary, perhaps the greatest mountaineer the world has ever seen, and the first man, along with Tenzing Norgay, to officially summit Mt Everest, famously said, 'It is not the mountain that we conquer but ourselves'.

At our epicentre is fear, which we must face and overcome – or at least take on at its own game.

The equation, therefore, is simple: take control of your fears before your fears take control of you. For much of my life, I allowed my fears to control me. I let them stifle my potential, dictate which road I took, or validate the excuses I made, all so that my courage could seldom shine. Most notably, although also partially governed by logic, fear sealed my decision not to pursue my childhood dream of becoming a professional football player in the UK. There is no doubt that this would have been a gamble at the age of 15 while studying for my O Levels in the UK, but my own doubts had already led me to it.

This was one of my two greatest regrets until I finally found redemption through facing my most debilitating fear – drowning. Through learning how to take on my fears consistently, I've come to realise that I am responsible for controlling my fear.

Imagining or visualising the worst-case scenario – like the Stoic practice – enabled me to rationalise, gain perspective and immediately minimise my fear. Having mastered this practice a long time ago, my immediate response to anyone who shares their fear with me is to ask, 'What's the worst thing that can happen?' To this day, nobody has responded with an answer that implicates them dying, which immediately discounts the most serious concern. Once the worst-case scenarios have been extinguished, I encourage the person to share the potential consequences that they envisage. Once established, we can then create a logical perspective and rationalise the threat, which is precisely what the Stoics would have practised. Rarely is the potential result ever as serious as contemplated.

The next step is to develop solutions and mitigation strategies that enable action. Beyond fear lies anything that you can dream of!

## UNDERSTANDING FEAR BIOLOGICALLY AND NEUROLOGICALLY

Now, let's take a deeper dive into the origins of fear, its impact on us, the physical and mental effects, and its influence on our lives, along with strategies and tactics anyone can apply to manage fear. Throughout my first life – my autumn, the one I lived for 35 years – fear was undoubtedly my life's captor.

Fear emanates from both the brain and the body, as part of a deeply rooted survival mechanism. It's a biological, psychological and emotional response to a perceived threat – real or imagined.

The amygdala, a part of the limbic system, plays a central role in processing fear. It scans sensory information for danger and sends signals to trigger a fight-or-flight response, even before you're fully conscious of the threat.

Once the amygdala senses danger, it signals the hypothalamus, which activates the autonomic nervous system. This leads to the release of adrenaline and cortisol (stress hormones), preparing the body to fight or flee, which increases heart rate, tenses muscles and breathing and redirects blood to survival-critical areas.

The prefrontal cortex evaluates the threat and helps regulate your response. In some cases, it calms the amygdala down, realising there's no real danger, such as public speaking. Often, public speaking terrifies people to the point that they will do anything to avoid speaking in front of an audience. However, under high stress, the amygdala can override rational thought.

Fear isn't always caused by physical danger. It often stems from past trauma or experiences, like failure or rejection, and it can create lasting fear patterns. This is because the brain 'remembers' pain and tries to avoid similar situations. Fear can also be learned (such as phobias) through repeated exposure to negative stimuli.

Humans can feel fear before anything happens, just by imagining failure, rejection, or danger. This is known as anticipatory anxiety or fear of the unknown.

## HOW FEAR AFFECTS MOST PEOPLE'S LIVES

Fear emanates primarily from the amygdala, the part of the brain responsible for detecting threats. It is activated by both real danger and imagined scenarios. Fear is a natural and necessary human response, designed to protect us. However, when fear is left unexamined or unchecked, it can significantly impact people's lives and hold them back in various ways.

Fear influences decisions, often leading people to choose based on avoiding discomfort or danger rather than pursuing their true desires. This can lead to outcomes such as staying in an unfulfilling job or relationship, or avoiding travel, change, or risk. Inevitably, this leads one to settle for 'safe' options rather than explore passions or dreams.

Fear also contributes to stress and anxiety. Chronic fear (especially fear of failure, judgment, or the unknown) can lead to constant worry and physical symptoms like insomnia, fatigue, or headaches. Further, it can also lead to long-term issues like depression or burnout.

Another common effect of fear is the formation of limiting beliefs. People start to believe internal stories like 'I'm not good enough', 'I'll never succeed', or 'People will laugh at me'. These beliefs become mental barriers that shape how people see themselves and what they believe they're capable of. Even if people do laugh at you, it's not the end of the world. With practice, you can convert such behaviour into motivation. This strategy has worked exceptionally well for me.

Fear of failure can prevent people from trying new things or starting something important. Some avoid taking action altogether as a way of avoiding potential failure and disappointment, such as not applying for a dream job out of fear of rejection.

Fear of judgment often leads people to minimise themselves. They may stay quiet, play small, or blend in as they're afraid of being criticised or not being accepted by others. A common example is someone who does not speak up in meetings, even when they have valuable input.

Fear of uncertainty keeps people stuck in comfort zones, even if they're unhappy, as the unknown feels scarier than a bad situation they already know. Typically, this leads a person to stay in a toxic environment rather than face the uncertainty of change.

Believe it or not, some people fear what success might bring – responsibility, pressure, or visibility. For instance, a person might self-sabotage due to fear of not meeting the expectations associated with success.

Understanding how fear operates is a crucial step in loosening its grip.

## SHAME

Shame and fear are closely linked emotions, and shame can significantly influence and intensify fear in several ways, often leading to inaction and paralysis.

At its core, shame often arises from the belief that one is flawed, inadequate, or unworthy. This belief leads to a fear of being judged, rejected, or exposed. When someone feels shame, they may become susceptible to how others perceive them, fearing social exclusion or ridicule. A person who feels ashamed of their background might avoid social situations due to fear that others will discover it and look down on them.

To protect themselves, many people attempt to hide their true selves in order to avoid further shame. This pattern gives rise to a fear of emotional vulnerability, as opening up could expose them to more shame or criticism. A typical example of this occurs when someone who was shamed for expressing emotion later avoids vulnerability in relationships, fearing a repeat of the same painful experience.

Having spent much of my life in a corporate finance environment where perceived strength is king, I've found that vulnerability has no place, as it's commonly regarded as the ultimate weakness in the corporate world. So, you quickly learn to toughen up and to hide any vulnerability you may feel, which comes with great consequences both for being a decent, compassionate human being and for growth. Now, away from the environment I existed in for 37 years, I've come to realise and accept that embracing my own vulnerability has enabled me to grow in ways I never imagined. Ironically, being vulnerable has become my ultimate strength and a catalyst for personal growth.

Past experiences of shame can create a deep-rooted fear of making mistakes or failing. The individual fears the emotional pain of shame returning if they fail. A typical scenario would be when a student who was publicly shamed for a poor grade might fear trying again, terrified of repeating the experience.

Over time, shame can create a distorted self-image in which a person fears not only external consequences but also their perceived defects. They fear their own identity – thinking, 'If people knew the real me, they'd leave.' Someone with internalised shame about their identity (e.g. related to sexuality, disability, or past trauma) may live in constant fear that others will find out and reject them.

Avoidance is another common response. By steering clear of situations that might trigger shame, people inadvertently reinforce their fears, as they never have the chance to disprove them. The more they hide, the more powerful the fear becomes. The most obvious consequence would perhaps be the avoidance of public speaking due to shame around one's voice, which leads to an increasing fear of ever doing it, compounding anxiety over time.

Ultimately, shame acts like a silent amplifier of fear. It adds a deep emotional layer, transforming fear from simple worry or caution into something personal and painful. While fear protects us from external danger, shame-based fear often protects us from internal exposure – from being seen, known, or vulnerable.

## OVERCOMING YOUR FEAR

Whatever the genesis of your fear, with consistent daily practice, you can influence and change this scenario to the point that your mindset transforms.

Like it or not, every action or reaction, whether positive or negative, is controlled by our brains. How we respond to situations, whether trivial or significant, is determined to a certain extent by logic and fact. For example, decades of research on how people make buying decisions suggests that decisions are formulated with 70 per cent emotional bias and 30 per cent logical bias. That's what it is to be human. Over the course of a lifetime, our decisions, actions and reactions contribute to hundreds of thousands of such incidents.

Our ability to survive or thrive in the face of daily challenges is greatly influenced by our mood, which is shaped by our state of mind and where we sit on the positivity scale at any given moment.

Hormones play a crucial role in shaping moods and promoting positivity by producing chemicals from various glands throughout the body. They travel through the bloodstream, serving as messengers and participating in numerous bodily processes. One of these essential functions is helping regulate our mood.

Several hormones are known to help promote positive feelings, including happiness and pleasure. These are often referred to as the body's 'happy hormones' and include:

- **Dopamine.** Known as the 'feel-good' hormone, dopamine is a neurotransmitter that's an integral part of your brain's reward system. It's associated with pleasurable sensations, learning, memory, and other cognitive functions.

- **Serotonin.** This hormone and neurotransmitter helps regulate your mood as well as your sleep, appetite, digestion, learning ability, and memory.
- **Oxytocin.** Often called the 'love hormone', oxytocin is essential for childbirth, breastfeeding and strong parent–child bonding. It can also help promote trust, empathy and bonding in relationships. Levels generally increase with physical affection.
- **Endorphins.** These hormones are your body's natural pain reliever, which your body produces in response to stress or discomfort. Levels may also increase when you engage in reward-producing activities such as eating, working out, or having sex.

Serotonin, dopamine, endorphins and oxytocin all help promote happiness and pleasure while reducing depression and anxiety. You can naturally boost these feel-good hormones with simple activities. With that in mind, let's look at practical ways to support the natural production of these mood-boosting hormones. Whatever you decide to implement, give it a shot today.

## GET OUTSIDE AND SEEK SUNLIGHT

Spending time outdoors, particularly in natural light, can boost your serotonin levels. Exposure to sunlight, with sufficient UV protection, plays an important role in regulating mood and emotional wellbeing. Being outside in the sunshine and around nature is my absolute favourite 'feel-good' pastime. The only activity that tops this for me is running in sunshine and among nature. For me, that cures anything and everything.

According to extensive research, exposure to ultraviolet (UV) radiation from the sun can increase serotonin production. You can try spending time outside at least a few times a week, for a minimum of 20 to 30 minutes each time. Try exploring a new neighbourhood, beach, or park if you're tired of the same old sights.

## MOVE YOUR BODY

Making time for exercise has multiple physical health benefits, which we will explore in more detail in Chapter 11: Movement. It can also have a positive impact on emotional wellbeing. If you've heard of a 'runner's high', you might already know about the link between exercise and endorphin release. I can assure you that a runner's high is very much a thing. But exercise doesn't just work on endorphins. Regular physical activity can also increase your dopamine and serotonin levels, making it a great option to boost your happy hormones.

## LAUGH MORE OFTEN

Laughing with a friend or simply laughing on your own or while watching a movie is an effective antidote to many negative states of mind. Who hasn't heard the old saying, 'Laughter is the best medicine'? Of course, laughter won't treat ongoing health issues, but it can help relieve feelings of anxiety or stress and improve a low mood by boosting dopamine and endorphin levels.

Life has dealt me some serious hands, not all of which I can share publicly, and I've had to overcome many situations and events that required laser-like focus and resilience. As a result, humour was rarely a priority, but Lisa has brought laughter to my life, and it has been life-changing at such an advanced age. One of my greatest pleasures these days materialises when I'm sitting next to Lisa on the couch at night, hearing her infectious, rapturous bouts of laughter as she scrolls through hilarious reels on Instagram.

Research has shown that social laughter can trigger endorphin release. So, share that funny video, dust off your joke book, or watch a comedy special with a friend or partner. There is also a bonus when you can bond over something hilarious with a loved one, which might even trigger oxytocin release.

## LISTEN TO OR MAKE MUSIC

Listening to music can also give more than one of your happy hormones a boost. Listening to any music, especially music that moves you, can increase dopamine production in your brain. The positive change that music brings about, elevating your mood, can increase serotonin production. You may also experience an endorphin release while performing music, especially in a large group. For example, a 2016 study by Trusted Source found that choir members experienced increased endorphin release during rehearsals.

While I have always loved music, Lisa has also brought a newfound obsession and love of music to my life, along with her irresistible, infectious humour. These days, we attend many live gigs – notably smaller, intimate settings where you are only metres from an artist – on average, once a month. Sometimes we fly around Australia or internationally to hear remarkable musicians; such experiences bring joy to our lives.

## MEDITATE

If you're familiar with meditation, you might already know of its many wellness benefits – from improving sleep to reducing stress. It comes in many forms, from traditional practices such as yoga to various other available formats, with many effective apps also available. Meditation, for me, is movement and exercise. That is my playground.

Not sure how to start? It's not as complicated as you might think. You don't even need to sit still, though it can help when you're first starting. Begin with a few quiet minutes of focused breathing or mindful movement and build from there.

## PRIORITISE SLEEP

Not getting enough quality sleep will most likely affect your health in multiple ways. For one, it can contribute to hormonal imbalances, particularly dopamine regulation. This can harm both your mood and physical health. Setting aside seven to nine hours each night for sleep can help restore the balance of hormones in your body, which will likely help you feel better.

If you find it challenging to get a good night's sleep, try:

- going to bed and getting up around the same time every day
- creating a quiet, restful sleeping environment (try reducing light, noise and screens)
- decreasing caffeine intake, especially in the afternoon and evening.

## MANAGE STRESS

It's normal to experience some stress from time to time. Managed stress can be beneficial as it creates an incentive to self-improve or take the next step. As discussed earlier, creating perspective is a highly effective technique in managing and contextualising stress and worry. But living with regular stress or dealing with highly stressful life events can cause drops in dopamine and serotonin production. This can negatively impact your health and mood, making it more challenging to cope with stress. If you're under a lot of stress, the American Psychological Association recommends:

- taking short breaks from the source of stress
- laughter
- taking 20 minutes for a walk, run, bike ride, or other physical activity
- meditation
- social interaction.

Any of these approaches can help relieve stress while boosting serotonin, dopamine and endorphin levels.

## GET A MASSAGE

If you enjoy a massage, as I do, there's one more reason to get one: massage can boost all four of your happy hormones. According to studies, massage boosts endorphins and oxytocin. Older research found that massage also increases serotonin and dopamine. You can get these benefits from a massage by a licensed massage therapist, but you can also get a massage from a partner for some extra oxytocin.

## LEGACY

For most humans, change is both confronting and challenging. As we age, many of us experience a decline in passion and appetite, along with reduced energy, which hinders our ability to pursue meaningful ambitions. It's almost as if we've come to accept our current state, recognising that our potential diminishes with age, and perhaps we should take our lot in life. My observation is that most of us begin our lives, or at least early adulthood, with ambitions and hopes for our future. As we ardently navigate the challenges that independence, career, relationships, health and fitness, family and life throw at us, each tenet of our life will have peaks and troughs. For the most part, we see an upward trend in many of these tenets.

Whether due to random circumstances, self-imposed constraints through poor choices, or the natural ebb and flow of our effort, not everyone will experience a steady upward rise. Eventually, some of these areas will flatline and then decline, unless there is serious self-intervention or support from those around us – or both. Sometimes, though, a moment comes when acceptance and a diminishing hope for better set in. As this occurs across various facets of our lives, the status quo becomes increasingly challenging to maintain, leading to emotional, psychological and physical decline.

I find these symptoms are easily identifiable in a person and are most evident in their eyes and demeanour. Conversely, the same can be said of a person who continues to aspire and strive in one or more of these areas as they age. Most times, you can see it in their eyes. Although the key tenets of our lives are inseparable due to their overlap and intersection with other areas, both positive and negative, they can be separated for analysis, focus, goal setting and development, and therefore improved with ardent focus and commitment.

During my corporate career in financial services, I was fortunate to encounter many remarkable individuals, including athletes, explorers and survivors of the most traumatic circumstances. Each of them found the courage and fortitude to thrive in the most devastating environments and circumstances. I would listen intensely and observe in awe, captivated by their stories.

As I saw a similar awe on each face in the audience when presenting at conferences, I wondered what others were feeling and thinking. Most often, you could hear a pin drop among the attendees, such was the intensity of the emotions that filled the air. Attendees sat transfixed, some busily writing notes. However, as I looked around and discussed the merits of the presentation afterwards with attendees, I realised that, despite the inspiration and goodwill, little action would occur once they returned to their everyday lives, when the status quo would prevail over their newfound enthusiasm. Essentially, no change! Their notes would be forgotten and eventually filed away as the conference notepad disappeared under the clutter of a desk or tucked away in a drawer.

My curiosity about this pattern of inertia and inaction – this strange disconnection between those in the audience and the remarkable humans who move them so deeply – has never faded. For decades, I wondered why so little truly changed once the applause died and life resumed. In searching for answers and recognising my own reflection in that same inaction, I stumbled upon my purpose, and crucially, I stopped measuring myself against others.

When I say 'others', I mean those extraordinary men and women whose stories of courage and achievement I've described in previous chapters. Over time, I came to understand that comparison is the thief of joy. Their greatness should never cast a shadow over your own potential. You must resist the urge to diminish your path by comparing it to theirs.

Ultimately, I learned to let go of comparison and turn my focus inwards – towards who I was and who I was determined to become.

Looking back for a moment, what would you tell your 18-year-old self, or your 30-year-old self? With hindsight and wisdom, I am guessing you might suggest, or possibly implore, your younger self to do a range of things that you did not do or didn't do enough of. Perhaps it would be to love more, to take some risks, to be more conscious of what you eat, to exercise more, to invest and save more of your income, or to go after the dreams and hopes that you harboured when you were younger – that youthful, optimistic, hopeful version of yourself. But of course, you can't, which is not the point of this life reflection.

The real point of this reflection is to harness these potentially regretful insights and emotions, which tend to grow over time, and to commit wholeheartedly to becoming a better you. Because if you don't, there is every chance that your regret will grow to the point that it can potentially create depressive bouts as you age.

Working in financial services for many decades, especially as a financial planner in the early years, I experienced varying degrees of regret, mental anxiety and depression suffered by many retirees at a time that should have been their golden years, with the freedom to do whatever they wanted. This consistent experience then inspired me to develop a reflective practice I termed 'the Armchair Test', a simple, profound practice that changed the entire trajectory of my life, which I practised to motivate action and change.

So, imagine for a moment that you are sitting in your armchair at age 65. If nothing really changed in your life between now and then, how would you feel about your life and legacy? Take a few minutes to reflect and make some notes, then allocate some time to describing the legacy that would fill you with pride and joy. That should reveal the essence of your future greatness and your renewed purpose.

If this approach does not yield a robust and meaningful outcome, consider revisiting your notes on what you would advise your younger self, as there is still time to take your own advice.

Once you have a clear vision of your future greatness, you can identify the next step to focus on, which is where you need to jump on your Greatness Bus.

## THE FOUR-SECOND RULE

The Four-Second Rule is deceptively simple: make the decision within four seconds.

When practised consistently, this time-bound principle can evolve into a life-changing habit. It is a powerful antidote to procrastination and inertia.

Of course, not every decision in life should be made within such a brief window. This rule is best applied to discretionary choices – those moments when you're standing at the crossroads between the easier path and the harder, more meaningful one.

The purpose of this practice is to eliminate apathy before it takes root and to deny procrastination even a moment to catch its breath. When you refuse to give yourself the luxury of hesitation, you remove the option of delay and, in doing so, strengthen your capacity for decisive action. Over time, this habit becomes a quiet form of discipline – a mindset that naturally leans into challenge rather than away from it.

Let me give you a simple example.

The alarm goes off at 5 a.m. on a cold winter morning. You have a run planned, but the warmth of your bed feels irresistible. In that moment, your mind will search for reasons to postpone, to justify, to wait. That's when you invoke the rule: count to four and move.

Before you know it, you're up, dressed and running through the crisp air. Within minutes, your blood is pumping, your mind is clear, and you feel an unmistakable surge of gratitude for having chosen movement over comfort. You've not only conquered the morning – you've taken one more step towards the seemingly impossible goal that once lived only in your imagination.

This used to be a daily battle for me – until it wasn't. Eventually, I no longer needed to count or negotiate with my inner resistance. I lived by a mantra I repeated countless times: *To be truly successful in life, you must first do what you don't want to do, when you don't want to do it – until you do.*

In time, that mantra became unnecessary. The hesitation was gone. The habit was formed. I no longer needed to think about it. I just did it.

Starting your journey towards greatness, jolting yourself out of your comfortable existence, maintaining your enthusiasm and discipline for a few weeks after starting, or overcoming setbacks when the wheels fall off are typically key inflection points in your journey towards greatness.

People face many barriers when implementing and adjusting to change. One of the most common obstacles to getting started is feeling inert or apathetic when the task or goal at hand seems impossible, which can be debilitating. When faced with such a situation, it's natural to feel overwhelmed and believe that there's no point in starting, especially when you sense that you'll be driven to find the courage and make sacrifices for a better future.

If you are faced with this paralysing scenario, you must park your purpose in the background because the enormity of the challenge will likely render you inert. In such circumstances, I will demonstrate in detail how to create a 90-Day High-Performance Plan in Chapter 5: Planning. Your plan should drill down to the clarity of what you must do, breaking your challenge down into manageable daily tasks and actions. Remember, this is the very first step, which, as in my case, can lead to a quarter of a billion steps and feats that once seemed impossible.

Take that first step and at the end of the day, recognise your bravery and commitment, and congratulate yourself, because you started your journey to greatness. Tell yourself you will get up tomorrow and keep your promise. Do the things you know, through your planning, will guide you towards your greatness.

## EXCUSES AND REGRET

Excuses; I have made more of them than I have had hot dinners – and when you reach 62, that is a lot of dinners! The vast majority, though, belong to my first life, before the age of 35, a period plagued by a litany of poor decisions, bad habits and quick fixes that led to dead ends. Each path promised relief or reward, only to lead to another dead end, followed by yet another attempt that was doomed to a similar fate.

Those poor choices were driven by hollow gratification – things that felt good for a short time, until the gratification quickly vanished, only to be replaced by another prospective: instant fix. Although I am not entirely sure how long this chapter of my life lasted, it was probably around 20 years. Not only was my potential squandered, but my legacy fell far short of being the shining example that I could proudly claim. Mainly, I chose the easier road, chasing after shiny things and a sense of validation that was as hollow as a log buried deep in an ancient forest. Grim, hey!

To provide context for the slow demise of my latent talent – a casualty of fear in its many disguises and my repeated decisions to evade risk and avoid discretionary effort – the origin of that long and unfulfilling chapter of my life can be traced back to a single pivotal moment.

As I've discussed earlier, at 15, I stepped away from a long-held dream of playing professional football (soccer) in England. Despite years of preparation, I chose the safer path of completing my high school education. It was a decision made in reason but rooted in fear.

In hindsight, it was one of the worst decisions I ever made. For the next two decades, I replayed that moment endlessly, trapped in a loop of regret that served no purpose and offered no peace. Each recollection was a painful reminder of potential left unrealised – a haunting echo of what might have been.

However, when properly harnessed, regret can become an influential teacher. Over time, I learned to silence those futile thoughts of the past, recognising them for what they were: distractions from the present and obstacles to the future. Eventually, I transformed that regret into fuel – into ambition, focus and an unshakable sense of purpose. What once symbolised failure became the foundation of my redemption.

If you can't change something, the only purpose of that experience now is to learn, modify, adapt and grow. Anything that serves no purpose or holds you back must be let go.

Once you are confident that you have learned what you needed to learn – whether that involved adapting, changing, or both – it's time to move forwards. In some cases, learning also requires accepting responsibility, which often precedes change. This may mean revisiting a situation, offering a genuine apology, or having a difficult but necessary conversation. This is wisdom.

Beyond that point, holding on serves no purpose. What remains will only weigh you down and limit your progress.

I have since come to see that decision – and the years of rumination and regret that followed – as the catalyst for profound change, including my decision to never again make excuses that enabled me to take the easier road.

So, let's talk about excuses versus reasonable reasons. It is not an exact science and, therefore, requires your own discretion. It is essential to identify them upfront, or at least be cognisant of them, so that you can start the process of evaluating what you identify as an excuse and what you accept as a reasonable reason.

This is a critical exercise that can yield widely disparate definitions, depending on the individual. Importantly, this analysis will serve as your guiding principles and source of truth, helping you maintain daily self-accountability. While I am sure you can instantly begin to list a bunch of typical excuses not to do something, such as going for a run or to the gym, the most common examples that I hear from most people include:

1. being too busy
2. not having enough time
3. being tired
4. not being able to run (when not injured).

Primarily, these excuses may serve as validation for taking the easier road. That is not to say, though, that being busy earning an income or looking after family, for example, is not necessarily easy and does not come with challenges. For most of us, life is often challenging, and opting for a choice that requires less discretionary effort will inevitably lead to a plethora of consequences sooner or later. For instance, neglecting physical wellbeing will, at the very least, hinder it, allowing issues to accumulate and worsen over time. This can lead to significant consequences later in life, particularly as cardiovascular health declines and essential strength is compromised.

Of course, there are genuine situations and mitigating circumstances that qualify as *reasonable* reasons. These should not be ignored or dismissed. The key is clarity. You must take the time to reflect and establish what you will and will not accept as a reasonable reason. Once established, this framework becomes your internal referee – a steady guide when strength and judgment are required.

In essence, this serves as your internal accountability and motivator to continue making choices that enhance your life and propel you towards greatness. This will serve as your guiding light, helping you build positive, purposeful habits.

## HARNESSING REDEMPTION

It would be reasonable to say that I've endured my fair share of failures, brutal accidents, serious illnesses and personal adversity. There have been times when I have fought for my life, my dignity and my sanity – in sport, in my personal life and in business. However, the struggle and hardship, epic failures and sometimes humiliation have served to inspire my determination to make them count for something meaningful. I refuse to be a victim of life's random cruelty, of my mistakes, or of my failures. So, I welded my purpose into my mind and my heart, and I refused to quit.

Above all else, redemption fuelled me. Daily, I envisioned my redemption to the point that I could see and feel the euphoria I was destined for as I crossed each finishing line, banishing those demons. And in those moments of redemption, I would be reborn. Nothing could stop me. Nothing!

One of my most epic failures was at the World Triathlon Long Distance Championships. It was also the failure that became the genesis of my greatness.

I arrived in Nice, France, in mid-June 2000 to compete in the World Championships. Despite my attempts to stay positive, I was seriously sick. While medication could have offered a partial solution, I had reservations about taking anything so close to such a significant race. I also held serious concerns about the safety of my health, as some drugs mask the symptoms of illness, as well as the risk of violating International Triathlon Union regulations by using unauthorised substances.

This was a serious race, both in terms of its world status and its degree of difficulty. It consisted of a two-kilometre ocean swim, a 120-kilometre bike ride, predominantly set over the Alps just inland from Nice, and a 30-kilometre run – not a race to be taken lightly when in perfect health. But I had sacrificed so much to train relentlessly over the preceding 12 months to earn my place there. I had even gone so far as to secure a personal naturalisation ceremony with the Mayor of the Sunshine Coast to become eligible to represent Australia.

I made every effort to rest in the apartment with my feet up, hoping for a miraculous recovery. As race morning arrived, though, my condition had worsened. A dry cough had developed, my throat was dry, my sinus congestion was extreme, and my breathing was laboured. Despite my best attempts to put on a brave face, I knew in my heart that my condition was far from ideal for a race of this magnitude.

After setting up my bike and running gear at the solitary transition area along the Promenade des Anglais, I joined approximately 2000 international competitors on the rocky beach. We were all gathered for a mass running start into the water.

As the cold round stones of the Nice beach bored into the soles of my feet, my breathing was already laboured, but I was determined to give this my best shot. The starter's gun sounded, and the 2000-strong human wave rolled and then crashed into the water. The melee of thrashing arms and legs turned the water white.

Much of the next 150 metres was a blur, except for the terrifying experience of being repeatedly forced underwater as thousands of competitors fought for space. Panic surged through me. One moment, I was swallowing salt water, then the next, I desperately sought oxygen. A sharp kick to my face focused me again. Head now down again, my arms turned over, another foot in my face. Another gasp of air. For the next 100 metres, this was my reality, my hell. My sick state colluded with my panicked, elevated heart rate. I knew I was in deep trouble.

As I hyperventilated, face towards the still dark sky, I reluctantly raised my hand in panic. Almost instantly, a dinghy pulled up at my side, and I was hauled over the edge and into the vessel.

As it raced ashore, my panic and sickness were already overwhelmed by shame and embarrassment. The indignity was palpable as I felt the stares of thousands of spectators watching as I was carefully helped off the boat and carried over the stones to the medical tent. I had suffered a significant failure on a grand scale.

After a thorough medical check, I made my way back to my bike and gear in the transition area. At this point, I not only felt physically ill but also mentally shattered and deeply distraught. In that moment, I knew that this had to count for something. I was feeling devastated. I quickly realised that I needed to absorb and bottle the devastating emotions, using them as fuel to motivate me to make amends for this monumental failure in the future. I was determined to find a purpose for my pain and avenge this catastrophic day.

Every fibre of my being urged me to immediately pack up my bike and gear and go back to the apartment and hide. But I knew that would only make me feel like I was running away like a coward. Instead, I sat down next to my bike and, over the next 45 minutes, watched as other competitors returned from their swim and continued towards their dreams. That stung hard.

Once everyone had finished the swim and embarked on the main course, I gathered my gear and headed back to the apartment to rest. As the bike leg neared its end and the elite athletes returned to Nice, I positioned myself near the transition area and watched as all the competitors returned over the next couple of hours.

After that, I sat in a café – consumed by disappointment and anguish – and watched thousands of competitors run past on the two-run loops that made up the 30-kilometre run. The pain was palpable as I watched everyone successfully achieve their dreams and goals on one of the biggest stages. This hurt. But then that was the point; it had to hurt.

Later that day, I sat down to dinner outside at a quaint restaurant in one of the back streets, surrounded by ecstatic people who were laughing and celebrating their adrenaline-fuelled accomplishments.

The final chapter of my ordeal entailed watching the embraces and effusive smiles as the athletes wandered around Nice, their shiny finisher's medals gleaming around their necks. Mission complete. I would draw on those emotions hundreds of times in the coming years.

Harnessing the power of redemption in the face of multiple failures and setbacks is a complex and multifaceted process that encompasses both psychological and spiritual aspects. Redemption is more than bouncing back – it's about transformation, reclaiming meaning and rewriting your story. Here are some thoughts about how to tap into it:

1. **Accept the wound without resisting it.** Redemption begins with owning our failures without shame, recognising that a failure is sometimes our own mistake. This isn't about blaming yourself or others, but about honestly acknowledging what's happened. Above all else, avoid denial, defensiveness, or distraction. Growth lives in the clarity of truth.
2. **Reframe the meaning of failure.** Setbacks are often interpreted as the end. Redemption reframes them as the middle – the turning point. My philosophy has always been that if you are pushing your boundaries and chasing your greatness, you will fail. If you don't, then you haven't pushed your boundaries far enough. Numerous historical examples demonstrate how the fall often precedes the rise and redemption.
3. **Reconnect to what matters most.** Failure often disconnects us from ourselves, but redemption reconnects us to our core values, purpose, or faith. When failure occurs, try reflecting – *Why am I still here? What do I believe in, even now?* Whether spiritual or secular, find a source of grounding, a reason to get up again. Most likely, this will be your purpose.
4. **Tell a new story.** Redemption requires a shift from 'I failed' to 'I'm becoming'. The story you tell yourself determines what you do next. Avoid being a victim or being labelled permanently, but instead, reset. Tell yourself that this is only one small chapter of your story, and that you will move on to write the chapter you have dreamed of.

5. **Take small but courageous steps.** Even tiny actions in a new direction have redemptive power. They signal to you that the story isn't over. They also signal that you have courage and resilience. They tell you that you have grown and will continue to grow, and they give you hope. Start with one commitment – journalling, reaching out for help, applying again, forgiving yourself. Progress does not and should not be perfection-only, but rather momentum and another small step on your road to greatness.
6. **Forgive yourself and others.** Redemption and forgiveness are often intertwined. Letting go of resentment (towards yourself or others) frees energy for rebuilding. You don't have to justify the hurt, but you can release its hold on you. Forgiveness is a gift to your future, not a reward for the past.
7. **Serve others or a cause.** One of the most powerful redemptive moves is to use your pain to help others. It gives failure a new, noble purpose. Utilise what you have learned and consider investing in mentoring someone, volunteering, or sharing your story so that others can learn from your experience and wisdom. I can attest that redemption is strongest when it ripples outwards.
8. **Hold onto hope (even if it's fragile).** Redemption doesn't require complete confidence, only a crack of hope. Sometimes, just staying in the fight is an act of redemption. Surround yourself with voices that speak life, not doom, and borrow belief from others if you have none yourself. Redemption isn't about erasing your past but transforming it into a foundation for a new future. The very fact that you're asking how to harness it means you've already started.

Find your courage. Work on the step to greatness that has made you stumble, and one day, redemption will be your proudest and most effusive moment in life.

I've felt that truth most vividly in the long miles of training – the ones that break you down until your thoughts are the only company you have.

In those moments, your mindset is exposed. There's nowhere to hide from it. If it's weak, it will turn against you. If it's disciplined, it will become your greatest ally. Over time, endurance becomes mental architecture. Every repetition strengthens belief. Every small victory builds resilience. Every failure, when faced with honesty, refines perspective.

I used to think mindset was something I had to build from nothing. But I've learned it's already within us, buried under doubt, fear and the noise of the world. Training, reflection and stillness aren't ways to create a mindset; they're ways to uncover it. Mindset is self-creation. It's the daily decision to choose growth over comfort, effort over ease, truth over illusion. It's what allows a man in a prison cell to feel free, a woman in open water to feel infinite, and a mechanic in a shed to feel immortal.

In the end, mindset is not merely one step in the pursuit of greatness – it is the gatekeeper. It is the quiet architect behind every triumph and every transformation. It is the unseen force that determines whether fear becomes a prison or a teacher, whether obstacles become excuses or invitations, and whether regret becomes an anchor or a catalyst. Every story of human ascent – King, Mandela, Munro, Nyad, the Stoics and millions of unnamed warriors – shares the same root: a mind trained to rise.

Mindset is the beginning of all beginnings. It is also the return point; the place you come back to when the world breaks you, when failure humbles you, when fear whispers its familiar lies. It is the internal compass that recalibrates you when storms distort your sense of direction. And because it lives within you, it is the one element of life that cannot be taken, only neglected.

Greatness does not require perfect circumstances, extraordinary talent, or a life free of suffering. But it does require a mind that refuses to surrender its authorship; one willing to examine itself honestly, confront its own illusions and sharpen itself against adversity instead of collapsing beneath it. Above all else, it requires a mind willing to choose the harder road that leads inwards before it leads upwards.

You cannot control who you were yesterday. You cannot control the mountain life places in your path. But you can control the stance you take towards it. You can choose the mindset that lifts you, steadies you and calls forth the strongest, truest, most courageous version of you – a mindset shaped not by fear, but by possibility; not by excuses, but by action; not by comparison, but by purpose.

And when – not if – the moment comes that you falter, when old doubts return, when your past tries to reclaim you, remember this: the mind you need is already inside you. It always has been. Every mile, every failure, every step into discomfort has been revealing it piece by piece. The work now is to keep choosing it – again and again, four seconds at a time.

Greatness doesn't care about talent, but it cares deeply about mindset. Because talent can fade and opportunity can vanish, but the mind – if trained, tended and tested – will carry you further than anything else.

## *REFLECTION, ACTION AND GROWTH*

### CHALLENGE THE STORY YOU'RE TELLING YOURSELF

**Reflection:** Where in your life are you currently telling yourself a story of limitation – 'this is just who I am' or 'this is as good as it gets'?

**Action:** Identify one small, specific situation this week where you will consciously replace that story with a growth perspective (e.g. 'I can learn or improve at this') and then act in alignment with that new story.

### CHANGE THE LANGUAGE THAT SHAPES YOUR IDENTITY

**Reflection:** Which words or phrases in your daily self-talk (hard, can't, I'm not good enough, etc.) are quietly shrinking your potential and reinforcing a fixed mindset?

**Action:** Choose one disempowering word or phrase to eliminate from your vocabulary for the next seven days and decide what empowering alternative you will use instead.

### ACT DESPITE FEAR AND SHAME

**Reflection:** What fear most often stops you from taking the next step towards your greatness? For example: failure, judgment, uncertainty, success or vulnerability. How has shame – or the fear of being 'seen' – amplified that?

**Action:** Identify one small action you've been avoiding because of this fear and commit to using the Four-Second Rule to do it within the next 24 hours.

## LIVE WITH THE END IN MIND

**Reflection:** If you were sitting in your armchair at 65 and nothing about your current mindset had changed, what would you most regret not thinking, believing, or daring sooner?

**Action:** From that imagined regret, extract one belief you need to adopt now (about yourself or what's possible) and one daily habit you will begin this week to honour the future you who refuses to settle.

SS GREAT
EATNESS G
SS GREAT
EATNESS G
SS GREAT
EATNESS G
SS GREAT
EATNESS G

# CHAPTER 5
# PLANNING

***'THE ONLY WAY TO ACHIEVE THE IMPOSSIBLE IS TO BELIEVE IT IS POSSIBLE.'*** *– CHARLES KINGSLEIGH*

No doubt you've heard of the age-old adage: 'People don't plan to fail; they just fail to plan.' I have failed before, in the corporate world, in my personal life and as an athlete due to poor planning, but I have also found my greatness through diligent and effective planning.

Planning is one of the most critical factors in achieving goals and ultimately greatness. It bridges the gap between vision and action. It creates clarity of direction, forcing you to define what you want and why it matters to your purpose. It turns all aspirations into concrete, measurable targets, optimises time so you minimise wasted effort and resources, and keeps you moving towards a meaningful purpose. Powerfully, it translates vision into action, as greatness is never achieved by chance but through consistent, deliberate effort.

Planning breaks a big vision into smaller, manageable steps, making even the most ambitious goals believable and achievable. It also helps anticipate challenges, which are inevitable in any ambitious journey towards greatness. This includes foreseeable potential setbacks such as financial issues, competition, fatigue, resource gaps and time constraints, as well as developing strategies to overcome them. This resilience ensures that challenges don't derail progress. Time, energy, money and talent are limited, but planning enables you to allocate them wisely for maximum impact. It prevents burnout by striking a balance between ambition and sustainability.

Building discipline and consistency are both highly effective outcomes of a well-structured plan that acts like a compass, reminding you of what matters most each day. It encourages persistence, because you're not just relying on motivation – which fades – but on a system of actions that compound over time. Greatness is built on disciplined consistency, and planning provides that structure.

Planning also sets benchmarks, enabling you to track progress and adjust if you fall behind or deviate from your planned schedule. For instance, if you fall behind, you can adjust your tactics without giving up on the goal. This adaptability is key: almost no outstanding achievement followed the original plan perfectly, but all relied on having a plan to adjust in the first place.

Having a well-founded plan instils a sense of control and belief that the goal is possible, inspiring confidence. This confidence fuels persistence through difficulties. Many great leaders, athletes, inventors and changemakers credit their faith in their plan as much as their talent.

## THE TWO PILLARS

Planning can be understood through two core formats, or pillars: strategic and tactical. Both are essential for achieving greatness, whether in your career, training, or any other significant endeavour. Understanding how each works, how they operate together and how you can optimise both is crucial.

Strategic planning refers to high-level, long-term planning that sets the overall direction, vision and goals of an organisation, project, or individual. Typically, the scope will be broad and directional, with a time horizon of three years or more and no maximum term. Strategic planning often involves setting a clear vision and purpose, establishing long-term objectives and aspirational goals. Typical examples may include a company deciding to expand into international markets, a sports team aiming to become a championship contender within five years, or an individual setting a goal to transition into a new career.

Tactical planning typically follows strategic planning, outlining shorter-term, more detailed plans that translate strategic goals into specific actions, processes and resources. Timeframes usually span weeks or months. The scope will likely be much narrower and often department- or team-specific. Examples include developing a marketing campaign to capture customers in a new region, creating a training program to improve players' skills for the season, or making tweaks to a marathon training program.

## ENGINEERING THE PATH TO GREATNESS

Martin Luther King Jr. understood planning intimately. His movement was not a spontaneous eruption of emotion; it was a masterpiece of strategy. Every march, every speech, every moment of civil disobedience was meticulously prepared. The timing, the tone and the symbolism were all deliberate.

He knew that without planning, passion could dissolve into noise. It was the structure that gave his purpose strength. The Montgomery bus boycott didn't last a day or a week – it lasted 381 days. Behind those headlines were logistics, meetings, maps and timetables. His faith gave him fire, but his planning kept it burning.

Greatness, I've learned, is never accidental. It's engineered through intention and patience.

Nelson Mandela's planning was of another kind, forged not in freedom but in captivity. Prison didn't give him access to action, only to reflection. But even within those walls, he was planning – not his escape, but his nation's. He studied his captors, learned their language and anticipated their fears. He planned for reconciliation before the world believed it possible. When freedom finally came, he was ready not just to lead, but to unite. His planning had prepared him not for revenge, but for peace.

Burt Munro's planning lived in the margins, drawn in grease-stained notebooks, etched into metal and tested through trial. His was the planning of precision, not politics. Every component he built was calculated to withstand the impossible. His small shed in Invercargill became a laboratory of persistence.

He didn't have blueprints from engineers or approval from institutions. He had intuition, observation and the discipline of detail. His planning was not a luxury; it was a matter of life and death. He planned because he had to. Because dreams, left unmeasured, die in the realm of fantasy. That's the truth about planning: it's not about control; it's about alignment. It's about ensuring that your daily actions mirror your deepest intentions.

Diana Nyad understood that. Before her final crossing, she spent years planning every element – from nutrition and pacing to crew shifts and navigation, as well as contingency plans. The ocean, unpredictable and cruel, does not respect improvisation. Planning was her armour against chaos. Every stroke, every breath, every mile was rehearsed in the mind long before it met the sea. And yet, her greatest strength lay in flexibility: the ability to adapt when the plan met reality. That's where true mastery lies in preparation deep enough to allow freedom.

The Stoics called this 'premeditatio malorum' – the premeditation of adversity. They believed that planning was not about eliminating uncertainty but about preparing the mind to face it. Epictetus taught his students to rehearse hardship in their thoughts so that when it arrived in life, they would not be taken aback. Seneca wrote, 'The man who has anticipated the coming of troubles takes away their power when they arrive.' Marcus Aurelius planned his days around virtue, reminding himself each morning to expect ignorance, selfishness and ingratitude – not to resent them, but to remain steady despite them. Their planning was spiritual – a daily rehearsal of resilience.

To the Stoics, planning was vital because it helped prepare the mind for obstacles and challenges, focusing on what could be controlled – primarily one's own actions and thoughts – and living intentionally, guided by virtue and reason. This enabled one to strengthen discipline to face life's hardships with courage, detach from outcomes and stay true to one's character. For the Stoics, greatness was not the result of flawless plans, but of a life guided by purpose, self-control and wisdom.

I've come to see planning the same way. For 12 months leading up to a huge race, I prepare diligently every day. Before a big race, I also plan routes, nutrition, rest and rhythm – every detail is accounted for. But the true purpose of the plan isn't to control the outcome; it's to anchor the mind. Because no plan survives first contact with reality; the weather shifts, the body falters, and the unexpected arrives. And when it does, the value of planning is not in the map itself, but in the clarity it gives you when the map falls apart.

That's what King, Mandela, Munro, Nyad and the Stoics all understood: plans are not cages – they are scaffolding. They give shape to effort, direction to courage and rhythm to chaos.

Soon, we will take a deeper dive into tactical planning through the implementation of a 90-Day High-Performance Plan, which has stood rock-solid as the nucleus of my accomplishments over the past 27 years – including in writing *Greatness Doesn't Care*. But first, let's analyse the essential practice and art of goal setting, to which we can apply this process.

## SETTING GOALS

Let's begin by exploring the fundamentals of goals and goal setting, and understanding why they are crucial, before we examine the characteristics within our control. These characteristics will provide you with the most likely inputs to achieve your aspirations. As I cover these fundamentals and the supporting tools, my primary focus will be on inputs rather than outputs. This is particularly important in business, as changing inputs is the only action that drives progress and predicts future results.

The significance of focusing on inputs increases when goals and objectives are longer-term, or the pipeline is longer-term, meaning that actions taken today may not yield a definitive outcome for three, six, or 12 months. Far too many businesses, sales leaders and individuals are obsessed with outputs and results. The same can be said for many people aspiring to be fitter or healthier, or to improve their physical performance.

Among the many examples I consistently observe when posting and helping people in various fitness communities, I notice two key groups: those who constantly aspire to and measure short-term physical performance during training, and those focused on weight loss. While periodic measurement is necessary and relevant, performance at your best is not. Once you take your focus off the daily inputs, there will be consequences at some stage.

It is impossible to consistently and infinitely achieve PBs, at least in sports. In fact, having trained on almost 9,000 days over the last 27 years, I can say with confidence that there will be many days when you feel so flat that you will question everything. You will wonder how you can be your best again or doubt how you achieved what you have before.

The number of times most humans can perform a maximum endurance effort in a year is limited – at least at peak performance – because various layers of training must be built over time to prepare for it. Furthermore, our bodies and minds need time to recover from maximum effort, as epitomised by a typical annual racing schedule that an elite, professional endurance athlete would design and implement – or any competitive athlete, for that matter. Additionally, it can take many years, and even decades, to achieve peak or optimum performance, which requires planning, patience, diligence and relentless dedication. Therefore, careful, diligent and structured planning is necessary to ensure that what you execute today aligns with your purpose and long-term goals.

It's likely not surprising to you that setting specific, measurable and time-bound goals, documented in writing, is a practice followed by only a minority of people. So, why do so few people seriously embark on the journey of setting goals? And among those who do, why does their resolve often wane so rapidly?

To avoid a similar fate, how can one stack the odds in their favour, increasing the likelihood of accomplishing their goals once they've been established? In essence, the issue I've observed is a gradual decline in motivation as initial enthusiasm wanes. At this point, individuals often opt for the path of least resistance. This situation can be exacerbated when people fail to develop a comprehensive plan, which prevents them from effectively following the daily routines necessary to achieve their goals. It's essential to recognise the value and significance of each day, even when working towards substantial long-term goals that may be one or two years, or even a decade, away.

## GOALS AND YOUR IMPOSSIBLE

Once I had found my purpose, then my courage, my first impossible goal materialised. And when I say impossible, I mean that my old identity could never have conceived of achieving such a herculean feat. I was inspired and motivated, yet clueless about how to realistically achieve something so far beyond anything I had ever accomplished. Consequently, it was imperative to create a belief and build a plan through which I could start moving, day by day, towards that goal with some modicum of confidence. To enable this, I developed a framework and a high-performance tool that I have utilised in sporting endeavours and in business to this very day.

The model I have followed is as follows:

1. Understand your 'why' (refer to Chapter 2).
2. See your goal.
3. Quantify your goal.
4. Create a date to achieve it.
5. Make your goal visible every day.
6. Build a 90-day high-performance plan and review it every 30 days.
7. Believe you can achieve your goal.
8. Be relentless, rise each day and carry out your planned tasks without making excuses.

## SEE YOUR GOAL

What is your purpose? What is your genuine desire? If you were to reflect on your life at the age of 60 or 70, what accomplishments would fill you with immense pride? These key questions should seed your goal-setting process.

A goal can be anything meaningful to you. It can encompass any aspect of life, such as career, family, personal development in education or the arts, contributions to the community, fundraising for a noble cause, or even sports achievements. Above all else, your goal should align with and support your purpose. When setting a goal, the only strict rule is that it should challenge you and hold deep personal significance. In fact, it might even appear insurmountable when you first envision it.

## QUANTIFY YOUR GOAL

It's essential to quantify your goal. Be specific about what you want to achieve and make sure it can be measured.

## CREATE A DATE TO ACHIEVE IT

Setting a specific date for your goal is non-negotiable, but the timeframe should not be overly restrictive. Larger goals may take several years to achieve, with various sub-goals or milestones to keep you on track. The date you set should motivate you to work towards your goal every day, keeping you committed to your daily actions. Often, my most significant goals were five to 10 years away.

## MAKE YOUR GOAL VISIBLE EVERY DAY

Life gets busy, right, and it's easy for other responsibilities to take precedence. To keep your goal alive, place a physical reminder in a prominent location. This reminder will serve as a regular prompt, reminding you of the daily sacrifices you are making and helping you stay motivated and committed to your goal, especially on challenging days.

Creating visible progress proves to your brain that change is happening and progressing, even if it's in small steps. Importantly, progress releases dopamine, which increases motivation and reinforces the belief that you can do this. Dopamine has been my saviour on countless occasions, maybe tens of thousands of times, and my mind is programmed automatically to find positive reinforcement every day in everything around me.

I have employed this tactic over the past 25 years. One of my most motivating practices was creating a visual countdown of the days until a primary race or event, which I displayed on my desk. The power of this tactic lay in realising that every day counted and that the day I had been training so hard for would arrive before I knew it.

Like interest in a bank account, small gains add up. A one per cent improvement each day can lead to a massive transformation over months or years. One of my favourite quotes by James Clear, author of the bestseller *Atomic Habits*, nails it: 'If you get 1% better each day for one year, you'll end up 37 times better by the end of the year.'

Gradual, incremental improvements are not only necessary but also essential, as shortcuts are never an option for achieving greatness. Shortcuts and easy wins negate greatness. Indeed, for physical achievements, greatness is virtually impossible without incremental physical improvements. My rule of thumb for the quantum of incremental improvements in fitness is to limit physical effort to no more than 10 per cent week on week, as the human body is generally incapable of consistently increasing physical effort by more than that amount indefinitely.

## BUILD A 90-DAY HIGH-PERFORMANCE PLAN

If your goal is one, two, three, or even 10 years away, it's crucial to establish measurable milestones or targets to keep yourself on track and maintain focus. Building smaller, achievable goals will help you stay motivated and ensure you're making progress towards your larger objective. I will share a method for creating a 90-Day High-Performance Plan (HPP), which can be applied to various aspects of your life, including health and business, in detail at the conclusion of this chapter. In addition to a daily HPP review of actions, a deliberate and robust monthly review of progress against your milestones is essential.

## BELIEVE YOU CAN ACHIEVE YOUR GOAL

Belief in your ability to achieve a significant long-term goal may not be immediately apparent from your current position. In many cases, such goals may seem unattainable. Building belief requires creating a plan, setting milestones and establishing the foundation for your journey. While setbacks and challenges are inevitable, both minor and significant, this framework can help you maintain and rebuild your belief in your ability to achieve your goals, even when it feels close to breaking. But you will get back on track with this framework. Remember, believing in yourself and your goals is a continuous process that you can nurture and strengthen over time, even in the face of seemingly insurmountable obstacles.

Setting ambitious goals that may take five or ten years – or even a lifetime – to achieve can be daunting for anyone. In fact, it can be very easy for the goal to seem elusive and out of reach, derailing all momentum and potentially making your goal seem out of reach. It's not unusual to unintentionally squander precious time when you feel you have endless time on your side, which can lead to stalling or derailing the completion of your goal. Achieving goals requires consistent focus and a clear understanding of the daily requirements to maintain progress.

Belief – particularly during tough days or prolonged setbacks, which you will inevitably experience – is a precious commodity in maintaining confidence when the shore is nowhere to be seen on the horizon. Minor incremental improvements are crucial for building belief in achieving big goals.

You can also build trust in yourself. Every time you follow through on a small promise, you build self-trust – and that trust becomes the foundation of belief. Small steps, powered by discipline, create proof points that show you you've got this.

## BE RELENTLESS

Developing resilience and discipline is essential when pursuing your goals. It's not just about toughening up; it's a skill that can be learned and honed. Resilience involves building confidence and self-belief so that when you face adversity, you have the mental strength to persevere. It enables you to transition from doubt to belief, shifting from being overwhelmed by problems to focusing on solutions. While the path forwards might not always be clear, your resilience helps you find a way. In extreme situations, such as during long races or challenging training sessions, you will repeatedly rely on your resilience.

Consistent small actions reshape how you see yourself: from someone who tries to someone who follows through. For decades, my desire to find greatness burned brightly within me, although I hadn't yet found my purpose. But my discipline was inconsistent, and my habits gravitated towards pleasure rather than sacrifice. Short-term gratification was my drug. Consequently, my identity was 'I could have'. That's who I saw myself as, but my shame grew as I projected an imposter to everyone else, believing that would protect my identity. In truth, I couldn't fool myself, and it was me who really mattered. There is no escaping yourself unless you change.

Change can be small and positive, as long as you start and keep doing exactly what you said you would do. For example, something as simple as doing 10 push-ups daily can evoke self-talk such as 'I work out consistently' and 'I'm a disciplined person'. The next thing you know, you will be increasing that to 15, then 20, and so on.

Big goals can feel intimidating, even if they trigger a quick dopamine hit that fades without small wins, leaving you to conclude that your goal is just a pipe dream. The most effective way to reduce overwhelm is to break them down into bite-sized, manageable steps that make them feel possible. For example, you can reframe a significant aspiration and plan from 'I want to run a marathon' to 'Today, I'll jog one kilometre'.

At the age of 35, when I finally found my purpose, inspired by watching the IRONMAN World Championship on television, I immediately proclaimed, 'I am going to qualify for and race the IRONMAN World Championship!' My declaration triggered a surge in dopamine, a sensation I had craved for many years, and it felt terrific. Until, that is, a few hours later, when the enormity of the challenge crashed my feet back to the ground. History had shown that previous aspirations have quickly faded and died in my life without significant action and a plan that included small steps and milestones.

But this time was different. I knew unequivocally that it had to be. So, I set about building a five-year plan that would show me the pathway towards my new, seemingly impossible goal.

Each step forwards makes the goal feel a little closer. Your belief shifts from 'Can I do this?' to 'I am doing this'.

David Goggins, the brother of my good friend Trunnis Goggins II, is an exemplary human who began his transformation with small steps: walking, then jogging, and eventually running ultras. Each tiny win helped him believe he could do more – even after growing up abused, overweight and insecure. As he puts it: 'I didn't run 100 miles on day one. I ran to the end of the block and built from there.'

As proven by many remarkable individuals who have taken small steps to get started, achieving minor improvements builds confidence because they make the process real, manageable and repeatable. They prove you're capable. And when belief is built on action, it becomes unshakable.

In my own life, the moments when I've grown most have not been those that went perfectly according to plan, but those that demanded adaptation – the long runs that veered off course, the races that unravelled, the projects that failed forwards, and the endless chain of brutal accidents and illness. But planning gives you structure. Life gives you improvisation. Greatness demands both. To plan is to declare your faith in possibility – to say, 'I am willing to prepare for a future that has not yet arrived'.

Martin planned for justice. Nelson planned for peace. Burt planned for perfection. Diana planned for endurance. The Stoics planned for virtue.

## THE POWER OF PLANNING

Planning, then, is not a dry exercise in spreadsheets and schedules. It is an act of self-respect. It is you declaring that your life, your work, your health, your relationships and your greatness matter enough to be designed, not left to chance. Anyone can dream. Anyone can talk about what they 'could have' done. The difference between the person who looks back with pride and the one who looks back with regret is rarely talent. It is almost always the presence – or absence – of a plan that was honoured.

When you commit your intentions to paper, when you break the journey to a distant summit into 90 days, then 30, then today, you are doing far more than organising tasks. You are casting a vote for the person you intend to become. Each small action in your plan is a quiet promise to your future self: *I will not abandon you. I will show up for you, even when it's inconvenient, even when it's uncomfortable, even when no one is watching.* Over time, those promises accumulate. They become your identity. They become your legacy.

Of course, no plan will ever unfold perfectly. Life will interrupt. Injury, illness, disappointment and chaos will appear uninvited. But this is precisely why we plan – not to control the world, but to steady us when the world refuses to be controlled. A thoughtful plan gives you something to return to when you're blown off course, a structure to adapt rather than a dream to abandon. It allows you to bend without breaking.

One day, you will sit in your own metaphorical armchair and look back on the years you were given. You will remember not only the finish lines, the promotions, the races, the milestones, but also the ordinary days when you chose to honour your plan instead of your excuses. The mornings you got up. The conversations you had. The kilometres you ran. The calls you made. The small, unglamorous actions that nobody applauded but that quietly changed everything.

## REVIEW THE SUCCESS MEASURES OF YOUR HPP EVERY 30 DAYS

In addition to your daily HPP review of actions, a deliberate and robust monthly review of progress against your milestones is essential. Each monthly review should centre on accountability and honest measurement, assessing how your actions have aligned with the targets you set for yourself.

This evaluation should begin by recognising the progress you have made, even if it falls short of your original expectations. Growth rarely occurs in perfect, uninterrupted strides. Progress – however incremental – deserves acknowledgement, because it reflects movement toward your purpose.

A monthly review is also a powerful opportunity to be completely honest with yourself about the discipline you have shown in honouring the commitments you made each day. Celebrate the areas where you executed well, where your actions reflected intention and effort. At the same time, examine with clarity where you fell short, not with judgment, but with curiosity and resolve.

## THE 90-DAY HIGH-PERFORMANCE PLAN

The 90-Day High-Performance Plan (HPP) is exactly what its name suggests: a focused, time-bound system designed to help you maintain unwavering concentration on measurable objectives over the next 30, 60 and 90 days. Each phase includes clear targets and specific actions that guide you daily towards meaningful progress.

The purpose of this plan is simple – to generate positive momentum by converting your ambitions into consistent, tangible results. By breaking larger goals into smaller, attainable milestones, you create a structure that builds confidence and belief. Every completed action becomes part of your daily rhythm, transforming intent into reality.

Every effective HPP consists of three essential elements:

1. **Objective.** Your objective is your end goal – the outcome you want to achieve, including your desired timeline.
2. **Targets.** Your targets are the measurable checkpoints along the way. They should be specific, time-bound and achievable within 90 days. To sharpen your focus, break them into 30-, 60- and 90-day segments. This creates clarity and enables you to regularly measure progress.
3. **Actions.** Actions are the daily or weekly tasks that drive you towards your targets. These are the habits and behaviours that, over time, compound into excellence.

When your ultimate objective is still a year or more away, small daily actions can sometimes feel mundane or insignificant. Yet these steps are the foundation on which long-term success is built. Especially when starting from scratch, embracing early, seemingly minor tasks is essential. They forge confidence, create momentum and strengthen your discipline – the cornerstones of sustainable performance.

With many years of practice and implementation, here is an example that was only possible because of the relentless application of my High-Performance Plan.

Picture this: you have been running for hours through unforgiving terrain, with mountains rising before you, darkness pressing in behind. You are exhausted, alone, every muscle trembling. Your body pleads for mercy; your mind whispers: *Stop. Just stop.* Each step feels like a negotiation between collapse and willpower. Between you and that glorious finish line lies another 80 kilometres of the same unrelenting hell.

The super glue holding your blisters together starts to break down. A fourth toenail is loosening, ready to join the three already lost to the trail. With every jarring descent, your toes slam against the shoe's edge, more than 100,000 steps still to come. And then the voice returns, sharper now, convincing, almost kind: *You'll never make it. You can come back another day.*

But you know the truth, there is no other day. This is the legendary Western States® 100-Mile Endurance Run. You've trained for years for this single chance. You recall the countless dawns and the nights of darkness spent running while the world slept, the long, lonely miles, the celebrations declined and the comfort forsaken. This pain has been earned; it is part of the price.

You remind yourself of your purpose, that current of meaning running through your veins, the why that outlasts fatigue. You are not a quitter. You are stronger than this voice that lies to you. *Left, right. Left, right.* You focus on a single tree up ahead, then another, breaking the impossible into the possible. Step by step, mountain by mountain, you endure.

To understand the depth of that experience, imagine you've already run 100 kilometres, your mind waging war with itself for hours. The voice that began as a whisper is now a roar. The finish feels galaxies away, too distant to grasp. In those moments, vision alone isn't enough, and survival depends on focus. You must shrink the mountain until it fits inside a single step.

Eleven hours later, minus two more toenails, you cross the finish line. The pain dissolves into euphoria. You are reborn. That moment is etched into your DNA – a truth no comfort or currency could ever replace.

I've met that voice thousands of times. Sometimes I've silenced it, sometimes I've fallen to it. A handful of races ended with the dreaded three letters: DNF – Did Not Finish. Each one cut deep, but even in those moments, I learned.

When you're stripped to your core, and that voice becomes deafening, the key is to reset – to set a micro-goal, something so small that your mind accepts it. Run for two more minutes. Reach the next hill. Touch the next tree. Then reset again. And again. That's how you survive the storm. That's how you win battles most will never see.

Whether you're on a mountain trail or facing life's invisible climbs, the same truth applies: there will be moments when belief falters, when doubt seduces, when quitting feels merciful. But that is when you must fight back, not with grand gestures but with quiet persistence. One breath. One step. One choice to keep going. That is how you conquer the voice. That is how you find greatness.

To demonstrate the diversity and application of this highly effective practice, let's run through two real-life examples from individuals I have coached on the HPP's construction and application.

## EXAMPLE: BOB'S 90-DAY HIGH-PERFORMANCE PLAN

Bob is one of three financial advisers in a well-established small practice. Most of his clients were inherited from Sally, a senior adviser who has since become the General Manager. Sally built a successful referral partnership with an accountant she knew from school and recently shared the firm's ambitious growth plans for the next three years. She tasked Bob with creating his own network of external referral sources.

After some reflection, Bob decided to set a clear objective and map out a 90-Day HPP to present to Sally.

**Objective:** Build a successful, scalable referral partnership that generates two new prospect referrals per month within 12 months.

| TIMEFRAME | TARGETS | ACTIONS |
|---|---|---|
| WITHIN 30 DAYS | Identify and establish initial contact with 40 proactive accountancy practices via email. | • Research and compile a list of 40 suitable accountancy practices within a defined radius.<br>• Draft a professional and compelling email template.<br>• Send 40 initial emails and follow up with phone calls to non-responders after seven days. |
| WITHIN 60 DAYS | Secure four meetings with accounting firms that express genuine interest. | • Follow up with all remaining non-responders.<br>• Refine and clarify the client value proposition (CVP) to ensure it is compelling and easy to understand.<br>• Prepare and rehearse the pitch for upcoming meetings.<br>• Conduct a minimum of four meetings with interested firms. |
| WITHIN 90 DAYS | Finalise agreements with two firms to refer at least one client each by the end of the month. | • Finalise agreements with at least two firms.<br>• Request an initial client referral from each firm to commence collaboration. |

By approaching his goal through a 90-Day HPP, Bob replaces vague intention with structured execution. Each day's actions contribute directly to a measurable outcome. Over time, these small wins accumulate, creating unstoppable momentum that transforms ambition into achievement.

## EXAMPLE: JILL'S 90-DAY HIGH-PERFORMANCE PLAN

At 38, Jill hadn't run since her high school days, yet those memories remained among her fondest. She often recalled the joy and freedom she felt during evening runs at the local park with her group of energetic friends. However, over the years, the demands of a career, raising children and managing the daily rhythm of family life had left her with little time and even less energy to focus on herself.

Then, by pure coincidence, a chance encounter reignited a long-dormant spark.

One afternoon, rushing to grab lunch to take back to the office, Jill bumped into Alice, a close school friend she hadn't seen in more than a decade. Alice, it turned out, was lacing up her shoes for a quick lunchtime run. They hugged, laughed and took a moment to absorb how much time had passed. Jill couldn't help but notice how radiant, strong and confident Alice looked.

Back at the office, Jill found her mind consumed by the brief reunion. She felt inspired – even a little envious – and couldn't shake the image of Alice's vibrancy and health. That evening, she messaged her old friend, suggesting they catch up properly over coffee.

When they met later that week, Alice shared her journey. She revealed that she was training for her fifth half-marathon, just two weeks away, as part of her build-up to her first full marathon scheduled three months later. Jill was in awe. 'How on earth do you find the time, with work and family?' she asked.

Alice smiled and explained that it all began a few years earlier when a colleague invited her to a local park run. At first, she joined for fun – a mix of running, walking and socialising over brunch afterwards. But something clicked. The simple joy of moving again awakened a part of her she'd forgotten existed. From there, she set small, achievable goals, creating a plan that made progress inevitable.

Jill left that lunch deeply inspired. That night, she decided to reclaim her own fitness, joy and confidence. To achieve this, she created her first 90-Day HPP, centred on her long-term goal: completing the Sydney Half Marathon.

**Objective:** Complete the Sydney Half Marathon on May 23, 2024.

| TIMEFRAME | TARGETS | ACTIONS |
|---|---|---|
| WITHIN 30 DAYS | Complete two fast walks and one run/ walk session by the final week. | • Schedule three 20-minute sessions per week and add them to the phone calendar.<br>• Share the goal and plan with Dave [her partner] for support and accountability.<br>• Research and purchase suitable running shoes.<br>• Weeks 1–2: Two fast walks and one run/walk session per week.<br>• Week 3: One fast walk, one run/walk, and one full run session.<br>• Week 4: One fast walk and two run sessions.<br>• Create a simple calorie and nutrition plan to support energy and recovery. |
| WITHIN 60 DAYS | • Build up to three 20-minute run sessions per week by the end of the second month.<br>• Complete one 20-minute core and strength session weekly. | • Week 5: Two fast walks and one easy run session.<br>• Week 6: Two 20-minute runs and one hill run/walk session.<br>• Week 7: Two regular 20-minute runs and one short sprint session.<br>• Week 8: Two fast walks and one easy run session.<br>• Complete one 20-minute core and strength workout each week. |

| TIMEFRAME | TARGETS | ACTIONS |
|---|---|---|
| WITHIN 90 DAYS | • Enter the Mother's Day Fun Run and finish within 45 minutes.<br>• Accumulate a total of 70 minutes of running within one week.<br>• Complete one 30-minute core and strength session weekly. | • Week 9: One 20-minute run/walk, one 20-minute run, and one 30-minute run.<br>• Week 10: One 20-minute run and one 30-minute run, plus two hill or endurance sessions.<br>• Week 11: Rest during the week leading up to the Mother's Day Fun Run; complete the race in under 45 minutes.<br>• Week 12: Recovery phase with two light fast walks. |

By structuring her plan into 30-, 60- and 90-day increments, Jill replaced vague aspiration with an actionable structure. Each week delivered a small, confidence-building win. Within months, running became not just an activity, but part of her identity again – a rediscovery of self through movement and discipline.

Her transformation is a powerful reminder that the journey to greatness begins not with a monumental leap, but with one deliberate step – and the decision to take it.

## THE ARCHITECTURE OF A LIFE YOU CHOOSE

Planning is not about predicting the future but preparing for it. It is the silent architecture behind every extraordinary life, the blueprint that transforms wandering into direction and desire into destiny. Without planning, even the strongest purpose drifts. With it, purpose becomes movement and movement becomes momentum.

King planned for justice. Mandela planned for unity. Munro planned for speed. Nyad planned for endurance. The Stoics planned for virtue. None of them left their greatness to chance. They engineered it, one step, one strategy, one deliberate action at a time.

So it must be with you.

A dream without a plan is little more than a wish, but a dream supported by structure becomes inevitable. When you commit your intentions to paper – when you shape them into objectives, milestones and daily actions – you are doing more than organising your life. You are declaring, with quiet conviction:

My greatness matters.

My time matters.

My future matters.

This is the true gift of planning: it transforms hope into honour. Each task you complete is a promise kept for your future self. And kept promises build identity. Identity builds belief. Belief builds greatness.

Of course, no plan unfolds without friction. Life will interrupt, as it always does, with illness, exhaustion, doubt, or unexpected storms. But planning is not armour against adversity; it is an anchor. When chaos arrives, a good plan holds you steady, offers clarity and provides a path back to centre. It allows you to adapt without surrender, to bend without breaking.

One day, perhaps years from now, you will sit quietly and look back on the life you have built. And what will give you the greatest pride will not be the grand achievements alone, but the accumulation of days in which you honoured your plan – the mornings you rose early, the miles you ran, and the actions you took when no applause echoed. Those seemingly ordinary days will reveal themselves as the bricks of your extraordinary life.

So, plan your path. Break your impossible into the inevitable. Build your 90-Day High-Performance Plan and follow it diligently, with humility and courage. Not perfectly, but consistently. Greatness doesn't respond to intensity; it responds to intentionality. It doesn't care how loudly you dream, only how deliberately you act.

Every great life is designed twice: first on the page, then in the world. Planning is where you stop wishing, start engineering and quietly begin constructing the life you will one day be proud to call your own.

# REFLECTION, ACTION AND GROWTH

## CLARIFY YOUR LONG-TERM DIRECTION

**Reflection:** If you zoomed out to the next three to 10 years of you life, what would you *most* want to be true? How clearly have you written that vision down?

**Action:** Set aside 10 to 15 minutes to write one clear, specific long-term objective (personal, professional, physical, or legacy-based) and assign it a particular date.

## TURN GOALS INTO PLANS

**Reflection:** Where are you confusing 'having a goal' with 'having a plan'?

**Action:** Choose *one* crucial goal and sketch a simple 90-Day High-Performance Plan, including:

- one objective
- three to five measurable targets (30/60/90 days)
- three to five weekly actions that, if done consistently, would make success almost inevitable.

## ALIGN DAILY ACTIONS WITH INTENT

**Reflection:** Do your daily actions currently reflect your deepest intentions or your easiest excuses?

**Action:** For the next seven days, track one key behaviour that aligns with your goal (e.g. training, writing, prospecting, study). At the end of each day, ask: 'Did I do what I said I would do?' and write yes/no followed by one sentence explaining why.

## COMMIT TO THE GOAL THAT WON'T LET GO

**Reflection:** What is one 'impossible' goal that quietly won't leave you alone? What is the smallest, non-negotiable step you can take towards it in the next 24 hours?

**Action:** Name that 'impossible' goal on paper and define one micro-step to take (a phone call, a 20-minute session, a piece of research, a written commitment). Schedule it with a time in your calendar today or tomorrow.

SS GREAT
ATNESS G
SS GREAT
ATNESS G
SS GREAT
ATNESS G
SS GREAT
ATNESS G

# CHAPTER 6
# DISCIPLINE

***'IF YOU HAVE ANY MENTAL TOUGHNESS, IF YOU HAVE ANY FRACTION OF SELF-DISCIPLINE; THE ABILITY TO NOT WANT TO DO IT, BUT STILL DO IT; IF YOU CAN GET THROUGH TO DOING THINGS THAT YOU HATE TO DO, ON THE OTHER SIDE IS GREATNESS.'*** *- DAVID GOGGINS*

Regardless of age, gender, faith, wealth, or geography, there is one universal truth that binds us all: each day grants every human being precisely 1440 minutes of life. In a world otherwise divided by circumstance, privilege and fortune, time remains the one accurate measure of equality. Apart from birth and death, it is perhaps the most level playing field we are ever given.

Of course, the total number of days we receive varies dramatically. Some lives are blessed with decades, while others are cut heartbreakingly short. Yet within each day we are granted, we are all given the same allocation of hours, minutes and seconds.

How we use those minutes, however, could not differ more. For millions across the globe, time is not a choice but a condition of survival, dictated by hunger, scarcity, or war. Every waking moment is consumed by the fight for the next meal, the next drop of clean water, the next breath of safety. In such circumstances, survival itself becomes the full measure of a day.

For the rest of us, time is a resource over which we hold far greater control, though we often fail to treat it as such. Our days are shaped by competing priorities and obligations, but within that complexity lies the freedom to decide how we spend the most finite currency we will ever possess.

The difference between a life of purpose and a life merely endured often lies in how deliberately we spend our time. Each day offers choices, moments when rigour, discipline and intention transform ordinary minutes into extraordinary meaning.

The art of discipline literally transformed my life. Driven by my purpose, I pushed my mind and body to places I'd never conceived as possible. Discipline transcended everything that life could throw at me.

Despite 35 hospitalisations, multiple operations and broken bones, I never missed a single planned training session in more than two decades – unless I was in hospital or physically unable to move. My discipline was driven by an unstoppable sense of purpose. Even then, what counted as 'unable' was often a matter of mindset. I trained in conditions most people would have avoided – and, in hindsight, perhaps wisely so.

There were days I would fly 2000 kilometres, land, change clothes and run 18 kilometres home from the airport just to complete the session I had scheduled. I would leave a function at 10 p.m., rush home, and head straight out the door after a quick bathroom break. I once swam four kilometres in an eight-metre hotel pool, lap after endless lap, until it felt like battling a choppy ocean swell.

No matter the circumstances, I did what I had planned to do – no excuses!

Okay, let me stir the pot a little and throw this contentious claim out there: discipline is a fundamental value that shapes character and fosters freedom. Yes, freedom – contrary to popular belief that discipline stifles life! We will explore this in greater detail shortly, but I was hoping you could hold that thought. Another popular concept is that discipline is the key tool, or enabler, to achieving goals, which it is. Moreover, it is a value that shapes character, serving as a fundamental value that leads to greater self-respect and respect from others, laying the groundwork for a life of honour.

Without discipline, even purpose drifts. Passion burns hot, then dies. Dreams dissolve into excuses. But discipline – quiet, persistent, invisible – builds the bridge between vision and reality.

## THE QUIET ENGINE OF MASTERY

Martin Luther King Jr. understood this idea better than most. His movement wasn't sustained by inspiration alone but by discipline, the unrelenting order of thought, preparation and principle. Every speech, every march, every act of nonviolence required self-control to meet hatred with calmness and aggression with composure. Discipline gave his courage structure. It allowed his faith to function in the face of fear. It kept his emotions from overpowering his vision. His greatness was not just in what he dreamed, but in what he practised.

Nelson Mandela's discipline was forged in confinement. Prison strips away illusion. It reveals what's real, what remains when freedom, comfort and identity are stripped away. Mandela understood that the only thing no one could take from him was how he used his time. He built structure into days that had no meaning. He exercised, studied and reflected. He treated each sunrise as an opportunity to strengthen himself, physically, mentally and spiritually. That discipline became his weapon. It prepared him for the freedom that would one day come.

When he emerged, he was not broken but sharpened, and years of order had tempered his will. He was not consumed by rage because discipline had taught him to govern his impulses. He had mastered the most complex skill of all: self-command.

Burt Munro's discipline was no less sacred. While others rested, he worked. While others gave up, he refined. His life was a study in repetition, marked by measuring, filing, testing, adjusting and starting anew. He didn't need external motivation because his discipline was internal, rooted in his love for the craft and respect for the process. That's the thing about discipline: it's not sustained by adrenaline, but by affection. When you love the work, repetition becomes reverence.

Munro's workshop was his cathedral. His tools were his prayer beads. Every act of labour was devotion, with the slow, deliberate construction of a dream.

Discipline is not dramatic. It's not the roar of victory; it's the quiet scrape of persistence. It's showing up when no one's watching. It's doing the work when there's no guarantee of reward.

That's what Diana Nyad embodied each time she entered the water. Discipline was her anchor – the years of training, the relentless conditioning, the quiet rituals before dawn. Swimming is repetition incarnate – stroke after stroke, breath after breath – and without discipline, the sea devours you. Nyad's achievement wasn't born of talent or luck. It was built through years of disciplined preparation. Every small act of consistency was a vote of confidence in a future that didn't yet exist. That's the heart of discipline – faith enacted daily.

The Stoics wrote of discipline as the ultimate virtue – the ability to govern oneself by reason. For Marcus Aurelius, discipline meant aligning one's actions with one's intentions. For Epictetus, it was freedom from impulse. For Seneca, it was the art of progress – small, deliberate steps towards excellence. They believed that mastery of the self was the foundation for every other virtue. A man cannot be brave without discipline, or wise without restraint. They taught that discipline is not about suppression, but about direction and redirecting energy towards a purpose.

They built daily habits of acting with justice, courage and honesty, even when it was costly or dangerous. Marcus Aurelius, as emperor, demonstrated discipline by resisting corruption, working tirelessly for the empire's stability and holding himself accountable for every decision.

They practised constant self-examination, checking whether their judgments were based on truth or fear, vanity, or bias. They used techniques like negative visualisation (imagining loss or hardship) to strengthen mental resilience. For example, Seneca began each day with a plan for virtuous action and ended each night by reviewing where he had fallen short – a disciplined mental audit.

The Stoics believed greatness came from long-term, sustained effort, not occasional bursts of inspiration. They kept philosophical journals, rehearsed responses to adversity and maintained strict personal routines. Their discipline was akin to that of an athlete's training, preparing them for any test of character.

The Stoics' greatness came from living each day as a disciplined exercise in virtue, guided by reason rather than impulse. By mastering desire, action and thought, they created unshakable inner freedom, a form of greatness that no war, misfortune, or ruler could take away.

I've learned that lesson through endurance. Training is repetition without glamour, often in the early mornings and late nights, with tired legs and quiet hours no one sees, all amidst the unrelenting demands of running a business and raising a family. It's the same route, the same rhythm, repeatedly. And yet, somewhere in that monotony, you find meaning.

## DISCIPLINE IS FREEDOM

There's something sacred about showing up day after day, regardless of mood, weather, or doubt. It's in those repetitions that character is built. You begin to realise discipline isn't the enemy of freedom, it's the door to it. Without discipline, the mind becomes fragile. With it, you become unshakable. Discipline steadies emotion, sustains focus and protects potential. It is the quiet strength beneath every great endeavour.

There have been hundreds, perhaps thousands, of mornings and evenings over the last 27 years when I really didn't want to train twice a day, but I did, always. There were nights when fatigue whispered that

I'd done enough. But every time I chose to move anyway, something powerful happened; I became less dependent on motivation and more reliant on integrity. But there was not a single occasion when I did not fulfil what I had planned to do, unless I was hospitalised or unable to walk, as happened from time to time. Discipline, I've discovered, is integrity in practice. It's keeping promises you made to yourself when they're hardest to maintain. It's holding the line between who you are and who you could become.

King disciplined his heart. Mandela disciplined his mind. Munro disciplined his craft. Nyad disciplined her endurance. The Stoics disciplined their souls.

And I, like them, continue to learn that discipline is not a punishment – it's a privilege. It's the opportunity to participate in your own becoming.

In the book *Those Who Live Without Discipline, Die Without Honor*, Modern Arjuna explores the profound relationship between discipline, personal integrity and the pursuit of a meaningful life. Through a combination of philosophical insights, practical wisdom, and real-life examples, Arjuna encourages readers to cultivate discipline as a foundation for honour and success. Here are 10 key lessons and insights I took from the book:

1. **Discipline as a fundamental value.** The book emphasises that discipline is not merely a tool for achieving goals but a core value that shapes character. Arjuna argues that a disciplined life leads to greater self-respect and respect from others, laying the groundwork for a life of honour.
2. **The connection between discipline and freedom.** Contrary to the belief that discipline restricts freedom, Arjuna illustrates that true freedom comes from self-discipline. By mastering oneself, individuals can make informed choices that align with their values and long-term aspirations.
3. **Consistency is key.** Arjuna highlights the importance of consistency in practising discipline. Small, daily actions build momentum over time, leading to significant transformation.

The emphasis is on creating habits that reinforce discipline in various aspects of life.

4. **Embrace hardship.** The book teaches that hardship and challenges are integral to the journey of personal growth. Embracing difficulties with a disciplined mindset can foster resilience and strength, enabling individuals to face future obstacles with confidence.
5. **The role of accountability.** Arjuna underscores the significance of accountability in maintaining discipline by establishing systems of accountability. Whether through mentors, peers, or self-reflection, individuals can remain committed to their goals and values.
6. **Mindfulness and self-awareness.** Arjuna encourages readers to cultivate mindfulness and self-awareness as essential components of discipline. Understanding one's thoughts, emotions and behaviours enables individuals to make conscious choices that align with their values and principles.
7. **Discipline in relationships.** The book explores how discipline extends beyond personal goals to encompass relationships. Practising discipline in communication, commitments and interactions fosters trust and respect, strengthening bonds with others.
8. **The dangers of instant gratification.** Arjuna warns against the pitfalls of seeking instant gratification, which can undermine long-term goals. The book advocates patience and delayed gratification as essential to a disciplined life.
9. **Honour as a lifelong pursuit.** Arjuna positions honour as a lifelong pursuit that is intricately linked to discipline. Living honourably requires consistent effort and adherence to one's principles, serving as a guiding light in decision-making.
10. **Legacy and impact.** Finally, the book encourages readers to consider the legacy they leave behind. Living a disciplined life not only honours oneself but also has a positive impact on others. It emphasises that true honour is reflected in the lives we touch and the values we uphold.

*Those Who Live Without Discipline, Die Without Honor* presents a compelling argument for the importance of discipline in achieving a meaningful and honourable life. The book encourages readers to embrace discipline as a fundamental value that shapes character and fosters freedom. Arjuna's emphasis on consistency, accountability and mindfulness highlights the transformative power of discipline in personal growth and relationships. Ultimately, the book serves as a potent reminder that the pursuit of honour is an ongoing journey, deeply rooted in self-discipline and integrity.

## THE MASTER OF DISCIPLINE

David Goggins, for those of you who may be unfamiliar, is an American ultra-endurance athlete, retired US Navy SEAL, former Army Ranger, motivational speaker and bestselling author of *Can't Hurt Me*. He is known for his extreme philosophy of mental toughness and personal accountability.

No one is born with exceptional levels of discipline. Neither do we magically become David Goggins overnight while tucked up in bed asleep. The good news is that inspiring and maintaining discipline becomes easier, almost instinctive, as the rewards we receive build a clear connection between applying discipline and the resulting reward. It is essential to note that 'reward' can encompass a broad range of benefits, including emotional rewards – the most potent and meaningful benefits.

We are all challenged, to some degree, to execute everything we have committed to. It would be fair to say that numerous mental, emotional, practical and physical states influence and weaken our resolve to carry out tasks and actions we have committed to. Additionally, we face endless, constantly competing demands on our time, energy and attention, including raising children, managing partnerships and balancing work and friendships.

Aside from the things we know we need to do, there is also the randomness and unpredictability of life. When you combine the various human states with a busy life, you frequently need to make decisions, and those decisions form habits that are either beneficial, detrimental, or neutral. These are tasks and actions that we know we need to accomplish to achieve our greatness. In essence, these greatness thieves tempt us to submit to the easier option.

So, let's unpack one of the world's most inspiring athletes, David Goggins, known for his intense mental toughness and relentless mindset, who describes discipline not as a talent or gift but as a cultivated, daily choice. His perspective on discipline is rooted in brutal honesty, consistency and voluntary suffering.

## DISCIPLINE IS DOING WHAT YOU DON'T WANT TO DO

Goggins repeatedly emphasises that proper discipline is forged when you do the things you don't want to do, especially when you don't feel like doing them. He believes discipline grows when you reject comfort and choose the hard path. As he puts it: 'You have to build calluses on your brain just like how you build calluses on your hands. Discipline is doing it regardless of how you feel.'

Central to this thinking is Goggins' rejection of motivation as fleeting, emotional and unreliable. In contrast, discipline is stable and dependable. In his blunt assessment: 'Motivation is crap. Motivation comes and goes. When you're driven, whatever is in front of you will get destroyed.' While deliberately provocative, the underlying message is simple: progress cannot depend on motivation alone.

To develop this level of discipline, Goggins intentionally puts himself in uncomfortable situations, such as ice baths, ultramarathons and 4 a.m. runs to sharpen his discipline. These experiences are designed to reduce the power of excuses and strengthen his response to resistance. As he explains, 'The mind is trying to sabotage you. You've got to beat the mind. Discipline is when the body says no, the mind says yes, and you go anyway.'

Accountability plays a critical role in sustaining this approach. Goggins created what he calls the Accountability Mirror, which forces him to face his flaws daily. This brutal form of self-reflection removes denial and forces responsibility, keeping discipline grounded in truth rather than self-deception.

Ultimately, for Goggins, discipline is not just something you do – it's who you are. Discipline, in this sense, becomes a way of being rather than a series of isolated actions. As he frames it: 'Be uncommon amongst uncommon people. That requires insane discipline every single day.'

At its core, this philosophy is about mastering the mind through consistent action – doing hard things regardless of one's emotions or circumstances, seeking discomfort and owning every weakness with relentless honesty.

## ONE IN 10, OR NINE IN 10?

The most prevalent, and perhaps therefore the most relatable, goals that require discipline are those that we set for health, as they demand time, and physical and mental exertion. In our minds, a potent adversary works tirelessly to convince us that something is hard. If we accept that voice, we seek out excuses, validating our tendency to choose the option that requires less discretionary effort.

One of the most common scenarios that exemplifies the downfall of many well-intentioned people is signing up for a gym membership or a running event. This process often starts with the best of intentions – to create an incentive for accountability. In other words, they know from experience that they lack discipline and need logical, psychological and intrinsic encouragement: 'I've paid my hard-earned money, and so I need to get my money's worth.'

So, what began with motivation to improve strength, physical fitness and mental wellbeing, followed by an enforced incentive, often ends in tears. Well, perhaps not tears, but disaster as visits to the gym quickly dwindle, and the habit becomes submission to options that require considerably less effort. There is ample research supporting this trend, with only one in 10 people eventually achieving their health and fitness goals.

Generally, the weakness in this process begins with insufficient purpose – the genesis of all greatness journeys. A common goal that I frequently hear, read and experience in my mindset coaching courses is: 'I want to lose weight or to get fitter and healthier.'

This goal is often well-intentioned, but it is frequently set as a token goal in moments of discontent with one's health or fitness rather than as a genuine purpose. For example, a general fitness goal for a 45-year-old is likely underpinned by a deeper dissatisfaction with how that person feels about themselves, which can be traced back to a much deeper emotional state of turmoil.

When I partner with a person to help them achieve their greatness, I will go much deeper to understand what is going on for them. Once understood, I ask them to create a purpose statement, which entails describing in writing what achieving their objective will do for their lives and how finding their greatness will transform them. So, the purpose of the aforementioned 45-year-old might be: 'I want to feel the best I have ever felt. I will be fitter and stronger so that I can live my life to the full, and add more days to my life and more life to my days.'

If you need a frequent reminder to stay focused and inspired, consider placing this purpose statement somewhere it is constantly visible. Alternatively, you can etch it in your mind to draw on when life's challenges arise and excuses come your way.

## WHAT MASTERY ACTUALLY REQUIRES

In reading *Mastery* by Robert Greene, I was struck by how clearly it dismantles the idea that extraordinary skill or success is the result of talent or genius alone. What stayed with me is Greene's insistence that mastery – the highest level of skill or understanding in any field – is built through sustained commitment, discipline and ongoing learning.

One of the most valuable takeaways for me is Greene's framing of mastery as a process rather than a destination. He describes three broad phases that most people move through, regardless of their field:

1. **Apprenticeship phase.** Every master starts as a beginner. Greene emphasises the importance of humble, focused learning, whether under the guidance of mentors or through self-guided

exploration, and states that one must be patient and invest time to absorb foundational knowledge.

2. **Creative/active phase.** After building a base of knowledge, you start to experiment and apply what you've learned in new ways. Creativity is fuelled by deep understanding and experience – not random inspiration.
3. **Mastery.** The highest level, where intuition and skill merge, is where you no longer follow rules; you see patterns, innovate and lead in your domain. He argues that this can only be achieved through years – often decades – of persistence and evolution.

Greene brings these ideas to life through biographies of individuals such as Leonardo da Vinci, whose curiosity spanned multiple disciplines; Charles Darwin, whose breakthrough followed years of patient observation; and figures such as Mozart, Temple Grandin, Benjamin Franklin and more, each illustrating different paths to mastery.

What I ultimately took from *Mastery* is a reassuring message: mastery is not reserved for the naturally gifted. It is available to anyone willing to prioritise depth over speed, practice over shortcuts and long-term commitment over fleeting gains.

## HACKS FOR IMPROVING YOUR SELF-DISCIPLINE

To get you going on the road to mastery, and this critical greatness step, I have created a focused, no-fluff guide to improving self-discipline, blending what works from psychology, Stoicism and practical habit-building:

- Clarify your 'why', as discipline collapses without a compelling reason. To support this, write down exactly why this goal matters to you – link it to a bigger purpose (health, freedom, service, mastery). For example – 'I'm not just going to the gym to look fit, I'm training to be strong enough to keep up with my kids.'

- Start smaller than you think, as the brain resists big or sudden change. Begin with the most miniature version of the habit that's easy enough that you can't say no. If you are planning to start running to improve your fitness and lifestyle, consider taking a more manageable approach. Instead of setting a goal like 'I'll run two kilometres daily', begin with a simple step – 'I'll put on running shoes and step outside.'
- Create friction for your bad habits, as willpower is limited. This will make temptation harder to reach. You could do this by hiding distractions, deleting time-wasting apps, or keeping junk food out of the house. If you want to read more, try leaving a book on your pillow so you see it before you go to bed.
- Use the 'two-minute rule', as starting is often the most challenging part. Commit to just two minutes of the task – momentum usually keeps you going. If you then commit to something along the lines of 'I'll write for two minutes', you may end up writing for 30 minutes.
- Plan for 'if–then' scenarios, because discipline cracks when you face unexpected challenges. This could involve pre-deciding your responses to common obstacles such as tiredness or lethargy. If you're too tired to exercise, try doing 20 push-ups at home as an alternative. Soon, before you know it, 20 push-ups per day will increase your strength and vitality, providing an incentive to increase your push-up count. Next thing you know, you will be motivated to set new push-up goals.
- Track progress visibly, as seeing it fuels motivation. Tracking can take many forms, such as a calendar, a habit tracker app, or a simple checklist. Imagine putting a big tick on your calendar for each day you succeed with the small task that you have set.
- Use self-compassion, not self-loathing or comparison with others, to avoid quitting altogether if you fail at one task. This is much the same as a coach treats an athlete – firm but encouraging. 'Okay, I missed yesterday. What's my plan to bounce back today?' This tactic also requires caution, as continuing this practice can

lead to the habit of making excuses and suggesting that you can do everything tomorrow.

- Lean on your environment and people, as willpower alone is overrated until habits are formed. Remember, structure beats raw discipline. Surround yourself with people who share your values and create an environment that supports your goals, so you will not be doing this alone.
- Practise delayed gratification, as discipline is largely about choosing long-term gain over short-term pleasure. An example of this might be pausing before indulging by counting to 10, breathing and visualising the benefit of waiting. Another example is waiting 24 hours to make a purchase. Often, you will realise that you don't really need that thing.
- Train daily in small ways to exercise the muscle that is discipline. It is a muscle that strengthens with frequent use. By adding small acts of discipline into your day that aren't tied to your main goal, you will form great habits in no time. When you wake up in the morning, make your bed immediately. When you want to quit, finish the last rep of an exercise set.

In the end, discipline is not about punishment, perfection, or performance. It is about liberation. It is the quiet, unglamorous, fiercely personal decision to take ownership of your minutes – those 1440 equal units of life that every human receives, yet so few honour. Discipline is the choice to turn those minutes into meaning, rather than memories of what might have been.

What King practised in the face of hatred, what Mandela cultivated in captivity, what Munro carved into steel, what Nyad repeated across endless oceans, and what the Stoics rehearsed through the centuries is the same truth available to each of us: discipline is the foundation of self-command. It is the daily refusal to be ruled by impulse, fear, or comfort. It is the quiet knowledge that while you cannot control the world, you can always control how you step into it.

At some point, you will reach a moment when motivation deserts you, when fatigue whispers its lies, when excuses dress themselves up as logic. And when that moment comes – as it always does – it will not be your talent or your inspiration that rescues you. It will be the commitments you made and the integrity you chose to honour when keeping those commitments became difficult.

Discipline is integrity in motion. It is self-respect expressed through action. It is choosing who you wish to become and then proving it – to yourself – one choice at a time.

If you live without discipline, you drift. You compromise. You hand your life over to circumstance, impulse and chance. But when you live with discipline, you reclaim your agency. You forge identity. You sculpt character. You build the inner architecture that greatness requires. With discipline comes the freedom to rise above old narratives, old habits and old limitations to become someone you can trust.

Greatness doesn't care how you feel in the moment. It doesn't care how busy your day is, how tired your body is, or how loudly your doubts protest. It cares about one thing: did you do what you said you would do?

Discipline is the bridge between who you are and who you could be, between intention and transformation, between the life you're living and the life you're capable of living.

Use it and every dream becomes reachable.

Neglect it and every dream remains a theory.

In the chapters ahead, you will learn tools, structures and practices that further strengthen the discipline muscle. But never forget the truth that underpins them all:

Discipline is not the enemy of freedom – it is the birthplace of it.

Discipline is not the weight – it is the wings.

Discipline is not the punishment – it is the path.

Once you step onto that path with conviction, your greatness ceases to be a possibility. It becomes inevitable.

# *REFLECTION, ACTION AND GROWTH*

## AUDIT YOUR DISCIPLINE

**Reflection:** If someone watched a silent film of your last week, what would they say you're *truly* disciplined about – and what would they say you only *talk* about?

**Action:** Conduct a quick time audit. List how you spent the past week in rough 30- to 60-minute blocks. Circle *one* 30- to 60-minute window you can reclaim each day for disciplined, purpose-aligned work (e.g. training, writing, building, or studying) and lock it into your calendar as non-negotiable.

## REPLACE MOOD WITH STANDARDS

**Reflection:** Where in your life are you still waiting to 'feel like it' when what I actually need is a standard, not a mood?

**Action:** Choose *one* behaviour that matters to your greatness (e.g. running, gym, prospecting, practice, study) and turn it into a daily or weekday rule: 'I do *X* at *Y* time, no debate.' Keep a simple 14-day streak tracker and don't let the chain break.

## EXPOSE YOUR EXCUSES

**Reflection:** What are your three most common excuses? What honest truths are they hiding?

**Action:** Write down your top three repeat excuses (e.g. 'too tired', 'no time', 'I'll start Monday'). Next to each, write a brutally honest translation (e.g. 'not a priority right now') and an If–Then replacement: 'If I'm "too tired" to train, then I will at least walk for 10 minutes or do 20 push-ups at home.'

## COMMIT TO A DISCIPLINE EXPERIMENT

**Reflection:** If you lived for the next 90 days exactly as you did last week, would you be moving towards mastery or mediocrity?

**Action**: Choose one domain (health, work, craft, relationship) and design a seven-day discipline experiment with:

- One clear objective (e g 'rebuild training consistency')
- One tiny daily action (e g 'minimum 15 minutes of deliberate effort')
- One end-of-day question – did i do what i said i would do today?'

At the end of seven days, conduct an honest review and decide how to scale it into a 30- or 90-Day High-Performance Plan.

SS GREAT
ATNESS
SS GREAT
ATNESS
SS GREAT
ATNESS
SS GREAT
ATNESS

# CHAPTER 7
# PRESENCE

**'REALISE DEEPLY THAT THE PRESENT MOMENT IS ALL YOU EVER HAVE.'** – ECKHART TOLLE

Presence is the art of being where your feet are. It is the discipline of attention and the quiet mastery of now.

It raises an uncomfortable question: Is there any real point to life without presence? I ask this because life goes so damn quickly, and at 62, I can attest to this with authority and certainty. This is a question I pondered countless times during my frenetic life as a corporate executive and CEO, juggling family care, constant travel and a relentless physical training schedule.

During those years, my days were defined by constant multitasking – often poorly – from 5 a.m. until well into the evening. Weeks blurred into months, and months into years. In that state of perpetual motion, I found myself repeatedly questioning the meaning of life. My saving grace became my solitary training regime, which served as my island in the sun, where I could process even the most extreme pressures, solve problems and develop solutions. Training immediately after work enabled me to leave my mind free to be present and focused on the people and things I loved before I arrived home. Whatever its form, creating a 'presence space' between work and home is a powerful practice for parking whatever has challenged you at work.

This meditative state, while running or moving, taught me how to be present. It taught me how to sift out everything that really didn't matter. The noise around me had a way of multiplying, as small concerns accumulated and threatened to overwhelm me, like storm clouds gathering before a downpour. Over time, I realised that most of it would not matter in a year. I would not remember it when I was 65 and retired. It was not worth letting it shape my days or define my life.

So, I worked on building interludes of presence into my day – small returns to my island in the sun, where everything became clear, and gratitude emanated from every pore of my skin.

## TEN YEARS OF MONDAYS

Here's another question for you: Have you ever said or thought any of the following, or similar:

- 'I can't wait until we go on holiday in three months!'
- 'This week can't go quickly enough!'
- 'I wish it were Friday!'

Of course you have! We all have. It's perfectly natural to look forward to exciting events or the weekend when most of us get the chance to unwind, relax and spend time with our family and friends – or at least do something other than work. During my first life, this was precisely my mindset, and so I wished time away – week after week, year after year. As my second life began to emerge from my life-changing purpose, I heard a quote from an inspiring speaker at a conference that went like this: 'By the time you reach age 70, you will have lived 10 whole years of Mondays, so imagine what you would do at age 70 to get back 10 years of your life? Learn to love Mondays!'

These words felt so profound that from that day 27 years ago, my mission has been to value every single day, no matter what it brings. To this very day, and every day, I remind myself that the day I am blessed with living will never come back and that I must make the most of it. For decades now, my daily mantra has been: 'Every day is a gift!'

## THE POWER OF BEING FULLY HERE

Presence is not passive. It is active engagement – the full immersion of mind, body and spirit in what's unfolding. This is where greatness becomes possible, because excellence cannot exist anywhere else but here.

Martin Luther King Jr. lived in the centre of storms, literal and metaphorical. Every day brought new threats, new crises, new demands. And yet, those who stood beside him said he had an almost unshakable calmness. When others panicked, he remained steady. When noise surrounded him, he listened.

This is what presence looks like – not stillness without motion, but motion without distraction. He was entirely *in* his cause, not just around it. His presence gave others courage because it radiated a sense of steadiness. For King, presence was faith made visible – the belief that the moment in front of you, however heavy, is the only place where change can begin.

Nelson Mandela embodied the same grace. In prison, time lost meaning. Days bled into years, years into decades. Yet he refused to drift into despair. He was fully present even within confinement. He studied his guards, learned their patterns and watched the sky from the same window each day. He found meaning in repetition and beauty in the ordinary. Presence turned prison into a classroom.

When he was finally released, he carried that same stillness into his leadership. He listened more than he spoke. He looked people in the eye. He made everyone – from presidents to prison guards – feel seen. His greatness came not just from vision, but from presence. Because presence is love translated into attention.

Burt Munro's life was an ode to this. Presence was his process. In the solitude of his shed, surrounded by tools and metal filings, he found a kind of meditation. Every sound, every scent, every spark was part of his world. There's a holiness in that kind of attention, in the way he lost himself in each small task, not thinking about records or fame, but about the feel of the metal beneath his hands. He wasn't chasing time; he was suspended within it. That's the essence of presence: the complete surrender to the task at hand, until the line between doer and doing disappears.

Diana Nyad found that same surrender in the water. When she swam, time dissolved. The rhythm of her strokes became the rhythm of existence. Pain, distance and exhaustion were all real and present but were no longer obstacles, just sensations to move through. In interviews, she said there were long stretches during her crossings when thought disappeared, leaving only movement. That's presence at its purest – when mind and body move as one and you are no longer performing an act but *becoming* it.

The Stoics understood this state deeply. They taught that the present moment is the only realm of human control. 'Confine yourself to the present,' Marcus Aurelius wrote. 'The task of life is to live it well – right now.' Seneca warned that most people waste their lives waiting to begin. They speak of living someday, not realising that someday never comes. Epictetus urged his students to cultivate awareness in every breath, every choice and every conversation.

The Stoics also placed great importance on presence, or what they often referred to as living in accordance with nature or dwelling in the present moment, as a foundation for achieving greatness. For them, Greatness was not fame, wealth, or external success, but the cultivation of virtue (wisdom, courage, justice and self-discipline), which required the ability to remain fully present.

They believed that presence anchors the mind in what can be controlled. The Stoics taught that we should not waste energy worrying about the past (which is gone) or the future (which is uncertain); greatness comes from directing attention to what is within our control right now – our thoughts, actions and character.

Epictetus said, 'Do not seek for things to happen the way you want them to; rather, wish that what happens happen the way it happens: then you will be happy.' This is the practice of presence.

Fear often arises from imagining future pain, while regret comes from clinging to the past. Presence reduces fear and anxiety. By focusing on the present moment, the Stoic cultivates steadiness, courage and calm – the qualities needed for great deeds. Marcus Aurelius reminded himself: 'Confine yourself to the present.'

Greatness requires persistence and self-control, but the Stoics believed this discipline is best exercised moment by moment. Instead of being overwhelmed by the magnitude of life's challenges, the Stoic asks: 'What is the right action I can take here, now?' In this way, small acts of virtue build up into a great life as presence strengthens discipline.

The Stoics believed that life's meaning is not abstract or distant – it's found in how we respond to situations, duties and opportunities. To them, being present enables a person to act justly towards others, exhibit courage under challenging conditions and make wise decisions.

They linked presence to inner stillness – a calm mind undisturbed by distraction or passion. Stillness, in turn, enables clear judgment and decisive action, which are essential for greatness. The Stoics saw presence as the groundwork for greatness. By living fully in the present, focusing only on what can be controlled, and acting with virtue moment by moment, a person rises above fear, distraction and desire – and builds a life of enduring greatness.

King found presence in chaos. Mandela found it in captivity. Munro found it in craft. Nyad found it in the current. The Stoics found it in contemplation.

## THE MORE OF LESS: FINDING THE LIFE YOU WANT UNDER EVERYTHING YOU OWN

Another great book that I was fortunate to stumble upon is Joshua Becker's *The More of Less: Finding the Life You Want Under Everything You Own*. It is an excellent read for anyone seeking to declutter their life of anything that robs them of presence and happiness.

In *The More of Less*, Becker argues that owning fewer possessions leads to a richer, more intentional life. Drawing on his own experience as a suburban dad who discovered minimalism almost by accident, Becker presents a compelling case for why letting go of material excess creates space for purpose, passion and freedom.

The core themes of his book centre on the idea that minimalism isn't deprivation but a deliberate removal of distractions to focus on what really matters. He demonstrates that all material possessions come with hidden costs – they require cleaning, maintenance, organisation and worry – and that freedom from consumer culture allows for more time, energy, money and peace. And the big one: living with less helps you focus on relationships, contribution and personal growth.

Becker includes personal stories and reflections from his life in the narrative, which eloquently demonstrate his key themes and practical steps to declutter your home and mind. Central to his approach is purposeful minimalism: not just reducing possessions but intentionally aligning what remains with personal values. He also challenges the idea of the 'American dream' of bigger, better, more, which is appropriate wherever you live, especially if you're consumed by the constant pursuit of more, overwhelmed by clutter, or living a life that feels unfulfilling. Ultimately, the book speaks to readers who want to simplify not just their closets or homes, but their whole lives. As Becker defines it: 'Minimalism is the intentional promotion of the things we most value and the removal of anything that distracts us from them.'

## HACKS TO FIND PRESENCE

Finding presence in a busy life can feel like trying to slow down a rushing river, but it's possible with the right approaches. Presence means being fully engaged in the present moment, rather than getting lost in distractions, past regrets, or future worries. Here are some practical tips:

| PRACTICE | DESCRIPTION |
|---|---|
| ENGAGE IN MICRO-MOMENTS OF AWARENESS | Even in the pressure of a packed day, pausing for 30–60 seconds can make a difference. Wait; notice your breath, posture, or what you can see and hear right now. These micro-pauses build the habit of grounding yourself. |
| BREATHE INTENTIONALLY | Try the 4-7-8 technique: inhale for 4 seconds, hold for 7 seconds, exhale for 8 seconds. This technique calms the nervous system and helps you refocus on the present. |
| PRIORITISE SINGLE-TASKING OVER MULTITASKING | Multitasking scatters attention, whereas presence thrives on doing one thing at a time. For example, if you're eating, eat. If you're writing an email, write the email. |
| ANCHOR DAILY ACTIVITIES | Turn routines (like walking, making coffee, or washing dishes) into mindfulness anchors. Also, try to notice sensations, sounds and movements while doing them. |
| LIMIT NOISE AND CLUTTER | Constant notifications and cluttered spaces can distract you from being present. The real villain these days is mobile devices, whether working or in your free time. Consider silencing unnecessary alerts and keeping your workspace organised and tidy. |
| TECHNOLOGY BOUNDARIES | Set 'no-phone zones' (such as during meals, in bed, or during conversations) and try replacing some screen time with mindful breaks or journalling. |
| GROUND THE BODY | Why not try doing a body scan? This can be achieved by deliberately and consciously moving your attention slowly from head to toe. Getting up and stretching, taking a mindful walk, or simply feeling your feet on the ground can really have a positive impact. |
| PRACTISE GRATITUDE IN REAL TIME | Instead of just listing things at night, pause during the day to notice something you're thankful for in the moment. This would have to be my favourite presence technique. |
| CREATE BREATHING SPACES IN YOUR SCHEDULE | Breathing spaces in your schedule do not have to be long; even 5–10 minutes between tasks without rushing to the next thing helps reset presence. |

| PRACTICE | DESCRIPTION |
|---|---|
| REFLECT AND RE-CENTRE | At the end of the day, ask yourself: 'Where was I truly present today? Where was I lost?' This daily reflection on awareness helps you catch yourself more quickly tomorrow. |

While you can achieve longer periods of presence during your non-working hours, the key is not to look only for hours of stillness at once, but to weave small threads of presence into your day until they become a natural rhythm. Investing time in finding your stillness will be one of the most significant steps you can take to achieve happiness, gratitude and contentment. Without stillness in your life, a form of greatness will diminish in meaning.

We live in a world obsessed with 'next': the next goal, the next win, the next distraction. That was my world. Yet all greatness is born in the present. The future is only shaped by what we give to this moment. Presence is not passive. It's active engagement, with the full immersion of mind, body and spirit in what's unfolding. It's how greatness becomes possible, because excellence can't exist anywhere but here.

## THE ONLY MOMENT THAT BELONGS TO YOU

In the end, presence is not a luxury reserved for monks, mystics, or those with quiet lives. It is the essential skill of being human. It is the lens through which life becomes vivid rather than blurry, meaningful rather than mechanical, lived rather than endured. The past is memory. The future is imagination. But the present – this breath, this step, this conversation, this sunrise – is the only territory where life unfolds.

Presence is the great equaliser. You can be in a boardroom or a prison cell, on a mountain trail or in a cramped aeroplane seat, surrounded by chaos or wrapped in silence. The opportunity to be fully here is always yours.

King used it to bring calm to storms. Mandela used it to turn confinement into an opportunity for learning. Munro used it to consecrate craft. Nyad used it to quiet the ocean inside her so she could swim through the one around her.

The Stoics used it to build a life of virtue, one conscious choice at a time. Each of them achieved greatness not despite their circumstances, but because they mastered the art of meeting each moment as it arrived.

Presence is not the absence of chaos; it is the ability to stand steady within it. It's how you stop the mind from racing ahead or spiralling backwards. It's how you reclaim the minutes that would otherwise be lost to distraction, worry, or regret. It's how you touch the fullness of your own life before it becomes memory.

As I look back on my own journey – the first life driven by pace, pressure and performance; the second life built on purpose, movement and meaning – I see clearly that presence was the hinge between them. It allowed me to separate the noise from the essential. It taught me that most of what feels urgent is irrelevant, and most of what is relevant is quiet. It gave me gratitude, clarity and the capacity to love my days rather than rush through them.

And here's the truth that echoes across every great life: presence is a choice – to slow your breath, to notice what matters, to move through the world awake rather than on autopilot, to refuse to wish your days away in exchange for some imagined version of happiness, and instead to honour the people in front of you, the work in your hands and the moment that will never return.

Presence is the birthplace of stillness. Stillness is the birthplace of clarity. Clarity is the birthplace of purpose. And purpose is the birthplace of greatness.

Greatness doesn't care how busy you are, how stressed you feel, how much noise surrounds you, or how much you've got on your plate. It cares only about how fully you inhabit the moment in front of you. Because that moment, not tomorrow's fantasy or yesterday's story, is where your life is happening.

So, breathe. Look up. Slow down. Be where your feet are.

If you can give your presence to this moment, you can provide your greatness to your life.

To be present is to be alive. To be fully alive is to be great.

## REFLECTION, ACTION AND GROWTH

### COME BACK TO THE DAY YOU'RE LIVING

**Reflection:** Where in your life are you consistently living ahead of yourself? Are you waiting for Fridays, holidays, or 'someday' instead of valuing the day you're living right now?

**Action:** Identify one recurring moment each day when you tend to rush, escape, or mentally time-travel. Commit to transforming that moment into a presence ritual (a pause, a breath, a grounding cue, a gratitude check).

### RELEASE WHAT WON'T MATTER

**Reflection:** What burdens, worries, or 'shit storms' am I carrying that I won't even remember in a year – and why am I letting them shape my days right now?

**Action:** Write down three things that have been weighing on you this week. Put a star next to the one that genuinely matters long term. Circle the others and deliberately release them – mentally or physically. (Ritual suggestion: scrunch and bin the paper.)

### RECREATE PRESENCE

**Reflection:** When was the last time I was truly present – fully absorbed, calm and awake – and what conditions allowed me to enter that state?

**Action:** Create a daily five-minute presence space inspired by that moment. This might include a quiet walk, conscious breathing, a no-phone zone, a mindful household task, or movement that brings stillness. Make it non-negotiable.

## LIVE TODAY ON PURPOSE

**Reflection**: If I lived today as if it were a once-in-a-lifetime day – one that will never return – how differently would I show up, listen, love, work, or move?

**Action:** Choose one behaviour you will elevate *today* (e.g. a deeper conversation, slower meal, gracious response, single-tasked focus, or moment of gratitude) and practise it deliberately.

SS GREAT
ATNESS G
SS GREAT
ATNESS G
SS GREAT
ATNESS G
SS GREAT
ATNESS G

# CHAPTER 8
# BELIEF

***'WHETHER YOU THINK YOU CAN OR YOU THINK YOU CAN'T – YOU ARE RIGHT.'* – HENRY FORD**

Belief is the fire that burns beneath everything else. It's what turns purpose into power, effort into endurance and failure into fuel. Without belief, greatness collapses under its own weight.

Belief is not certainty. It's not naïve optimism or wishful thinking. It's faith, not in what is easy, but in what is possible. It's the decision to trust something you can't yet see, and the courage to keep trusting when every visible sign tells you not to. The most powerful beliefs are not shouted, they're lived. They are the quiet affirmations written into action, repeated day after day, until the world has no choice but to believe with you.

The most powerful aspect of belief is its capacity to liberate you from your neurological captors. Alongside courage, belief serves as the optimal antidote to fear and doubt. It interrupts negative cycles and redirects them in a healthier, more constructive direction. As belief takes hold, the downward spiral created by self-doubt and fear begins to reverse, generating upward momentum instead. Each positive outcome – whether small or significant – adds another layer of confidence. Over time, this becomes a reserve that you can draw upon when times get tough or when there seems to be no light at the end of a dark tunnel.

Creating belief and confidence that you can achieve something isn't just about positive thinking – it's about building evidence, controlling focus and managing your state. In a short while, I will share with you a practical psychological framework to help you build that belief and confidence from the ground up. First, I would like to share the transformational shift that occurred in my life, enabled by courage and powered by belief.

In 1998, I finally broke the spiral of addiction in my life. Addiction, essentially, is to anything that would bring instant pleasure and gratification with the least amount of effort. Consequently, any gratification was fleeting and lacked real meaning. My constant evasion of the fears that held me back led me to continually seek the next quick fix. But I found purpose, then courage, and I realised that the next key step was to create belief.

Having insufficient 'belief' in this instance was a big deal because the consequence of failure could result in death by drowning. Sounds dramatic, right? Well, it was real. As mentioned in Chapter 3, my life pivoted in a different direction, forever changed, when I finally chose to face my greatest fear: drowning. Initially, I had to build the belief that I could survive the 300-metre swim during my first triathlon, which I did.

The first seemingly impossible goal I set for my second life was to qualify for – and race – the IRONMAN World Championship in Hawai'i. Compared to the Noosa triathlon, this would require swimming 13 times the swim distance, cycling 16 times the bike distance and running 14 times the run distance! Even after completing the BRW sprint triathlon, the scale of the feat felt almost incomprehensible. Moreover, to qualify for Hawai'i, I would need to race fast enough to be among the best in my age group worldwide, not just complete the distance. From that moment, I applied the same principle to my training framework, gradually building distance and confidence over the next nine months in preparation for my first IRONMAN race.

From that day onward, this became the essential blueprint for believing I could accomplish every seemingly impossible feat I set my sights on.

## BELIEF PRECEDES BECOMING

I am immensely proud of an accomplishment that, to me, embodies every one of the 14 steps to greatness. It could justly belong in any chapter of this book, yet it finds its home here in 'belief' because at its core, this achievement is not about talent or triumph but endurance.

Courage was the enabler. Courage to chase another impossible dream, to leave behind the security of a senior executive role and devote four months entirely to training. Courage to persevere through a crippling injury (a severe medial meniscus tear) that shadowed me for a year and well beyond. Courage to rise above the ridicule and disbelief of others. Resilience was the companion that never left my side.

In 2005, a friend handed me a book that would ignite a fire I could never have anticipated – *Ultramarathon Man: Confessions of an All-Night Runner* by Dean Karnazes. As I devoured its pages, I felt both awe and fear stirring within me. Among the stories, one race captured my imagination like no other – the Western States® 100-Mile Endurance Run. As the oldest and most revered 100-mile trail ultramarathon in the world, it winds through the rugged mountains of California from the snow-covered peaks of the Palisades Tahoe ski resort to the track at Auburn's Placer High School – one hundred miles of brutal beauty, with 18,000 feet of ascent and nearly 23,000 feet of descent, through snow, scorching heat and darkness. Through the entirety of this great race, every runner must endure the debilitating effects of high altitude.

At the time, I had set aside my IRONMAN triathlon career to pursue ultramarathon running, with a dream of representing Australia at the elite World Championships. But Western States® was a different beast entirely. I had never run a trail, never trained at altitude, and never run more than 100 kilometres. The odds were unthinkable, which made it irresistible.

Entry to the race is a privilege few achieve. From thousands of qualified ultrarunners around the world, only 360 to 370 people are selected each year. Of those, roughly two-thirds finish within the 30-hour cut-off, and only a quarter of those finishers earn the coveted silver belt buckle, awarded to those who finish in under 24 hours. Few Australians have ever achieved this accolade.

I wanted to become one of them, but I had never even visited anywhere of notable altitude, let alone attempted to run extreme distances. Neither had I ever run a trail race of any description.

Training began nine months out, and with it came pain – a sharp, persistent ache in my left knee, the result of years of relentless mileage. My weekly training increased to 200 to 250 kilometres, with six-hour runs every other day and three-hour sessions in between, running up and down a total of 18,000 steps, non-stop. Each step was a constant conversation in my head between pain and purpose.

To prepare for the race's notorious heat, I endured four 90-minute sauna sessions at 55°C per week, conditioning my body to survive the desert furnace. I trained for altitude by repetition and relentlessness, running up and down a 1.5-kilometre hill 20 times a day, alternating with three-hour sessions climbing 70 stairs in the midday sun. My home sat barely 25 feet above sea level; my race would begin at 6000 feet plus and climb to 11,000 feet. I could not replicate the air, but I could simulate the suffering.

For weeks, I weighed my options, the risk, the cost, the time, knowing full well how rare it was to be accepted into Western States®. Regret, however, is heavier than risk. I remembered the pain of walking away from my boyhood dream two decades earlier. I would not repeat that mistake. I resigned from my job and committed fully to the mountain.

By race week, my knee was in agony. Doubt whispered daily, and every training session sent jarring pain up my left leg. But I had learned how to silence that voice, not through denial, but through belief.

Five days before the race, a documentary crew interviewed me. When asked which 100-mile races I had previously run, I answered honestly: 'None. This will be my first. Actually, this is my first trail race of any description.' The pause that followed was thick with disbelief.

Laughter broke the silence – not cruel, but dismissive. As I walked away, embarrassment burned through me. I sat alone for a few minutes, gazing up at the white summit above the valley, 4500 feet above me. Then I remembered my purpose. I had done the work. I had sacrificed. I had endured. Within 15 minutes, the laughter – and my doubt – were gone. I was ready.

The race began at dawn beneath a cobalt sky. Only six miles in, pain erupted in my knee – fierce, unrelenting. The voice returned, telling me to stop, to save myself, to come back another day. But I knew there would be no other day. Not for this race. Not for this moment. So, I ran on, through snow, through heat, through rivers up to my waist, then trails that shredded my feet. I ran through the night as exhaustion and hunger clawed at me. Every blister, every nail lost, every scream of pain was a declaration: *Not today. I will not quit today.* And I didn't.

That day, I discovered that greatness is not a medal or a finish line – it's the quiet victory over the voice that tells you to give up. Its courage made visible through pain. It's resilience, written into the body, etched into the soul.

## THE EPITOME OF BELIEF

Martin Luther King Jr. envisioned a world that had yet to come into existence. He believed in justice when the law denied it, in peace when violence surrounded him, and in love when hatred ruled the streets. That belief was not passive. It was forged in fire.

Every step he took, every sermon he preached, was an act of belief, not just in the cause, but in the capacity of humanity to evolve. He said, 'Faith is taking the first step even when you don't see the whole staircase.' That line is not a metaphor. It's a map. Belief was his compass when vision blurred. It allowed him to see possibilities beyond pain, meaning beyond suffering. And that is what belief truly does – it bends reality towards hope.

King believed that belief must be practised daily through action. Nonviolence required enormous discipline: resisting hatred, restraining retaliation and responding with dignity even when beaten or jailed.

This practice trained him and his followers to embody belief under pressure – turning faith into lived greatness.

Nelson Mandela's belief was tested in ways few could endure. There were days when the walls of Robben Island were all he could see, and the sound of the ocean – just beyond reach – mocked the freedom he no longer had. But even then, he believed. He believed that one day, freedom would not only return but would belong to all. His belief was not naïve; it was disciplined. He once said, 'I am fundamentally an optimist. Whether that comes from nature or nurture, I cannot say. But part of being optimistic is keeping one's head pointed toward the sun, one's feet moving forward.'

Belief, for Mandela, was not a feeling. It was a practice, a daily choice to orient himself towards light. That's what separates dreamers from doers: belief that persists beyond inspiration.

Burt Munro's belief was quieter, but no less fierce. He believed that an aging man, working alone in a shed, could defy the limits of engineering and time. He believed in the beauty of precision, the poetry of persistence. No one else saw what he saw. And that's what makes belief rare – it often begins in solitude. He had no corporate sponsor, no professional team. He had rusted tools, worn hands and a relentless conviction that effort could bridge any gap. Every late night, every small victory, every setback refined his faith, not in luck, but in work. And that's the purest form of belief: faith in the process when results are still invisible.

Diana Nyad's belief was forged in failure. After decades away from the sport, she returned to the ocean at 60, not because she needed to prove something, but because belief still whispered that she could. The sea, vast and cruel, punished her. Jellyfish stings, storms, hallucinations, exhaustion – each attempt ended in defeat. But belief doesn't die in failure. It feeds on it.

Nyad's belief evolved from ambition into devotion. She stopped chasing the swim as conquest and began treating it as communion – a conversation between her will and the world. When she finally made the crossing, it wasn't belief rewarded; it was belief fulfilled.

The Stoics believed in reason – the quiet certainty that the mind could be stronger than circumstance. Marcus Aurelius expressed this simply: 'Your mind will take the shape of what you frequently hold in thought.' Epictetus took the idea further, teaching that our beliefs are the architects of our reality. As he wrote, 'If you want to improve, be content to be thought foolish and stupid.'

Stoic thinkers like Epictetus, Seneca and Marcus Aurelius viewed belief not as blind faith or optimism, but as a rational trust in nature, virtue, and the power of the mind. For them, greatness was not about fame, wealth, or conquest, but about living with wisdom, courage, justice and self-mastery.

Here's how they found and practised belief. The Stoics believed the universe is governed by *logos* – rational order. Their belief was rooted in the trust that everything unfolds according to nature, and that our task is to align ourselves with it. By accepting this, they practised belief as a calm confidence in the flow of life, even during hardship.

Belief wasn't abstract; it was cultivated through daily exercises, including morning reflection to prepare for the day's challenges, evening journalling to review actions and thoughts, and negative visualisation to build resilience by imagining loss or hardship. These practices turned belief into lived strength, not just philosophy.

Many Stoics lived under extreme conditions – exile, slavery, or tyranny. Epictetus was enslaved; Seneca lived under Nero; Marcus Aurelius ruled through wars and the plague. For them, hardship became the testing ground of belief. If virtue could hold under pressure, then belief was genuine. This gave them a deep, practised faith that adversity reveals character, rather than destroying it.

Epictetus taught, 'You may not control events, but you control how you respond.' Belief was practised by choosing freedom within, training the mind not to be enslaved by fear, anger, or desire. This inner independence was the Stoics' pathway to greatness.

For the Stoics, greatness meant contributing to the common good. Marcus Aurelius constantly reminded himself, 'What is not good for the hive is not good for the bee.' To them, belief was not a wish but a discipline – the mental training to see truth over illusion and trust virtue over vanity. They believed that while fate controls circumstance, character controls response.

I've come to see belief that way too – not as magic, but as mastery. Belief doesn't remove difficulty; it redefines it, teaching you to see obstacles as part of the path and pain as part of progress.

Every endurance race has taught me that belief begins where the body ends. There's a point where muscles fail, lungs burn and the mind starts whispering reasons to stop. And that's where belief begins, in that small, stubborn voice that says: *one more step*. Belief is what carries you through the invisible miles – the ones between where you are and where you want to be. It's not loud or dramatic. It's a quiet, steady pulse that says, 'This matters'.

King's belief changed the laws. Mandela's changed nations. Munro's changed the boundaries of both speed and age. Nyad's changed human limits. The Stoics' changed minds.

## SELF-BELIEF IS YOUR SUPERPOWER

Tory Archbold's *Self-Belief Is Your Superpower* is another book that guides readers (especially women seeking empowerment) to deepen their confidence, align with their purpose and live more boldly. Archbold draws on her own journey – and on spiritual, entrepreneurial and mindset principles – to help people break free from doubt, judgment and inertia.

The book offers a holistic framework that brings together inner work and outward action. Key elements include:

1. **Intuition and inner guidance** – learning to trust your internal compass amid external noise
2. **Mindset shifts and narratives** – identifying limiting beliefs and reframing stories you tell yourself
3. **Action and alignment** – taking practical steps that blend purpose, intention and forward movement
4. **Spiritual/energetic perspectives** – viewing life through a lens of abundance, connection and possibility

5. **Real-life stories and reflection tools** – examples from Archbold and others, showing how these shifts play out in business, relationships and everyday life.

In short, the book's message is that self-belief is not a soft ideal but a dynamic force. When cultivated, it becomes a lens through which you attract, create and live the life you're meant for.

What stood out to me the most were the following core themes and takeaways:

| THEME | TAKEAWAY |
|---|---|
| BELIEF PRECEDES BECOMING | The book argues and illustrates that before you can become who you're meant to be, you must first cultivate the belief that you can become it. Belief is the foundation, not a byproduct. |
| YOUR STORY MATTERS | The narratives you tell yourself about your worth, your past and your potential are powerful. One of Archbold's tools is helping readers re-author those stories in a way that makes space for possibility. |
| JUDGMENT IS A BARRIER | The fear of judgment - by others and yourself - is a recurring obstacle. The book encourages readers to step beyond their fears and act, despite the inner voice that says, 'What will they think?' |
| ACTION IS GROUNDED IN ALIGNMENT | It's not just about force of will, but also about aligning your values, energy and actions. When what you do is resonant with who you are, momentum grows more effortlessly. |
| SUCCESS IS HOLISTIC | The aim isn't just external achievement (career, wealth, status) but integrated flourishing: in relationships, purpose, daily habits and inner peace. |
| TOOLS AND RITUALS ANCHOR THE SHIFTS | Archbold doesn't leave readers in the realm of abstractions. She offers rituals, frameworks and practices (e.g. morning routines, reflection prompts, story exercises) to anchor the shifts. |

## HACKS TO BUILDING BELIEF

There are many other methods you can implement to build your confidence in any aspect of life, so here are several helpful exercises that are worth trying.

### START WITH IDENTITY, NOT OUTCOME

Instead of saying, 'I want to achieve X', start with, 'I am the kind of person who can achieve X'. Over time, this identity-based belief becomes the foundation, reinforced through repetition and consistent action.

### GATHER EVIDENCE (EVEN SMALL WINS)

Confidence grows from proof, not just hope, which validates progress. So, break your goals into micro-goals that feel like regular, consistent progress, leading to positive forward momentum. There will be days, as there are for all of us, when movement, even by the smallest margins, is elusive, and you will experience setbacks. Sometimes the setbacks are minor, and other times they can feel like the world has come crashing down around you.

During many of my darkest times, when I was seriously injured, even in life-threatening situations, when I was reduced to crawling, or unable even to move, I found that setting the most micro of goals helped me to evoke positivity.

### TRACK PROGRESS

Seeing measurable progress reinforces the belief that success is happening. You can also reflect on past wins, even unrelated ones, such as times when you followed through, challenges you overcame, or skills that you developed. This practice is potent if you harboured doubt that you could achieve any of these accomplishments at any prior point in life.

There were many times in my life when things got tough, or I faced new challenges, and I would draw on my accomplishments in one field to boost my confidence in another. For example, if speaking in front of an audience of 500 successful people for the first time daunted me, I would say to myself, 'You raced an IRONMAN, against all odds, Jason. So, you can do this!'

Remember, every win is a data point that says, 'I can do hard things'.

## CONTROL YOUR INNER VOICE

Your self-talk creates your reality, regardless of what challenge you are facing. Therefore, positive affirmation has a significant positive impact. Instead of saying to yourself, 'I don't know what I'm doing', say, 'I am figuring this out'. This isn't about lying to yourself or false hope; rather, you're framing things in a way that helps you move forwards. In fact, it is the voice that beguiles you into believing you are not capable or worthy that is the liar.

## VISUALISE WITH SPECIFICITY

Visualisation works best when you see yourself doing the work, not just receiving the reward. Even more powerfully, imagine the emotions you'd feel when succeeding at what you set out to do. This mental rehearsal builds neural patterns like those experienced in real life.

## PRACTICE UNDER PRESSURE

Confidence is built by doing things before you feel fully ready. This means taking small, real-world risks, such as speaking up in meetings, sharing your project publicly, or attempting a miniature version of the big goal. With each cxperience, your comfort zone expands, and your beliefs follow.

By managing your state, you become aware of your body's signals. You can use posture, breathing and movement to signal strength – for example, by standing tall, adopting open body language and breathing deeply. Social psychologist Amy Cuddy's research has shown that deliberately adopting confident physical postures can influence physiology, temporarily boosting testosterone and reducing cortisol, the body's primary stress hormone.

Surrounding yourself intentionally also helps. Spend time with people who believe in you or model success, and you will discover that confidence and belief are contagious. Conversely, reduce time with those who reinforce self-doubt or belittle your accomplishments.

## THE SPARK THAT MAKES THE IMPOSSIBLE INEVITABLE

In the end, belief is not a loud declaration. It is not a motivational poster or a fleeting surge of adrenaline. Belief is quieter, deeper, steadier. It is the internal shift that takes place long before the world ever sees a result. It is the moment you stop negotiating with your fear and start aligning with your future.

Belief is not certainty; it is commitment. It is not confidence; it is courage. It is not the absence of doubt; it is the decision to move anyway.

Every great life is built on this paradox: belief often begins in the dark, long before any evidence exists. King believed long before change seemed possible. Mandela believed long before freedom seemed nearby. Munro believed long before machinery agreed with him. Nyad believed long before the sea relented. The Stoics believed long before peace surrounded them. And you believed long before you became who you are today – even if you didn't realise it at the time.

Belief is born at the edge of your limits. It begins where comfort ends. It grows in the gap between who you've been and who you're willing to become. It is sustained not by applause, but by action – the small, consistent, daily vote that says: I am still in this. I am still becoming.

Every time you take a step towards an impossible goal, you are teaching your mind a new truth: I am capable of more than I believed.

Every small win is a brick on the path. Every setback survived is a strengthening. Every moment of fear faced widens identity.

Belief compounds. It gathers proof, layer by layer, until what once felt unreachable becomes inevitable.

This is why belief precedes becoming. You do not wait to become the person capable of the goal – you believe yourself into that person by your actions.

In my own life, belief was not a gift I was born with. It was forged – sometimes painfully – through discipline, courage, movement and the willingness to confront myself. It began with four shaky laps in a swimming pool and expanded into a life of impossible races, impossible distances and impossible transformations. Each achievement was not the victory itself, but the evidence that belief had taken root.

And this is the truth that greatness whispers to anyone willing to listen: the world does not believe in you first. You believe in yourself first – and then you show the world why.

Belief does not eliminate hardship. It reshapes it. It turns pain into information, setbacks into strategy, fear into fuel. It transforms the voice that says, 'I can't' into the voice that whispers, 'Try again'. It gives meaning to suffering and direction to chaos.

When you understand this, you stop waiting for perfect conditions, timing and clarity. You begin to act, and through action, belief strengthens. Through belief, identity changes. Through identity, outcomes follow.

One day, you will look back at the life you built and realise that every chapter, every race, every storm, every victory began the same way: with a moment when you chose to believe just enough to take the next step.

That is the fire beneath greatness.

Greatness doesn't care how much anyone else believes in you. It cares about the belief you are willing to cultivate within yourself and the actions you are eager to take to honour it.

Because belief is the seed of every transformation, it must be nurtured and protected. In time, it will grow into everything you once thought impossible.

# REFLECTION, ACTION AND GROWTH

## STRENGTHEN YOUR BELIEF

**Reflection:** Where have you let past failures, labels, or addictions become the ceiling on what you believe is possible for you now?

**Action:** Write down one old story you've been telling yourself (e.g. 'I'm not a runner', 'I always quit', 'I'm just not that type of person'). Rewrite it as a new identity-based belief:

'I am the kind of person who ________.'

Finish that sentence and take one small action in the next 24 hours that proves the new story true.

## COMMIT TO THE GOAL THAT SCARES YOU

**Reflection:** What is the 'impossible' goal that quietly scares you because, deep down, you actually want it?

**Action:** Name that goal clearly, then sketch a simple 90-day belief plan:

- one 30-day milestone
- one 60-day milestone
- one 90-day milestone.

Decide on one tiny action you will take this week to start building evidence (your first deposit into the confidence bank).

## CHOOSE THE VOICE YOU LISTEN TO

**Reflection:** When doubt shouts the loudest – when the knee hurts, the crowd laughs, or fear grips – what voice do you listen to?

**Action:** Create a 'belief ritual' for those moments with:

- one phrase you will say (your version of 'not today, I will not quit today ')
- one physical shift (stand tall, deep breath, shoulders back)
- one question you'll ask yourself – 'What is my next step, not my perfect step?'

Commit to using this ritual the next time you feel like backing away.

## SHAPE AN ENVIRONMENT THAT SUPPORTS BELIEF

**Reflection:** Is your environment feeding your belief or fuelling your doubt?

**Action:** List three people, places, or habits that *drain* your belief, and three that *strengthen* it. Then:

- choose one drain to reduce your exposure to
- choose one strengthener to lean into more often (a person, a practice, a place)
- schedule a concrete action with that strengthener in the coming week.

SS GREAT
EATNESS G
SS GREAT
EATNESS G
SS GREAT
EATNESS G
SS GREAT
EATNESS G

# CHAPTER 9
# SACRIFICE

***'GREAT ACHIEVEMENT IS USUALLY BORN OF GREAT SACRIFICE.'* - NAPOLEON HILL**

Every great life is built on something given up. Sacrifice is the quiet currency of greatness, the price paid in private for what the world will one day call extraordinary.

We tend to glorify the rewards of achievement, such as medals, records and moments of triumph, but the real story unfolds in the hours unseen: the early mornings, the lonely choices and the quiet refusals. Sacrifice is never dramatic. It's not about grand gestures or martyrdom. It's the steady discipline of choosing what matters most over what feels easiest now.

Time is finite. Every day, we are gifted the same number of hours, minutes and seconds, regardless of who we are, where we are, or how much money we have. We all receive exactly 1440 minutes – of that, we can be certain.

Discipline enables efficiency, as we have previously addressed, freeing up more of those minutes to do more and live more. Often, circumstances outside our control dictate how we spend some of that time. Still, with the remainder of our time at our discretion, we must choose how to spend it.

Sacrifice is both a decision and an action: the choice to forgo something in favour of something else. Every sacrifice carries consequences, whether we give up a pleasurable, relaxing activity or a more challenging one. The difficulty lies in timing. The cost is paid today, while the benefits are usually future-oriented.

Until sacrifice becomes habitual, reaching a decision first requires evaluating the benefits versus the cost of making that choice. In many ways, it is like considering the purchase of a product or service. Although I say 'cost' in the context of the sacrifice evaluation, I mean the consequence to yourself and potentially others around you, either at work or home, of the activity you will be forgoing. Once you can satisfy yourself that the benefits are greater than the cost, then you will be more predisposed to make that all-important sacrifice.

This evaluation process is similar to a traditional value equation used when making a buying decision for a product or service. Purchasing decisions almost always combine logical, factual and emotional elements. It is widely accepted that most people apply an approximate 70 per cent emotional and 30 per cent logical ratio when making buying decisions. This is commonly referred to as the value equation.

The same applies when deciding to sacrifice one thing for another, though the choice is often more complex. What you are sacrificing may be far more comfortable than what you plan to do instead – the very action that will move you towards greatness. The sacrifice itself may involve comfort or pleasure, making it considerably easier than the alternative, which often demands greater discretionary effort, discomfort, or even confronting fear. More often than not, it is a combination of all three. As a result, sacrifice typically presents a much tougher decision, one that must be supported by a strong and rational case.

To tip the balance in favour of the more strenuous path, a clear incentive is needed. This begins with an honest evaluation of future benefits weighed against the immediate gratification you are choosing to forgo.

The first and most important step is to define your purpose logically and emotionally, as discussed in Chapter 1. All outstanding accomplishments align with your purpose statement, which should remain visible in the places where you spend most of your time, serving as a constant reminder. The more time you invest in exploring and clearly defining your purpose statement and why it should transcend many other aspects of life, including comfort, the more likely it is that your purpose will outweigh the easier, more comfortable activity you are sacrificing. Of course, on occasion, there will be reasonable reasons not to undertake the activity that underpins or supports your pathway to greatness. These reasons may include family or work commitments that you have already defined.

One of the most obvious scenarios that exemplifies these principles relates to a specific form of exercise. Let's work through a typical scenario that I encounter every day when offering advice to people in various Facebook fitness groups.

For the sake of illustration, consider this familiar and relatable scenario that I've encountered countless times. You are 45 years old, married with two children, and deeply immersed in a demanding career. Time is your most precious commodity. Exercise, once part of your routine, has slowly faded from view. Over the past 15 years, you've made several well-intentioned attempts to return to it – a few sessions here, a short burst of motivation there – but each effort has burned out within a few weeks.

Four times, fitness has been at the centre of your New Year's resolutions, each beginning with conviction and ending in quiet resignation. Your days are full, your energy divided. Meals are often chosen for convenience rather than nutrition and are frequently consumed on the go. You know these choices are not ideal, yet in the rush of modern life, they feel inevitable.

This situation, what I call the 'sacrifice equation', can be viewed from two perspectives.

The first perspective is through the lens of gain, focusing on the short-, medium- and long-term benefits of choosing health, vitality, strength, energy and an extended, more vibrant life. These are the rewards of consistency, the dividends of discipline. But they come at a cost: time, effort and the temporary discomfort of change.

The second perspective is through the lens of loss, examining the short-, medium- and long-term consequences of neglecting health, including fatigue, diminished strength and a reduced lifespan, all for the fleeting comfort of convenience.

Both perspectives can be powerful motivators; it simply depends on which language your mind responds to – the promise of what can be gained, or the cost of what will be lost. And of course, this equation extends far beyond health. Every area of life – from relationships to purpose, from personal growth to legacy – is defined by what we choose to sacrifice now for the life we wish to build later.

## THE ULTIMATE SACRIFICE

Martin Luther King Jr. understood that kind of sacrifice better than anyone. He gave up not only comfort but certainty. Every time he stepped onto a stage, he knew it might be his last. He sacrificed peace for purpose, safety for service, self for society. He didn't seek pain, but he accepted it as part of the path. His greatness wasn't in avoiding suffering, but in giving it meaning. He knew that change demands cost, and he was willing to pay it.

That's the truth about sacrifice: it's not about loss, but investment. It is what you give up that shapes what you gain.

Nelson Mandela's sacrifice stretched across decades. He gave up freedom, family and time – the three things most of us spend our lives protecting. Yet he never treated that loss as a tragedy. He reframed it as preparation. Prison became a forge – each year refining his purpose, strengthening his patience, tempering his soul. He didn't waste his suffering; he used it.

When he was finally freed, he could have claimed vengeance. Instead, he offered forgiveness. That was the ultimate sacrifice – ego surrendered to peace. His greatness was not in what he endured, but in what he chose not to become because of it.

Burt Munro's sacrifices were quieter but no less profound. He sacrificed security for passion, convention for conviction. While others built careers, he built a dream. He worked in solitude, often broke and doubtful, but never bitter. He gave up leisure, comfort and approval, not because he loved hardship, but because he loved the work more.

Sacrifice, for him, wasn't punishment; it was expression. Every scar on his hands, every sleepless night, every unfinished meal was proof of devotion. When he finally stood on the Bonneville Salt Flats, the roar of his motorcycle echoing against the desert sky, he wasn't just racing for speed. He was racing for everything he'd ever given up, and for the man he became because of it.

Diana Nyad's sacrifices were physical, emotional and spiritual. She gave her body to the sea again and again. Each failed crossing left her weaker, older and more bruised. But she refused to see sacrifice as suffering. She saw it as an offering. Every hour she spent in the water was a surrender of comfort, vanity and control. In return, she gained something the world rarely understands – peace through persistence.

When she finally reached the shore after 53 hours of swimming, she said, 'Never, ever give up.' What she didn't say – but her body did – was 'Never stop giving'. Because at its core, sacrifice is an act of love for what matters enough to cost you something.

The Stoics wrote about this long before modern ambition had a name. Seneca observed, 'No man can live a happy life, or even a tolerable one, without the study of wisdom, for the only true freedom is found in the control of the self.'

Sacrifice, in Stoic thought, was an act of self-mastery – the conscious decision to give up indulgence in favour of virtue, and impulse in favour of integrity. Marcus Aurelius reminded himself daily to forgo ease: 'The impediment to action advances action. What stands in the way becomes the way.' They understood that nothing of value comes without cost, and that to live meaningfully is to give meaning to what you relinquish.

The Stoics trained themselves to let go of destructive emotions, such as anger, envy and grief, even when circumstances did not warrant them. Epictetus, once a slave, sacrificed resentment against his master. Instead of letting anger consume him, he transformed suffering into philosophy. By sacrificing destructive passions, they achieved inner greatness, characterised by peace of mind and self-mastery.

This commitment to sacrifice was not accidental, but by principle. They gave up comfort, wealth, power, reputation and even life itself when these stood in the way of virtue. For them, true greatness came from living according to reason and justice, even at the cost of everything else.

In my own life, sacrifice has been both teacher and test. Every training cycle, every race, every period of sustained focus has required the same exchange – comfort for commitment, ease for excellence. You can't chase endurance and cling to convenience. You can't pursue greatness and hold on to everything that makes you feel safe. I've missed gatherings, lost sleep and endured injury, but what I've gained is deeper: clarity, gratitude and self-respect. Each sacrifice strips away the trivial and reveals what truly matters.

That's the paradox of sacrifice: it looks like loss, but it's how we gain alignment. It reminds us that time is finite, energy is sacred and greatness comes at a price, making it rare.

King sacrificed safety for justice. Mandela sacrificed freedom for unity. Munro sacrificed comfort for craft. Nyad sacrificed ease for endurance. The Stoics sacrificed distraction for wisdom.

## *WILLPOWER*: REDISCOVERING THE GREATEST HUMAN STRENGTH

*Willpower*, by Roy Baumeister and John Tierney, is a fascinating book that explores the science of self-control, arguing that willpower is one of the most important predictors of long-term success – more significant than intelligence, talent, or opportunity.

Their core finding is that self-control draws from a single, limited pool of mental energy. They argue that when this pool is depleted, people make poorer decisions, lose discipline and revert to short-term gratification. This phenomenon is known as ego depletion.

Baumeister and Tierney show that willpower functions like a muscle: it becomes fatigued with overuse but can be strengthened through consistent training. They reveal that every act of self-control draws from a single pool of mental energy, which is why decision fatigue, stress and emotional strain weaken our capacity to resist temptation, make good choices and stay focused on long-term goals. The authors also highlight the physiological foundation of willpower, including the role of glucose as a key fuel source, and they demonstrate how low energy levels, poor nutrition and insufficient rest undermine our ability to regulate behaviour.

The book also offers practical strategies for developing stronger self-control and creating environments that foster long-term success. By setting clear goals, monitoring progress, practising small daily acts of discipline and building strong habits, individuals can conserve willpower and reduce the cognitive load that leads to poor decisions.

Perhaps their most powerful insight is that people who build systems – pre-commitments, routines, accountability and structure – ultimately outperform those who rely solely on moment-to-moment willpower. With the proper habits, a strong 'why' and intelligent management of one's mental energy, self-control becomes a renewable, transformative strength that supports everything from health to relationships to peak performance.

## HACKS FOR TRADING SACRIFICE FOR GAIN

There are a limited number of hours in a day, and so many competing priorities. This is often the very excuse most people use to justify not doing something tough or challenging they need to do to find greatness.

Achieving greatness requires sacrifice. Making these choices in a way that serves your future benefit calls for a thoughtful, strategic and emotionally intelligent approach. Here are the key steps to guide you:

1. **Define your purpose.** Purpose is the beginning of everything. It is the spark that turns movement into momentum, struggle into sacrifice and time into meaning. Without it, even success feels hollow. With it, even failure becomes a source of fuel.
2. **Clarify your long-term goals.** Define what you truly want in five, 10, or 20 years (e.g. financial freedom, good health, deep relationships) and write these goals down. Revisit them regularly.

If your goals lack a clear purpose, I recommend reviewing and refining them to create a well-defined objective.

3. **Evaluate the trade-offs.** Begin by asking yourself, 'What am I giving up now?', 'What will I gain in the future?' and 'Is the long-term gain significantly more valuable than the short-term comfort?' For example, skipping a party to study may lead to a better job later.
4. **Use delayed gratification.** Train yourself to resist short-term pleasure in favour of long-term rewards. Use techniques like the 10-10-10 rule – how will this decision feel in 10 minutes, 10 months and 10 years? And practise small sacrifices to build discipline – for example, saving $10 instead of buying coffee.
5. **Visualise the outcome.** As with any positive visualisation technique, take quiet moments to picture the future you want, vividly and emotionally. Store these powerful mental images to fuel motivation when sacrifice feels difficult. Practised consistently, this approach can become intuitive. For me, I would frequently envision myself crossing the finish line of major races, drawing on the euphoria I had experienced from other successful race finishes.
6. **Prioritise based on values.** Align your decisions with your core values, such as integrity, growth and responsibility. Sacrifices based on values feel more meaningful and less painful.
7. **Set clear boundaries.** Not all sacrifices are wise. Avoid ones that cause burnout, resentment, self-neglect, or neglect of others around you. Regular practice will enable you to know when to say no to protect your long-term sustainability.
8. **Track progress and reward yourself.** Stay encouraged by monitoring the results of your sacrifices. This evokes a natural, healthy reward process that continually reinforces your choices.
9. **Surround yourself with support.** Sharing your goals with trusted people who hold you accountable can motivate you to make choices that will benefit your future. Avoid environments or people that tempt you towards short-term thinking.

Sacrifice is not about what we lose. It is about what we choose to build. It is the quiet declaration that your future matters more than your comfort, that your purpose outweighs your impulse, and that who you want to become deserves more from you than ease can ever offer.

Every great life has required this exchange.

King surrendered safety for justice. Mandela surrendered freedom for unity. Munro surrendered comfort for mastery. Nyad surrendered ease for endurance. The Stoics surrendered indulgence for virtue. None were chasing suffering. They were chasing meaning, and meaning always costs something.

Sacrifice strips away the unnecessary so the essential can emerge. It rearranges your priorities until the trivial falls silent and the true rises to the surface. It reveals what you value not by what you claim, but by what you're willing to give up.

Most people fear sacrifice because they mistake it for loss. But sacrifice, at its highest form, is alignment. It is the conscious choice to exchange who you are now for who you have the potential to become. It is the bridge between intention and embodiment.

Perhaps the most profound truth is this: every sacrifice is a vote for your future.

A vote that says, *I believe something greater is possible.*

A vote that says, *I am willing to pay the price my dream requires.*

A vote that says, *My life will not be governed by fear, distraction, or convenience.*

Sacrifice reveals character long before success does.

In my own life, every mile, every dawn session, every hour spent confronting fear rather than feeding it has taught me the same lesson: you cannot hold on to comfort and reach for greatness at the same time. Something must be set down so something larger can be lifted.

Sacrifice is how you cross the invisible gap between potential and proof. It is how you earn the life you want to live. It is not a punishment but a privilege to choose with intention, to shape your days rather than drift through them, and to place your future self ahead of your present cravings. It is a privilege to give yourself a real chance to see what you are capable of.

Greatness will never demand perfection from you, but it will require investment. It will ask you to trade what is easy for what is essential, what is fleeting for what is foundational and what is comfortable for what is true.

So, the question is no longer, 'What must I sacrifice?' but 'What is my future worth to me?'

If the answer is 'everything', then you are ready. Ready to choose the harder path today so you can stand taller tomorrow. Ready to give up the distractions that dilute you. Ready to walk away from the stories that shrink you. Ready to embrace the discomfort that will refine you.

Sacrifice is not the end of something – it is the beginning of everything that lasts.

And greatness, as you will soon discover, does not care what you gave up. It cares about who you become because of it.

## REFLECTION, ACTION AND GROWTH

### NOTICE THE SACRIFICES YOU'RE ALREADY MAKING

**Reflection:** What are you already sacrificing – without realising it – by choosing short-term comfort over long-term gain?

**Action:** Conduct a quick audit of your 1440 minutes:

- List three ways you regularly choose ease (e.g. scrolling late nights, skipping movement, saying 'yes' to everything).
- For each, write what you are *sacrificing* (health, energy, respect for yourself, time with those you love).
- Circle one you will consciously trade, just for this week, for a harder choice that serves your future.

### CHOOSE THE SACRIFICES YOUR PURPOSE DEMANDS

**Reflection:** If you truly honoured your purpose, what would you *have to* let go of?

**Action:** Write down your core purpose or a primary long-term goal (five to 20 years out), then:

- list at least three sacrifices that the goal demands (habits, comforts, distractions, even certain expectations from others)
- choose one specific sacrifice you will make in the next seven days (e.g. one early morning, one social event declined, one hour reclaimed from TV) and schedule it.

## LISTEN TO THE VOICE THAT PROTECTS YOUR FUTURE

**Reflection:** When you face a sacrifice decision, which voice do you usually listen to: the one chasing relief now, or the one protecting your future?

**Action:** Think of a decision you're sitting with right now (health, work, relationships, money). Use the 10–10–10 rule. How will this choice feel:

- in 10 minutes?
- in 10 months?
- in 10 years?

Write down your answers, then make one decision today that favours your 10-year self over your 10-minute self.

## SHAPE YOURSELF THROUGH INTENTIONAL SACRIFICE

**Reflection:** Are your current sacrifices shaping you into who you want to become – or into someone you won't recognise or respect later?

**Action:** List five things you are currently sacrificing most (e.g. sleep, health, time with family, learning, solitude, integrity, play). Mark each as:

- aligned with your values and future, or
- misaligned/costing you too much.

Commit to one adjustment this week: either deepen an aligned sacrifice (double down) or begin to reverse a misaligned one (set a boundary, ask for help, say 'no').

# CHAPTER 10
# STILLNESS

***'NOWHERE YOU CAN GO IS MORE PEACEFUL – MORE FREE OF INTERRUPTIONS – THAN YOUR OWN SOUL.'* – MARCUS AURELIUS**

Stillness is not the absence of movement. It is the presence of awareness – the quiet centre of motion, the calm beneath the waves, the breath between storms.

In a world that worships speed, stillness feels radical. But all extraordinary lives, all great acts, are rooted in it. Without stillness, courage becomes recklessness, effort becomes exhaustion and thought becomes noise. Stillness is where we gather ourselves before we give ourselves.

So let me ask you, 'Did you find the state of *stillness* yesterday?' If not yesterday, when was the last time that you saw and existed in your stillness, set your phone aside, removed all distractions, sat quietly and immersed yourself in a state of presence and reflection?

As you read this, I invite you to take a moment to find your stillness. As you immerse yourself in peace and calm, jot down your thoughts and reflections on paper.

How long did you remain in that state of stillness? Your propensity to reflect on that question for at least a few minutes should yield telling insights. If you literally turned the page to begin reading again, then there's some work to do to increase your stillness.

What reflections did you experience? How did it feel, and how long has it been since you last immersed yourself in your own stillness without distractions? Perhaps the most insightful question of all is: when did you last set your mobile device aside for a day without checking it? Or when did you last decide – unmotivated by necessity – to set it aside, or turn it off for even a few hours? I have every confidence that you are currently aware and contemplating a modicum of change.

It seems to me that we rarely find stillness anymore. Sure, much of our day is spent not moving – mostly seated – but seldom is this a state of intentional stillness without distraction. So why does distraction consume us so thoroughly? Distraction from meaningful presence. Distraction from everything around us. Distraction from people, our loved ones, from the moment and the things that matter most in life.

I completely understand that staying plugged in often feels necessary these days. But there was a time – not so long ago – when we lived, loved and communicated beautifully without mobile phones, computers, or the constant hum of notifications. In fact, we were more connected then than we are now.

We spoke to one another, face to face, uninterrupted. We gathered around dinner tables, sharing stories, laughter, problems and solutions. As children, we played outside in the streets, parks and wild corners of our neighbourhoods. Through these moments of pure, unfiltered human interaction, we learned what it meant to belong, to listen, to collaborate, to care. We grew because we were present.

Back then, stillness was not an indulgence; it was a natural part of life. There were pauses between tasks, silence between conversations and long stretches of undistracted attention. For rest and creativity, we read books, made things with our hands, stitched, baked and built.

In many homes, these simple crafts were everyday rituals, as they were in mine when I was growing up.

But with each passing generation, these skills – and the deep connections they created – seem to slip a little further away. Today, far too often, we trade engagement for convenience. We sit for hours, eyes fixed on screens, minds scattered, hearts elsewhere. And in the process, we lose not just the craft, but the connection, the intimacy and the stillness that once shaped who we were.

Tragically, research estimates that fewer than half of US citizens read a book for pleasure each year, and I suspect the same is true in most developed nations. I wonder, then, how many of those who haven't read a book in the last 12 months have read a book in the previous 10 years, or since leaving school.

If you're not convinced yet, consider hopping on a train, taking an elevator in an office block, or simply spending a day observing our collective obsession with distraction. We are constantly distracted from where we are in the moment. We seem obsessed with being somewhere else, often to avoid the simple act of interacting with another human, because it feels easier. I have come to believe that we deliberately bury our attention in our mobile devices as a form of escape.

Of course, there are times when we need to be available. But the amount of time we now choose to be unavailable says a great deal about our capacity for presence and stillness. I appreciate that some readers may question this view, so I urge you to consider one simple fact: since the first Sumerian civilisation, human civilisation has existed for 99.9963 per cent of its history without mobile devices or internet connections.

Stillness holds profound importance for humans – physically, mentally, emotionally and even spiritually. In a world full of noise, distraction and constant motion, stillness offers a counterbalance that promotes clarity, healing and inner growth.

Stillness reduces mental clutter, allowing the mind to rest and detach from overstimulation, such as social media, news and multitasking. It also enhances focus because when distractions quiet down, it's easier to concentrate and think clearly. Stillness also fosters insight. Many people report that their most profound realisations come during moments of quiet reflection.

As an athlete who trained twice a day, six days a week, while immersed in a high-pressure, frenetic corporate world, exercise was my time of stillness, even as I moved. And during this season of my life, which began 27 years ago, the time I spent alone while training – often 25 hours every week – was the most valuable and practical time I have ever experienced. No matter the pressure in my frantic life, I would reflect and find solutions with presence and clarity of mind. Stillness, therefore, does not always require you to be physically still and can be effectively found while sitting quietly alone or walking. Aside from running, my preference is to remove myself from civilisation, surrounded by nature, whether at the beach, by a body of water, or in a forest or park, and walk, run, or read.

Emotional regulation derived from stillness is invaluable, as it creates space between stimulus and reaction. This enables you to pause before responding emotionally, leading to better decision-making. By pausing before reacting emotionally, stillness enables you to make better decisions and fosters stronger, more meaningful interpersonal relationships. Stillness also helps us to process emotions: quiet time allows buried emotions to surface and be understood, rather than suppressed or ignored.

Being still, primarily through practices like meditation or deep breathing, activates the parasympathetic nervous system ('rest and digest'), lowering stress hormones like cortisol. Stillness is highly effective in reducing stress, which not only benefits happiness but also contributes to extending our longevity. Another significant benefit is that it supports healing, as when the body isn't in a constant state of fight or flight, it can't effectively repair itself or restore balance.

Stillness opens imaginative, creative space. Many artists, scientists and thinkers emphasise the importance of silence and solitude for creativity and breakthroughs. I can attest to this, as many of my most creative or solution-oriented moments have emerged from my stillness.

Nearly all spiritual traditions emphasise stillness – whether through meditation, prayer, or contemplation – to connect with a more profound sense of self or a higher power. While I would never classify myself as a spiritual person from a religious perspective, I am in many other ways, and connecting with nature is my spiritual nirvana, my proper happy place. Merging exercise and nature, such as trail running or swimming in the ocean, brings me into an elevated state of consciousness that nothing in this world can match. Undoubtedly, stillness helps cultivate presence, allowing you to experience life more fully in the moment.

Without constant external input, you position yourself to tune into your inner voice and values. Stillness enables you to reflect on your life direction, relationships and choices without the pressure of external opinions. Stillness is not the absence of activity – it's a deliberate turning inward. It's where humans can restore balance, find meaning and reconnect with their true selves. In an age that rewards speed and noise, stillness is a quiet rebellion that leads to wholeness.

## WHERE GREATNESS FINDS ITS QUIET

Martin Luther King Jr. found his stillness in prayer. Behind every speech that stirred a nation were hours spent alone, searching for clarity in silence. He knew that noise could inspire, but only stillness can align. In those moments of solitude, he wrestled with fear, doubt and exhaustion, and emerged with peace. That peace became his strength. It gave him the composure to face hatred without reciprocating hatred, to meet chaos with grace. That is the purpose of stillness: not escape, but preparation.

Nelson Mandela learned stillness through necessity. In prison, there was nothing but time – long, unending stretches of silence broken only by routine. Many men went mad in that space. Mandela went inwards. He used silence as a study, reflection as a strategy, and stillness as survival. He learned that calm is a form of power – that self-control disarms even those who seek to provoke it. His stillness was not submission. It was strength at rest, patience embodied.

When he emerged after 27 years, his composure stunned the world. They expected rage. They found serenity. That stillness became the foundation of reconciliation.

Burt Munro found stillness in movement. His workshop was a world of constant sound – tools, metal, engines – but inside him, there was quiet. Precision requires presence, and presence involves stillness. To shape metal so that it sings instead of shatters, you must listen. You must feel. That's what Munro did. His focus was complete, his mind undivided. During the noise, he found silence. That's the paradox of stillness: it's not always about stopping. It's about awareness within action.

Diana Nyad's stillness was born in chaos. The ocean is never still. It moves, breathes, shifts without pattern or mercy. Yet amid that constant motion, she found her calm. When she swam for hours, then days, she entered a state where thought dissolved. Pain, fear and fatigue were all still there, but somehow irrelevant. She wasn't fighting the water anymore; she was part of it.

That's the essence of stillness: when you stop resisting life and begin to move with it.

The Stoics built their philosophy on this. Marcus Aurelius wrote his *Meditations* amid war and chaos, yet his words read as if written in perfect calm: 'Nowhere can man find a quieter or more untroubled retreat than in his own soul.'

Seneca taught that peace isn't the absence of trouble, but the mastery of it. Epictetus, crippled and enslaved, wrote of serenity as the ultimate freedom – the power to remain composed regardless of circumstance.

The Stoics taught that emotions such as anger, fear, envy and greed can cloud judgment. Stillness – the disciplined quieting of these passions – allowed the mind to act with reason. By maintaining emotional equilibrium, a Stoic could respond wisely rather than impulsively, even under pressure. As Marcus Aurelius said: 'If you are disturbed by anything external, the pain is not due to the thing itself, but to your estimate of it.'

Stillness enables a person to see things as they truly are, not as distorted by desire or fear. In this clarity, a person could make decisions grounded in virtue, such as justice, courage, temperance and wisdom, which was the Stoic definition of greatness.

For the Stoics, greatness required being self-contained, not dependent on the praise of others or the outcome of events. Stillness fostered 'autarkeia' – self-sufficiency – a calm rooted in internal control, rather than external fortune.

In short, the Stoics saw stillness not as withdrawal from life, but as the foundation for living it bravely, wisely and well. In stillness, they found the space to align their actions with their highest values and to become truly great.

King found stillness in prayer. Mandela found it in patience. Munro found it in creation. Nyad found it in flow. The Stoics found it in reason.

## STILLNESS IS THE KEY

Ryan Holiday's *Stillness Is the Key* is an excellent guide to cultivating calm, clarity and presence in a noisy, distracted world. It draws on Stoic philosophy, Buddhism, Christianity and lessons from history, showing how great leaders, thinkers and athletes mastered stillness to achieve excellence. Here are the key messages from what I regard as the most enlightening book on the art of stillness:

1. **Stillness of the mind (clarity of thought).** Holiday emphasises that distractions, worries and noise constantly pull the mind, and that true clarity comes from slowing down, focusing and refusing to be consumed by endless thoughts. He also encourages practices such as journalling, meditation, solitude and limiting information overload. For example, Marcus Aurelius wrote in his journal to steady his mind amid the demands of ruling an empire.
2. **Stillness of the spirit (peace within).** A restless spirit leads to anxiety, envy and dissatisfaction, argues Holiday. He defines peace as living with integrity, aligning actions with values, and letting go of what we can't control. Additionally, gratitude, forgiveness and humility are essential.
3. **Stillness of the body (balance and discipline).** Rest, health and physical routines ground us, allowing for greater focus, as overwork and excessive stimulation can compromise clarity. Holiday also impresses upon us that

movement – walking, exercise and nature – helps the body reset and quiets the mind. He notes that Churchill balanced his intense work with painting and walks to maintain composure.

4. **The power of presence.** Life is lived only in the present moment – not in regrets of the past or anxieties of the future. Therefore, stillness means being fully engaged with what's in front of us, and that presence enables better decisions, stronger relationships and more profound joy.
5. **Resisting the urge to react.** Stillness creates space between stimulus and response, which I struggled with for much of my life. Greatness, therefore, often comes from restraint, patience and thoughtful action rather than rash reaction. He exemplifies this by citing John F. Kennedy's calm deliberation during the Cuban Missile Crisis, which avoided nuclear war.
6. **Simplicity and essentialism.** Holiday explains that complexity, excess possessions and endless busyness create chaos, and argues that a simpler life – fewer commitments and clear priorities – leads to greater peace and focus. Consequently, stillness isn't inactivity but deliberate, purposeful action.
7. **The intersection of wisdom traditions.** Holiday powerfully ties together Stoicism, Buddhism, Taoism and Christianity, showing that they all point towards stillness as the foundation of wisdom and strength.

Throughout *Stillness Is the Key*, Holiday impresses that stillness is not about doing nothing – it's about cultivating clarity, presence and peace so that when we do act, we act with strength, focus and wisdom. If it is stillness that you seek to develop, I highly recommend this great book.

## HOW TO FIND YOUR STILLNESS

Stillness, with purpose, can seem elusive in our fast-paced world, where information and communication are readily available at our fingertips 24/7. With employers expecting increasing productivity from their employees, alongside our predilection for distraction and communication, it can be challenging to put our phones down, out of sight, or turn them off. Eventually, screen time becomes addictive for a plethora of reasons.

So, here are some practical tips for finding stillness along your pathway to greatness – the kind of calm focus that allows clarity, resilience, and purpose to emerge even when life feels overwhelming.

| CATEGORY | PRACTICE |
|---|---|
| MINDSET SHIFTS | **Redefine stillness:** Stillness doesn't always mean doing nothing; it means creating inner calm while life continues around you. |
| | **Detach from noise:** Recognise that greatness doesn't come from constant motion, but from well-directed action. |
| DAILY PRACTICES | **Start your day quietly:** Even five minutes of silence, mindful breathing, or journalling can anchor your mind and foster creativity, gratitude, problem-solving and presence. |
| | **Practise mindful pauses:** Before a big decision or in the middle of stress, take three slow breaths to reset. |
| | **Limit stimulation:** Reduce unnecessary notifications, background noise and distractions that pull you away from focus. This is particularly important before attempting to sleep. |
| BODY AND ENVIRONMENT | **Use movement for stillness:** Walking, stretching, or slow exercise (like yoga or tai chi) can calm the mind while engaging the body. |
| | **Create a stillness space:** Choose a spot in your home, no matter how small, where you go for silence and reflection. For me, this is my garden and oasis. |
| | **Connect with nature:** Time outdoors naturally quietens the mind and restores perspective. In fact, if you can make this a daily priority, even for just 10 or 15 minutes, it will be transformative. If you think you don't have time, get up 15 minutes earlier or go for a walk during your lunch break. Immersing yourself in nature's beauty, even in a small city park, will create stillness, presence, clarity and perspective. |

| CATEGORY | PRACTICE |
|---|---|
| **REFLECTION AND PERSPECTIVE** | **Journal your thoughts:** Writing helps untangle mental clutter, turning noise into clarity. It also enables further reflection on previous journal entries, reminding you how you felt during a specific situation, or how you overcame a challenge, doubt, or fear. |
| | **Embrace solitude:** Spend time alone, not as loneliness but as an opportunity to recharge and listen to your inner voice. Finding solitude has a profound positive impact on life and mindset. Being alone does not necessarily mean being lonely, which is primarily a state of mind. Utilising this time to come to terms with who you are and who you desire to be will be transformative. |
| | **Practise gratitude:** Shifting focus to what's meaningful brings peace and steadiness, which I will cover in depth in the next chapter. Gratitude, beyond all doubt, is the most essential element of happiness and positivity. |
| **LONG-TERM INTEGRATION** | **Schedule stillness:** Treat quiet time as essential as meetings or workouts. Scheduling quiet time in your diary signals its importance, making it as crucial as any other event or gathering that fills your calendar. This ensures you commit to it. |
| | **Focus on the present:** Greatness isn't achieved in the future; it's built in the present, through mindful choices. As I have already addressed, presence is the elixir of life. Without presence, you diminish your connections with other humans. An absence of presence will be the thief of joy and of living. Without it, life will pass in a flash – until you have all the time in the world to reflect and regret living in the moment throughout your life. |
| | **Accept imperfection:** Stillness comes when you let go of the need to control everything. |

For me, stillness has often come only after exhaustion. In the aftermath of a long run or race, when the noise fades and the world feels wide and quiet, I find that moment of complete awareness. The breath deepens, the mind clears, and for a brief time, there is no separation between self and life.

It's not empty. It's full – of gratitude, humility, peace. Stillness doesn't remove motion; it refines it. It teaches you to move deliberately, to act from clarity rather than chaos.

In these moments, we reconnect with why we began. Purpose, belief, courage – all of it returns to focus. That's why every great leader, thinker and athlete, whether consciously or not, learns to build silence into their lives.

I find it in the breath between steps, in those fleeting moments when effort gives way to awareness, and the noise of striving fades into the hum of being alive. Stillness is not retreat. It's readiness.

Stillness is not the absence of effort, but the grounding that makes effort purposeful. It allows you to act with clarity, persistence and courage – the very qualities needed for greatness.

Greatness doesn't care how loud you are, how fast you move, or how busy you seem. It cares how deeply you listen and how often you return to stillness to remember who you are before the world tells you otherwise.

Because the most extraordinary power in life doesn't come from movement itself, but from the stillness that shapes how and why we move.

# REFLECTION, ACTION AND GROWTH

## PRACTISE INTENTIONAL STILLNESS

**Reflection:** When was the last time you sat in intentional stillness – no phone, no screens, no noise – for at least 10 minutes? What did you notice rising to the surface when the distractions fell away?

**Action:** Choose one time in the next 24 hours to sit in complete stillness for 10 minutes. Set a timer, put your phone in another room and notice your thoughts and feelings without trying to change them. Afterwards, jot down three words to describe how you felt.

## INTERRUPT THE PULL OF DISTRACTION

**Reflection:** In what moments of your typical day do you most often reach for your phone or another distraction instead of allowing yourself to be present with yourself, your work, or the people around you?

**Action:** Pick one of these moments – commuting, waiting in a queue, before bed – and declare it a distraction-free zone for the next seven days. During that time, keep your device out of reach and practise simply observing your surroundings, your breath, or the person in front of you.

## FIND STILLNESS IN MOTION

**Reflection:** When have you last experienced a sense of inner calm while moving (e.g. walking, running, swimming, or being in nature), when your mind felt clear and your body felt connected rather than rushed?

**Action:** Schedule one short 'stillness-in-motion' session this week (e.g. 15 to 30 minutes of walking, easy running, or gentle movement without headphones). Use that time to tune in to your breath, your body and the environment. Afterwards, write down one insight or idea that emerged.

## PAUSE BEFORE YOU RESPOND

**Reflection:** Think of a recent situation when you reacted quickly from emotion – anger, frustration, or anxiety. How might that moment have unfolded differently if you had created even a few seconds of stillness before responding?

**Action:** For the next three days, practise a simple rule: whenever you feel emotionally triggered, pause and take three slow, deliberate breaths before you speak or act. At the end of each day, note one moment when this pause changed your response – or when it could have.

SS GREAT
EATNESS G
SS GREAT
EATNESS G
SS GREAT
EATNESS G
SS GREAT
EATNESS G

# CHAPTER 11
# MOVEMENT

***'PHYSICAL FITNESS IS NOT ONLY ONE OF THE MOST IMPORTANT KEYS TO A HEALTHY BODY, IT IS THE BASIS OF DYNAMIC AND CREATIVE INTELLECTUAL ACTIVITY.' – JOHN F. KENNEDY***

Movement is life. Before we speak, we reach. Before we think, we breathe. Before we dream, we move.

To move is to participate in existence, to declare, 'I am still here'. It's our first act as infants and our final act before death. Every heartbeat, every inhalation, every step is proof of our aliveness.

Movement is more than motion. It's the physical expression of spirit, the outward shape of inner intention. When we move, we turn thought into being.

Movement became my life. In fact, movement saved my life! Once I found my purpose and got going, it set in motion my pathway of discovery, happiness and greatness. It became addictive on so many physical, emotional, spiritual and psychological levels that it pervaded every element of my life. Movement and strength gave me confidence and took me places – geographically and emotionally – that filled my happiness bucket to the point of overflow.

While movement, fitness, physical strength and excellent health are not prerequisites for achieving greatness – as countless people throughout history have shown – they are essential to fully experiencing and sustaining it. When you cultivate physical wellness, your emotional and psychological wellbeing is far better positioned to follow. And I guarantee you that when those elements align, they will elevate your potential to achieve greatness.

## MORE LIFE TO YOUR DAYS AND MORE DAYS TO YOUR LIFE

Movement and exercise will improve your health and, in most instances, minimise sickness and ill health. While many illnesses and physical ailments can affect your quality of life, or even your chances of staying alive, I will focus only on the leading cause of death in the USA for more than 100 years, as well as in many developed countries: heart disease.

Dr Benjamin Levine, a renowned cardiologist and exercise physiologist, has conducted pivotal research demonstrating that regular, appropriately dosed exercise can prevent – and even reverse – age-related changes in heart structure and function. His studies, particularly those published in the journal *Circulation*, have significantly contributed to our understanding of how exercise affects cardiac aging.

Key findings from Dr Levine's research include the following:

1. **Reversing cardiac aging in middle age.** In a landmark study, Dr Levine and his team investigated whether a structured exercise regimen could reverse heart aging in sedentary adults aged 45 to 64. Participants engaged in a two-year program that included high-intensity interval training (HIIT) once weekly, moderate-intensity aerobic exercise two to three times per week, one weekly strength training session, and a weekly long-duration

aerobic session. The results were compelling – participants showed an 18 per cent improvement in maximal oxygen uptake ($VO_2$ max) and a 25 per cent enhancement in left ventricular compliance, effectively reversing decades of sedentary-induced cardiac stiffening. These benefits were not observed in a control group that performed only flexibility and balance exercises.

2. **Optimal exercise 'dose' for heart health.** Dr Levine's research highlights the importance of both exercise frequency and intensity. His findings show that engaging in aerobic exercise four to five times per week is necessary to maintain or improve cardiac elasticity. Casual exercise (two to three times weekly) was insufficient to produce these benefits. This 'dose' of exercise appears to be most effective when initiated in late middle age, before the heart loses its plasticity.
3. **Long-term endurance training and heart health.** Further studies have shown that lifelong endurance athletes have cardiac structures similar to those of much younger individuals. Their hearts remained more compliant and less stiff than those of sedentary peers, suggesting that consistent, long-term endurance training can preserve youthful heart function. These facts I can wholeheartedly validate, as at the age of 62, testing shows that I have maintained the heart function and blood pressure of an 18-year-old.
4. **Exercise and coronary artery calcium.** Addressing concerns about high levels of exercise potentially increasing coronary artery calcium (CAC) scores – a marker of atherosclerosis – Dr Levine levine conducted a study involving over 8700 participants aged 40 and older. The research concluded that high levels of physical activity did not accelerate CAC progression over time. Instead, baseline CAC levels were the strongest predictor of future CAC scores, indicating that regular intense exercise does not inherently increase heart disease risk.

Dr Levine's extensive research underscores the profound impact of regular, appropriately dosed exercise on cardiac health. His findings advocate integrating structured aerobic and resistance training into daily routines, particularly starting in middle age, to prevent or even reverse age-related cardiac changes. These insights have been instrumental in shaping exercise recommendations for cardiovascular health.

## MOVEMENT AS REBELLION AND REDEMPTION

Martin Luther King Jr. understood movement not only as a metaphor, but as a mandate. His marches were not spontaneous; they were sacred. Each step through Montgomery or Selma was an act of prayer, a living sermon about justice in motion.

Those marches changed laws, yes, but more importantly, they changed people. They reminded the world that transformation begins with movement – the courage to take a first step when the destination is still unseen.

'Faith,' King said, 'is taking the first step even when you don't see the whole staircase.' That step is everything. It's when purpose becomes proof.

Nelson Mandela, confined for years in a cell, never stopped moving. Even when his body was trapped, his spirit moved. He ran in place, exercised and kept rhythm with the beat of his own heart. Movement was his rebellion. It was his way of saying, 'You can imprison my body, but not my will'. When he was finally freed, his first steps through the gates of Robben Island were not merely physical; they were symbolic. Each stride was a bridge between the man he had been and the world he was ready to rebuild. That's what movement does – it transforms us. It changes not just where we are, but who we are.

Burt Munro's movement was mechanical but no less human. His hands, stained with oil, moved with precise, ritual devotion. Every stroke of the file, every adjustment of a piston, was part of a dance that required patience, rhythm and love. The roar of his motorcycle on the Bonneville Salt Flats was not noise; it was expression. It was years of small, deliberate movements culminating in one significant motion; a life's purpose set free.

Diana Nyad found her movement in water, immersed in vast, cold seas without an end. Her strokes were slow, steady, eternal. For 53 hours, she moved towards a horizon she could not see. That's the most valid form of motion – not the chase for speed, but the surrender to persistence.

She didn't fight the ocean. She became part of it. Movement became meditation. Pain became rhythm. The act of swimming became a dialogue between will and nature. When she finally touched land, her first words weren't about conquest but about connection: 'Never, ever give up.' It wasn't advice – it was embodiment.

The Stoics saw movement not as chaos, but as harmony. To them, the universe itself was movement, the turning of the stars, the cycle of birth and decay, the constant renewal of time.

Marcus Aurelius wrote that we must 'observe how all things are continually being born of change'. Movement, to the Stoics, was the natural state of everything. Resistance to change was resistance to life. Epictetus taught that we should move in accordance with nature – not fight against what is, but flow with it. Movement, in that sense, becomes wisdom: the grace to evolve without fear.

The Stoics saw the body and soul as interconnected. Movement keeps the body in its natural state, preventing it from becoming sluggish, and sharpens the mind. Seneca warned against both neglecting the body and obsessing over it. Movement was valuable because it served higher moral purposes.

The Stoics considered movement not an end in itself, but a means of strengthening resilience, aligning with nature and preparing both body and soul for virtuous action. In this way, movement enabled greatness through virtue, endurance and service.

For me, movement has always been both escape and arrival. Running began as release – a way to quiet the noise – but it became revelation. Somewhere between the start and the finish, I discovered that the run itself was the destination.

There are moments, deep in a long race, when thought disappears, and only rhythm remains – breath, stride, pulse. The world narrows to the sound of footsteps and the beat of life itself. That's when movement becomes prayer. It's there that I feel closest to the truth. That greatness isn't found in speed or victory, but in the decision to move forwards despite fatigue, doubt, or fear. Movement reminds me that progress is not always visible, but it is always possible.

King moved for justice. Mandela moved for freedom. Munro moved for creation. Nyad moved for transcendence. The Stoics moved for harmony.

## BORN TO RUN

As an ultrarunner and IRONMAN athlete, Christopher McDougall's *Born to Run* sits among my top five books of all time, not because it's about ultramarathon running – though it is – but because it speaks to something far deeper: the connection between movement, health and human potential.

At its core, *Born to Run* reminds us of something we've largely forgotten – that humans are built to move, not in short, frantic bursts, but through steady, rhythmic endurance. The book argues that we evolved as endurance animals, capable of travelling long distances through persistence rather than speed. When movement is natural, consistent and joyful, it isn't destructive. It's restorative.

This philosophy comes to life through the Tarahumara people of Mexico. This reclusive tribe lives long, healthy lives free from many modern diseases. Their longevity is linked to a combination of constant physical activity, simple diets (including corn, beans, chia and vegetables) and a stress-free community life.

Rather than wearing the body down, and contrary to the advice of many general practitioners, consistent natural movement preserves vitality into old age. This is exemplified by the many Tarahumara who run ultramarathons well beyond 60 miles.

When the shy, reclusive Tarahumara arrived at the Leadville Trail 100, they rewrote the limits of what humans believed was possible. Running in simple huarache leather sandals and flowing robes, carrying themselves with an almost childlike ease, they floated through the thin Colorado air while seasoned ultrarunners laboured behind them.

In their first year, the 55-year-old Victoriano Churro finished among the top competitors, hinting at the depth of their extraordinary ability. When they returned the following year, they delivered a performance that stunned the ultrarunning world. Juan Herrera surged through the mountains to win the race in 17 hours and 30 minutes, breaking the course record with a calm, almost effortless composure.

Their achievement wasn't just a victory; it was a revelation. It was proof that joy, simplicity, community and a lifelong devotion to movement could outperform technology, gear and many modern training doctrines. Greatness is achieved not by obsessing over performance, but by embracing movement as a natural and playful part of life.

The book emphasises that true greatness is not in avoiding struggle, but in embracing it. Ultrarunners (and the Tarahumara people) endure pain, uncertainty and vast distances with an acceptance mindset. Greatness is framed not as elite achievement, but as reconnecting with our shared human gift of endurance, adaptability and community.

In short, *Born to Run* teaches that health comes from natural movement, longevity from living simply and joyfully, and greatness from resilience, humility and the embrace of our human design for endurance.

## HACKS TO FIND MOVEMENT, VITALITY AND LONGEVITY

Claiming that movement saved my life might, on the surface, sound like an oxymoron – especially when you consider the brutal toll my body has endured through training-related accidents. Yet, given the same choice, I would take the same path again without hesitation. It is infinitely better to live with purpose and struggle than to drift through a life that counts for little – a life choked and paralysed by regret, born of choosing the easier road.

So, how do you add more life to your days and more days to your life? My intent, unlike in writing *UNLIMITED*, is to share a beginner's insight into getting moving. By defining your health and wellness purpose, getting started and building a solid fitness base and foundation, you can take this anywhere – perhaps even 250 million steps over the next 25 years.

For now, though, here are some practical tips to help you on your way to greatness, whether in a physical pursuit or any other form of greatness:

1. **Start small.** Begin with five to 10 minutes of walking, stretching, or bodyweight movements. Focus on building the habit first, moving slowly rather than with intensity.
2. **Schedule it.** Treat exercise like an appointment and schedule specific commitments in your calendar – perhaps a morning walk or jog. Morning is my favourite time, as it gets the blood pumping around your body and brain. Alternatively, I enjoy a lunchtime stretch and walk, or an afternoon callisthenics session, and another run.
3. **Set simple goals.** Use smart goals that are specific, measurable, achievable, relevant and time-bound. That way, you can aspire to a smaller target and feel validated when you achieve your goal. Remember, muscles require rest. To recover and to help you feel the improvement in strength and fitness, a day's break between sessions.
4. **Make it enjoyable.** Choose a movement you look forward to, such as dancing, cycling, hiking, swimming, or yoga, as fun matters more than 'perfect' workouts.
5. **Break it up.** Movement doesn't need to be one long session and can be broken down into three 10-minute sessions instead of a full 30-minute workout.
6. **Find accountability.** Exercise with a friend, group, or class, of which there are many. This practice will create an incentive to show up and to give your best shot. Sharing this experience with like-minded individuals can enhance your enjoyment and

strengthen social connections. You can use one of the many apps available today, some of which are free, as well as trackers and even journalling, to stay motivated.

7. **Build gradually.** The most common mistake humans make when starting is taking their newfound motivation to extremes, which can lead to exhaustion or injury. Ultimately, they end their fitness journey as quickly as they began it. So, increase time, intensity, or frequency slowly to avoid burnout or injury. Over the last 27 years, I have gradually increased my workout volume and intensity to ensure sustainable growth. My simple rule of thumb is to limit week-on-week increases to 10 per cent, and to follow the body's recovery cycle with an easier week, say 50 per cent, every three to four weeks. The added benefit of this process is that steady progress feels motivating.
8. **Add incentives.** Try listening to music, podcasts, or audiobooks – perhaps even *UNLIMITED* – while moving. This is a fantastic way to learn and find inspiration. You can also reward yourself after workouts with healthy snacks that replenish vital nutrients, as your body is like a sponge for 15 to 20 minutes after exercise. This will promote a faster recovery and greater strength. Scheduling downtime can also serve as a reward for your effort.
9. **Remove barriers.** Lay out your exercise clothes or shoes the night before and keep all necessary equipment at home, such as resistance bands or dumbbells.
10. **Shift your mindset.** Reframe movement as energy-giving rather than energy-draining. Within a short time, that is precisely what it will become. Reframe it as self-care, not a chore.

I move for meaning, to remember that life – at its core – is motion, that stagnation is death disguised as comfort, and that every step taken towards purpose is an act of becoming.

## THE PULSE OF BECOMING

In the end, movement is more than exercise, fitness, or the mechanics of the body. It is the pulse of life, the physical declaration that we are alive, awake and participating in our own story. Every step, every breath, every motion is a reminder that we are not finished yet.

Movement frees what stagnation suffocates. It lifts the fog from the mind, the weight from the spirit and the fear from the heart. It reconnects us with the simple truth that progress is not always profound or dramatic – sometimes, it is a single step taken when staying still would have been easier. Sometimes, it rises when comfort whispers 'not today'. Sometimes, it is choosing to participate in your own life rather than watching it drift past.

King marched to move a nation. Mandela moved in a cell to keep his spirit free. Munro moved with his hands to turn a machine into a miracle. Nyad moved through darkness to prove that persistence can outlast pain. The Stoics aligned with nature to stay in harmony with wisdom.

Movement has always been both rebellion and redemption – the refusal to be defined by fear, age, injury, doubt, or circumstance.

And for me, movement became a lifeline. It saved me from regret, paralysis, addiction and the numbness of an unlived life. It carried me across continents, seasons and finish lines. It gave me back my confidence, my clarity, my peace and, ultimately, my purpose. Through movement, I learned who I was. Through movement, I discovered who I could become.

That is why movement matters – not because it makes us fitter or faster, but because it makes us *freer*. It is a physical vote for the life you want to live and the person you want to be. Every time you move – even gently, even slowly – you cast that vote.

So, move.

Move for your health.

Move for your mind.

Move for your spirit.

Move for the version of you who refuses to settle.

Move because stagnation is the slowest death, and movement is the purest life.

You do not need to run ultramarathons. You do not need to conquer mountains or cross oceans. You simply need to begin with one walk, one stretch, one breath that reminds your body it was built for motion.

Because movement is the bridge between who you were and who you can still become.

Greatness doesn't care how far you go or how long it takes. It only cares that you keep moving towards your truth, your potential and your purpose.

To move is to be alive. To move with intention is to be transformed. And to move, day after day, with courage is the quiet, powerful beginning of your greatness.

# *REFLECTION, ACTION AND GROWTH*

## REFRAME WHAT MOVEMENT MEANS TO YOU

**Reflection:** What does movement currently mean in your life (e.g. escape, obligation, avoidance, expression)? How does that meaning shape your wellbeing?

**Action:** This week, choose *one* short movement session (five to 15 minutes) and approach it with a new intention – not for fitness or goals, but simply to feel alive. Afterwards, write one sentence describing how the movement changed your state.

## MOVE WITH DELIBERATE PRESENCE

**Reflection:** When was the last time you moved your body with purpose – not hurried, not distracted, but deliberately – and what impact did it have on your emotional or mental clarity?

**Action:** Schedule one intentional movement moment in the next 48 hours (e.g. a walk, stretch, run, swim, or cycle). During it, silence notifications and tune in to your breath, your body and your rhythm. Afterwards, note one insight or idea that surfaced.

## USE MOVEMENT AS A BRIDGE

**Reflection:** If movement is a bridge between who you were and who you can become, what part of your life or identity are you trying to reach or leave behind?

**Action:** Identify one barrier (e.g. time, fear, habit, comfort, self-doubt, or overthinking) that stops you from moving more. Today, remove *one* friction point: lay out clothes the night before, schedule a walk, ask a friend to join, or prepare your shoes by the door.

## COMMIT TO CONSISTENT MOVEMENT

**Reflection:** How would your physical, emotional and spiritual health change if you committed to even a modest, consistent movement practice for the next 30 days?

**Action:** Set a simple, achievable 30-day movement goal (e.g. 'exercise for 10 minutes daily', 'walk three times a week', or 'stretch before bed'). Track each completed day on a calendar or journal. At the end of each week, write one sentence describing how your energy, mood, and confidence shifted.

SS GREAT
ATNESS G
SS GREAT
ATNESS G
SS GREAT
ATNESS G
SS GREAT
ATNESS G

# CHAPTER 12
# RESILIENCE

***'DO NOT JUDGE ME BY MY SUCCESSES. JUDGE ME BY HOW MANY TIMES I FELL DOWN AND GOT BACK UP AGAIN.' – NELSON MANDELA***

Resilience is the echo of courage, the quiet strength that rises after the fall. It's the decision to begin again when the world believes you're finished. It doesn't announce itself with noise or glory. It reveals itself in silence, in the small, unseen moments when you refuse to surrender, when you choose to keep moving even as everything inside you begs to stop.

Greatness doesn't exist without resilience, because every meaningful path will break you in some way. And what you do with the pieces is what defines you.

Resilience is a process: purpose, courage, plan, sacrifice, fail, then get back up, learn, adapt and go again.

Chances are, during your pursuit of purpose and greatness, building exceptional resilience will be essential. And if you don't need to call upon your resilience, perhaps what you aspire to is not your true greatness. A good friend of mine, Martin, said to me over 40 years ago when I began to water ski: 'If you don't fall off, Jas, then you are not trying hard enough.'

I have carried that gem with me for more than 40 years, reminding myself that failure is only an inevitable step on the way to greatness.

The measure of resilience you will require depends on many factors, including the difficulty of your purpose and goals, and the degree of adversity and trauma you face. As I have learned the hard way, the severity of events – and their timing and frequency – is largely unpredictable. That is life. You can either accept it and move on or be undone by it.

I've had that mindset for almost as long as I can remember. Many setbacks arrived without warning, like a steam train blasting out of a tunnel. Yet time and again, my resilience had armed me with the physiological and emotional tools to respond. Each time, I was tested and brought to my knees, quite literally, but I knew how to respond. I never doubted that redemption would be the sweetest moment of all.

Resilience is the psychological, emotional and sometimes physical capacity to adapt well in the face of adversity, trauma, tragedy, or significant stress. Adapting well, I want to stress, is not simply the act of surviving such adversity, trauma, or significant stress to make it through another day, at least not beyond the initial impact. It also doesn't mean burying the trauma without processing grief and moving on, or moving too quickly so as not to reflect, review, acquire wisdom and adapt. These are essential steps as you reframe and adjust to move forwards as a stronger, improved, more capable, more determined version of yourself.

Building resilience often takes time. Each layer is formed through experience, gradually creating an invisible fortress of strength. With every layer built, confidence grows – not that hardship won't return, but that you can withstand it and rebuild again, as you have before. Resilience does not eliminate grief, struggle, or distress. It allows you to recover and rebuild more quickly and effectively.

So, let's start by looking at the different types of resilience.

# EMOTIONAL RESILIENCE

Emotional resilience is the ability to manage your emotions effectively, remain calm under pressure and recover from emotional setbacks such as loss, failure, conflict, or stress. It's not about avoiding emotions but being able to feel them without being overwhelmed or shut down by them. The six key characteristics of emotional resilience are:

- **Emotional regulation** – the ability to stay calm and composed in stressful or emotionally intense situations, such as taking deep breaths and pausing before reacting during an argument
- **Self-awareness** – understanding your emotions and how they affect your behaviour; for example, recognising feelings of anxiety and identifying the source
- **Optimism** – maintaining a hopeful, positive outlook, even in difficult times, such as believing that things will improve after a job loss or that your loss is a potential blessing in disguise
- **Empathy** – the capacity to understand and share the feelings of others, strengthening emotional connection, communication and support systems
- **Self-compassion** – treating yourself with kindness during times of failure or stress instead of beating yourself up for making a mistake, focus on learning from it and building wisdom
- **Adaptability** – adjusting to changing emotional demands without losing stability, so that you cope constructively with unexpected changes or disappointments.

Emotional resilience plays a vital role in mental health. It supports healthier relationships through improved communication and conflict resolution, increases tolerance for daily stressors and enables faster recovery from emotional trauma by enabling more effective processing and healing.

It can be developed and strengthened through a range of practical habits. Mindfulness and meditation increase awareness of emotions and reduce impulsive reactions. Exercise, journalling, talking to a friend, or creative expression can help develop healthy coping strategies. Reframing negative thoughts is also an effective way to challenge irrational beliefs and focus on what you can control.

By surrounding yourself with people who provide empathy and encouragement, you can foster supportive relationships and boost your emotional resilience and confidence, rather than isolating yourself or blaming yourself excessively. Another effective tactic is to set realistic goals that yield small wins, which in turn build trust and emotional strength.

## PSYCHOLOGICAL RESILIENCE

Psychological resilience is the mental capacity to cope with stress, adversity, or trauma and still function effectively. It's the inner strength that enables someone to adapt, recover and grow in response to challenges such as loss, illness, failure, or life changes.

The key characteristics of psychological resilience are:

- **Cognitive flexibility** – the ability to shift thinking and adapt beliefs or behaviours when circumstances change, such as adjusting expectations after a significant life transition like job loss or divorce
- **Self-efficacy** – the belief in one's ability to manage life's challenges, often expressed through positive affirmation or self-talk, such as 'I can get through this and figure out a solution'
- **Optimism and hope** – maintaining a realistic yet positive outlook about the future, including viewing setbacks as temporary and solvable
- **A sense of purpose** – meaning derived from goals, values, or a belief system, which strengthens resilience by motivating during difficult times, such as focusing on family or a long-held career dream
- **Perseverance** – the ability to keep going, even when facing repeated obstacles, setbacks or periods of uncertainty.

The benefits of psychological resilience are extensive and life-changing. They include the reduced risk of depression and anxiety, improved problem-solving and decision-making, quicker recovery from trauma, grief, or stress, and greater adaptability to change or uncertainty. By enhancing your psychological resilience, you will experience greater overall life satisfaction and wellbeing.

Here are some helpful practices to help build physical resilience:

- **Challenge negative thinking.** Using cognitive-behavioural techniques to reframe unhelpful beliefs can strengthen resilience in the face of both physical and mental strain. Breaking challenges into smaller, manageable parts can also improve problem-solving skills and reduce overwhelm
- **Adopt a growth mindset.** Viewing failure as an opportunity to learn and grow helps you move forwards with confidence. Reframing setbacks was a significant part of my own mindset shift, diminishing fear and allowing me to take failure in stride, adapt quickly and maintain positive momentum.
- **Practise self-reflection and structure.** Self-reflection or journalling can deepen insight into your thoughts and behaviours, both in the moment and over time. Consistent routines and structure also play a critical role in creating stability and a sense of control, particularly during challenging periods.

## SOCIAL RESILIENCE

Social resilience is the ability to build and maintain strong relationships and social networks that provide support during difficult times – for example, by relying on friends and community after a job loss or natural disaster – and to demonstrate key traits such as communication, empathy and collaboration.

## COMMUNITY RESILIENCE

Community resilience refers to the ability of a group of people living in the same area or sharing common interests to withstand, adapt to and recover from disruptions – whether from natural disasters, economic hardship, public health crises, or social conflict – while maintaining their core functions and identity.

It's about more than just bouncing back; it's also about bouncing forwards by learning from adversity and becoming stronger. The key components of community resilience begin with preparedness and planning, which include access to resources and the deployment of systems before a crisis occurs.

Social cohesion, fostered through trust, collaboration and strong relationships among residents, creates strong community resilience. Strong local leadership and governance are invaluable, bringing responsive leadership that coordinates efforts and communicates clearly. The availability of resources, such as access to housing, healthcare, food, education and economic opportunity, which are unevenly distributed, will ensure a strong sense of resilience in any community. Community engagement and participation will be built on residents' involvement in planning, decision-making and problem-solving.

Community resilience is vital for a faster recovery from disasters and crises, reducing long-term damage to lives, property and local economies, and fostering stronger social support networks and improved mental health outcomes. Another benefit is the enhanced preparedness for future challenges.

## KEY CHARACTERISTICS OF RESILIENCE

There are many significant benefits to building one or all the various types of resilience:

- **Emotional strength.** Resilient individuals can manage their emotions during stressful events. They experience pain, sadness, or frustration, but they don't allow these feelings to paralyse them.
- **Cognitive flexibility.** They can shift perspectives, reframe negative experiences, and find meaning in hardship, allowing them to adapt to changing circumstances and maintain a sense of control.

- **Optimism.** Resilient people tend to maintain a hopeful outlook. They believe that challenges can be overcome and that the future holds possibilities, not just threats.
- **Problem-solving skills.** Rather than being overwhelmed by problems, resilient individuals focus on solutions. They take proactive steps and make thoughtful decisions even under pressure.
- **Support systems.** Strong relationships – with family, friends, mentors, or communities – are vital to resilience. Social support offers encouragement, perspective and practical assistance during challenging times.
- **Sense of purpose.** A clear sense of meaning or direction – through personal goals, faith, values, or commitments – can act as an anchor when everything else feels uncertain.
- **Self-efficacy.** Resilient people have confidence in their ability to influence outcomes. They believe in their capacity to cope and solve problems.

Fortunately, resilience can be learned. While some people may naturally be more resilient due to temperament or upbringing, resilience can be developed by building emotional awareness, practising mindfulness and stress management, cultivating strong relationships, learning from setbacks, setting realistic goals, developing problem-solving skills and reflecting on past successes and strengths.

Resilience is not about avoiding pain, but rather about facing it with strength, adaptability and a purposeful approach. It allows individuals to bend without breaking, and in many cases, to grow through their experiences.

## RISING EACH TIME THE WORLD PUSHES YOU DOWN

Martin Luther King Jr. faced defeats that would have crushed lesser men. His efforts were met with hatred, his marches with violence and his dream dismissed as naïve. Yet every time the world tried to silence him, he came back stronger. His resilience wasn't just endurance; it was grace under pressure. It was the strength to keep loving in a world determined to teach him hate. That is the hardest kind of resilience – not to harden, but to remain open.

He said, 'Darkness cannot drive out darkness; only light can do that.' Those words are resilience distilled – the courage to stay soft when the world grows sharp.

Nelson Mandela's resilience was tested beyond comprehension. After 27 years of imprisonment, isolation and loss, he emerged not bitter, but luminous. As he once said, 'Do not judge me by my successes; judge me by how many times I fell and got back up again.'

That's the truth of resilience – not perfection, but persistence. Mandela's power came from his refusal to let pain become identity. He transformed it into wisdom, patience and empathy. He didn't just survive prison; he repurposed it. He used adversity as education, turning confinement into refinement. That's the secret the resilient know: every hardship is either destruction or instruction, and the choice is ours.

Burt Munro's resilience was mechanical and spiritual. His dreams were bigger than his means. For decades, he faced failure, ridicule and mechanical disaster. But every setback became material. Every mistake became an instruction.

He didn't measure progress by success, but by persistence. If a part broke, he built another. If an attempt failed, he recalibrated. His resilience was iterative – the relentless devotion to improvement, no matter how small. In his shed, resilience sounded like the rhythm of tools – the hum of creation despite limitation. His story reminds us that resilience is not only surviving the storm but learning to build in the rain.

Diana Nyad's resilience, like the ocean she swam, was infinite. Four times she tried and failed to cross from Cuba to Florida. Each time she was forced out of the water, she was defeated and broken. But defeat didn't define her. It refined her. She studied what went wrong, strengthened what had weakened, and when the world moved on, she prepared in silence.

Five years later, she entered the water again. When she emerged 53 hours later, she was salt-stung, sunburned and victorious. Her resilience wasn't physical. It was spiritual. It was a belief made visible through motion. When she reached the shore, she said, 'I have three messages: never, ever give up; you're never too old to chase your dreams; and it looks like a solitary sport, but it takes a team.' That statement holds the full spectrum of resilience: persistence, humility and gratitude.

The Stoics taught that resilience is the art of adapting to what is. Marcus Aurelius wrote, 'The impediment to action advances action,' and 'What stands in the way becomes the way.'

Epictetus, once enslaved and crippled, found freedom through philosophy. He taught that suffering is unavoidable, but misery is optional. He said, 'It's not what happens to you, but how you react to it that matters.'

Seneca echoed him: 'Fire tests gold; adversity tests the brave.'

To the Stoics, resilience was not a reactive quality but a practised one – the deliberate shaping of perception until hardship becomes a teacher. Building resilience was not merely important; it was essential to living a Stoic life. Resilience was the shield that protected virtue, the training ground of character, and the path to inner freedom. Hardship wasn't something to avoid, but the very arena in which resilience, and therefore greatness, was forged.

I've lived that lesson more times than I can count. Endurance sport teaches you that resilience is rarely loud. It's not the roar at the finish line; it's the silence between breaths, the moment you decide to take one more step when everything inside you says you can't.

Some runs have broken me – physically and mentally. There were moments when my body screamed for mercy and my mind whispered to *stop*. But resilience speaks more steadily: *not yet*.

That's what keeps you alive in motion – that quiet insistence that you can still move, still try, still become.

Over time, resilience stops being a reaction and becomes a rhythm. You begin to trust that pain will pass, that failure will teach, and that falling is not the opposite of progress but part of it.

King's resilience changed nations. Mandela's changed hearts. Munro's changed possibilities. Nyad's changed limits. The Stoics' changed philosophy.

## CONSISTENCY

Consistency is just as integral to achieving greatness as persistence, but it works in a slightly different way. If persistence is about not giving up, then consistency is about showing up – day after day – with focused effort. It transforms ambition into steady progress, ensuring that greatness is built on a solid foundation rather than fleeting bursts of effort.

Here's why consistency plays such a central role:

- **Compounding small actions into big results.** Greatness isn't achieved in one giant leap; it's built through countless small steps. Consistency allows those steps to accumulate, compounding over time into mastery, strength and impact.
- **Creating habits of excellence.** When you act consistently, effort becomes automatic. Training, learning, practising, or leading no longer relies on bursts of motivation but on disciplined habits that sustain progress even when motivation fades.
- **Establishing reliability and trust.** For leaders, athletes, or creators, consistency builds trust in themselves and others. People begin to believe in you when they see steady dedication and results over time.
- **Sustaining momentum.** Momentum is one of the most powerful forces in achieving greatness. Consistency keeps the wheel turning; even small daily actions prevent stagnation and make it easier to maintain progress.
- **Refining skills and deepening knowledge.** Actual expertise requires repetitive practice and reflection. Consistency provides the framework for gradual, incremental improvement, allowing individuals to refine details and reach mastery.
- **Outlasting talent alone.** Many people start with talent, but without consistency, it quickly plateaus. Those who are consistent, even if less naturally gifted, often surpass the talented because they steadily build and adapt.

# PERSISTENCE

Persistence is one of the most integral parts of achieving greatness because it acts as the force that bridges vision and reality. Almost every person who has accomplished something extraordinary – whether in sports, science, leadership, art, or personal growth – has done so not because the path was smooth, but because they refused to stop when obstacles arose. Persistence shows up through a series of behaviours that compound over time. Here's why it matters:

- **Overcoming obstacles.** Greatness always comes with setbacks, failures, rejections, disappointments, and resistance from others. In fact, greatness is born from every one of these impediments. Persistence enables a person to push through barriers rather than be defeated by them.
- **Turning effort into mastery.** Talent alone is never enough. Persistent, repeated effort refines skills, builds knowledge and transforms raw potential into mastery. Every repetition compounds over time until excellence is achieved.
- **Building resilience.** Persistence strengthens character. Each time a challenge is faced and endured, a person develops resilience. This resilience becomes the foundation to withstand even greater challenges.
- **Maintaining focus on purpose.** Greatness often takes years, even decades, to materialise. Persistence ensures that someone doesn't lose sight of their long-term purpose when immediate rewards are lacking.
- **Separating the extraordinary from the ordinary.** Many people have dreams, but only those who persist, even when progress is slow or results seem invisible, achieve them. Persistence is the differentiating factor between those who quit and those who make history.
- **Transforming failure into fuel.** Persistence reframes failure as feedback. Instead of giving up, persistent individuals learn from mistakes, adapt and continue moving forwards, turning each failure into a stepping stone towards success.

## HABITS

As mentioned earlier, historian Will Durant said while summarising Aristotle, 'We are what we repeatedly do. Excellence, then, is not an act, but a habit.'

A habit is a behaviour or action that a person performs regularly and often without thinking, because it has become automatic through repetition. It typically develops over time as the brain learns to associate specific cues, such as the time of day or emotional states, with corresponding responses.

In simple terms, a habit is something you do often, so often that you don't even have to think about it – it just happens. The challenge with most habits is that they form unintentionally and usually have a harmful impact. In fact, it seems that good habits are only implemented and practised with discipline, whereas negative habits are reactions to stress, poor decisions and coping mechanisms for life's situations.

For the first two decades of my adult life, I found myself drawn to the easier option: poor habits born from procrastination and inaction. They were comfortable and easy to maintain, but sooner or later, they would become uncomfortable and eventually rob me of my greatness. Those habits didn't just shape my behaviour; they became my identity.

Be warned: poor habits snowball into a mountain of regret. I know, because that's what happened to me. Until you find purpose, you must find the courage to take the more challenging road, to act and to wake each day to your new identity, shaped by your new, better habits.

Your life today is essentially the sum of your habits. How in shape or out of shape are you? A result of your habits. How happy or unhappy are you? A result of your habits. How successful or unsuccessful are you? A result of your habits.

What you repeatedly do – what you spend time thinking about and doing each day – ultimately shapes who you are, what you believe and the personality you portray. Everything I write about – from procrastination and productivity to strength and nutrition – starts with better habits. When you learn to transform your habits, you can transform your life.

Waking up at the crack of dawn and going for a run can be intimidating when you're trying to make it a habit. Weaving a significant new activity such as this into your routine obviously takes determination and time. But how much time is really needed to make that habit stick?

One popular idea suggests that it takes 21 days to solidify a habit. A three-week timeframe can sound easily achievable when making New Year's resolutions – or during major life transitions such as a career change, a move, the birth of a child, or the end of a relationship – when motivation is high, and the desire for reinvention feels urgent. Yet by 21 January, very few people can boast of having kept their resolutions, and without repetition and structure, any initial resolve rarely translates into lasting change.

Everyone has a unique habit-building timeline. Repetition, however, is the key to making it work, regardless of how long the process takes. Research led by Phillippa Lally, a senior lecturer in psychology at the University of Surrey, suggests that habits are strengthened through consistent repetition and personalised strategies that gradually turn intentional behaviours into automatic ones.

Habit formation can take anywhere from a few weeks to several months. The origin of the so-called 'three-week theory' has little to do with habits themselves. It traces back to the 1960 self-help book *Psycho-Cybernetics*, in which plastic surgeon Maxwell Maltz observed that his patients took about 21 days to get used to their new appearance after surgery. No formal experiment was conducted to verify this, but the book applied this 21-day timeline to self-transformation in many other wide-ranging aspects of life. For instance, the book also suggests that three weeks is the time needed for people to get accustomed to a new house or reconsider their beliefs.

Even without substantial research, the 21-day myth gained widespread acceptance. It likely persisted because it seems like such a reasonable amount of time. Behavioural economist Colin Camerer argues that timeframes need to feel believable in order to motivate change. Establishing a regular exercise habit in just three days feels too quick and implausible, whereas a year can seem too long and daunting.

Camerer suggests that people are more likely to succeed when they choose a realistic and achievable timeframe, such as 21 days.

Almost a half-century later, researchers finally gathered substantial evidence that countered this idea. Lally's hallmark 2009 study on habit creation found that habits developed in a range of 18 to 254 days; participants reported taking an average of about 66 days to reliably incorporate one of three new daily activities – eating a piece of fruit with lunch, drinking a bottle of water with lunch or running for 15 minutes before dinner. Lally confirmed that consistent daily repetition was the most significant factor influencing whether a behaviour would become part of an automatic daily routine.

## ATOMIC HABITS

There is probably no better modern reference for behaviour change than James Clear's *Atomic Habits*. The book is a *New York Times* bestseller that has sold more than 20 million copies worldwide. It explores how small, consistent actions – rather than dramatic transformations – lead to lasting change.

Here are the key themes I took from this transformational book:

- **Small changes compound.** Lasting change comes from consistent, incremental improvement. Getting one per cent better each day may feel insignificant, but over time those gains accumulate into meaningful transformation.
- **Identity drives behaviour.** Instead of focusing solely on goals or outcomes, cultivate habits that align with the person you aspire to become. For example, don't say, 'I want to run,' say, 'I'm a runner.'
- **Environment shapes outcomes.** Behaviour is often dictated by what is visible, convenient and familiar. Designing your environment intentionally makes good habits easier and bad habits harder.
- **Systems matter more than goals.** Goals define outcomes, but systems determine progress. Focusing on processes reduces

pressure, discourages shortcuts and supports sustainable improvement.
- **Tracking and accountability sustain momentum.** Measuring behaviour and involving others increases awareness and follow-through, reinforcing habits over time.

*Atomic Habits* teaches that lasting change doesn't come from massive overhauls, but from small, smart decisions made consistently. It's about mastering the process, not just chasing the outcome.

The power of tiny changes – small habits – when repeated consistently, compounds over time and leads to remarkable results. The key message is to focus on improving by just one per cent each day.

## HACKS TO BUILD GREAT HABITS

Building great habits is about turning intentional actions into automatic behaviours that support your goals. Here are some practical, research-backed tips you can try:

- **Start small (make it easy).** Begin with a habit so simple it's almost impossible to fail (e.g. two push-ups, reading one page) remember, small wins create momentum and confidence.
- **Anchor new habits to existing routines.** James Clear talks about this one too; use habit stacking – 'After I brush my teeth, I'll floss one tooth,' or, 'after I make coffee, I'll write one line in my journal.'
- **Focus on identity, not just outcomes.** Another one from *Atomic Habits*, instead of saying, 'I want to run a marathon', think, 'I am a runner.' Habits stick more when tied to who you want to become, not just what you want to achieve.
- **Use clear triggers and cues.** Environment shapes behaviour. Keep water on your desk, place running shoes by the door, or keep fruit in sight. Reduce cues for habits you want to break (e.g. remove junk food from the house).

- **Make habits attractive.** Try pairing something you want with something you need (e.g. listen to an audiobook only while exercising).
- **Track your progress.** Use a journal, calendar, or app to track your streaks visually. 'Don't break the chain', for example, is a powerful motivator.
- **Build accountability.** Share your goal with a friend, join a group, or work with a qualified and experienced coach. You will also find that public commitment raises follow-through.
- **Reward progress.** Celebrate small wins. While external rewards help, intrinsic rewards – feeling stronger, calmer or more focused – matter most.
- **Focus on systems, not goals.** Goals set direction, but systems create progress. If your goal is to write a book, the system is writing 200 words every morning.
- **Accept imperfection.** Missing once won't undo your progress, but missing twice in a row will. Consistency, not perfection, builds great habits.

## NEVER FINISHED

Resilience is not a gift given to a lucky few. It is a muscle, forged in friction, strengthened in the very moments you would most prefer to avoid. It is the quiet decision – again and again – to rise, not because you are unbroken, but because you are not finished.

You will fall. You will fail. You will be misunderstood, doubted, criticised and, at times, forgotten. Plans will unravel. People will leave. Circumstances will blindside you from angles you never anticipated. That is not a sign that you are on the wrong path; often, it is proof that you are walking a meaningful one. A life without resistance is rarely a life of greatness – it is usually a life of avoidance.

Martin Luther King Jr. did not become who he was because his journey was easy, but because he refused to let hatred harden his heart. Nelson Mandela did not emerge from prison powerful despite his suffering, but because of what he chose to do with it. Burt Munro did not create history because the parts never broke, but because every failure became a blueprint for the next attempt. Diana Nyad did not cross the ocean without fear, but with a faith that outlasted it. The Stoics did not write of resilience from ivory towers, but from exile, illness, oppression and war. Different lives, same lesson: resilience is not the absence of pain – it is the transformation of it.

In my own life, the races that shaped me most were not the ones that went to plan, but the ones that came apart. The days when my body screamed to stop. The seasons where injury, loss, or catastrophe reduced me to a crawl. Each time, resilience did not arrive as a heroic surge – it came as a small, stubborn voice that said: *Not yet. One more step. One more day. One more try.* Over time, that whisper becomes a rhythm. You begin to trust that you can bend without breaking; that you can be brought to your knees and still rise taller than before.

That is the true power of resilience: it turns setbacks into teachers, scars into stories and obstacles into origins. It does not erase grief or pretend away hardship. It allows you to feel deeply and still move forwards. It permits you to fall without letting you stay down.

And this is where consistency, persistence and habits intertwine with resilience. You won't always *feel* strong, but you can still *act* in alignment with strength. Tiny disciplines – the early alarm you honour, the training session you complete when you'd rather quit and the honest conversation you have instead of avoiding – are all quiet votes for the person you are becoming. Each small, repeated act of courage lays another brick in the foundation of your resilience. Over months and years, those bricks become a fortress.

You do not need to 'be resilient' in some grand, cinematic way. You just need to choose, in this moment, not to surrender the part of you that still wants to grow. You need to learn from the fall, adjust the plan, refine the habit and step forwards again, however slowly, however shakily. Resilience is less about bouncing back to who you were and more about bouncing forwards into who you could be.

So, when the next storm comes – and it will – remember this: you have been here before, in some form. You have survived every dark night of your life so far. You carry within you a record of comebacks, a history of hard things already endured. That is your evidence. That is your proof. Draw on it. Add to it.

Because greatness doesn't care how many times you hit the ground. It cares about the number of times you rise.

Resilience is that rise.

Persistence is the ability to rise again.

Habit is the scaffolding that helps you keep rising, even when belief wavers.

You will not always choose perfectly. You will not always respond bravely. But if, each time you fall, you can summon enough courage to stand a little wiser, a little kinder, a little more committed to your purpose, then you are already walking the road to greatness.

Resilience is not reserved for heroes in history books. It is available to you – right now, in the life you are living, with the pain you carry and the dreams you hold.

When the world pushes you down, let that be your cue. Take a breath. Feel the weight. Learn what you must.

Then get up.

And go again.

# REFLECTION, ACTION AND GROWTH

## LEARN FROM WHERE YOU'VE FALLEN

**Reflection:** Where in your life have you fallen? What did you do next?

**Action:** Choose one setback that still lingers in your mind:

- Write down what happened, how you responded at the time and what you wish you had done differently.
- Then add one line – 'If this happened again, my resilient response would be…' and finish the sentence.

## LET PAIN INSTRUCT YOU

**Reflection:** When pain arrives now, do you let it define you or instruct you?

**Action:** Take a moment to examine how you respond to difficulty:

- List three current or recent challenges (big or small).
- Next to each, write – 'Destruction or instruction?' and briefly note one lesson that the challenge might be trying to teach you.
- Circle one of those lessons and turn it into a simple commitment – 'Because of this, from today I will…'

## LEAN ON WHAT LIFTS YOU BACK UP

**Reflection:** Who and what makes you stronger when you're on your knees?

**Action:** Map the supports that help you recover and continue:

- Draw three columns – people; practices; beliefs.
- Under each, list what (or who) genuinely helps you get back up – a person, a practice (running, journalling, walking, prayer, meditation), a belief or a phrase.
- Choose one person to contact this week to thank for their support, and one practice you will deliberately use next time you feel like quitting. Put both in your diary.

## STRENGTHEN RESILIENCE THROUGH HABIT

**Reflection:** What habit, when done consistently, would most strengthen your resilience over the next 90 days?

**Action:** Define the habit that will quietly harden you over time:

Complete this sentence: 'If I did ____ every day (or most days) for 90 days, I would be harder to break.' Name a specific habit (e.g. 10-minute walk, five-minute journal, one tough conversation each week, cold shower, reading five pages).

Design your 'resilience system' for that habit:

- Cue – when and where will you do it? (After coffee, before bed, after work, etc.)
- Make it easy – what is the most miniature version you will do, even on bad days?
- Accountability – who will you tell, or how will you track it (tick box, app, calendar)?

Commit to not missing twice. If you miss a day, your job is to show up on the next one.

# CHAPTER 13
# GRATITUDE

**'GRATITUDE IS AN ANTIDOTE TO NEGATIVE EMOTIONS, A NEUTRALISER OF ENVY, HOSTILITY, WORRY AND IRRITATION. IT IS SAVOURING, IT IS NOT TAKING THINGS FOR GRANTED, IT IS PRESENT-ORIENTED.'** – SONJA LYUBOMIRSKY

Gratitude is the quiet completion of greatness. It is the humility that balances ambition, the grace that steadies strength. Without it, success corrodes. With it, even suffering becomes sacred.

Gratitude, therefore, is the greatest enabler of happiness and human positivity.

It was 18 July 1981. I awoke in a dazed, almost catatonic state. Just 24 hours after emerging from seven hours of life-saving surgery, my first instinct was to raise my fingers to my hideously swollen, unrecognisable face – much as I had when I first regained consciousness 36 hours earlier, in the back of the ambulance.

That time, though, I had felt, with horror, the carnage inflicted by the out-of-control car driven by a drunk driver which had collided head-on with mine, leaving me no chance to brake or brace for impact.

Consequently, the violent collision forced my head and face to violently hit the steering wheel, among other bodily impacts. My only clear recollection of the accident was the sharpness of my broken teeth, which had pierced through my skin and were now perversely protruding from my chin, along with fragments of my jawbone that had also broken through below it.

This time, when instinct drove me to assess my condition, my fingers encountered something different: the softness of bandages encasing my head and face. Bizarrely, the smooth surface that I touched seemed to be a few inches from my skin, courtesy of the excessive facial swelling and the depth of bandages after the mammoth operation.

In the days following surgery, I drifted in and out of a morphine-induced state. Sleep was broken only by brief flashes of consciousness and moments of self-pity, as I grappled with the inescapable question: 'Why me?' But that afternoon, something shifted – a moment that would alter my perspective for life.

Still in intensive care, I became aware of other patients being admitted, transferred or wheeled away for emergency tests and scans. As I surveyed the constant procession of broken humans, my thoughts turned to each of them, their circumstances, and what life had in store for them beyond that moment.

Suddenly, a realisation struck me with startling clarity: countless others I had observed were far less fortunate than I, enduring circumstances far more harrowing than my own. Some, I suspected, would never leave that hospital alive. Others might survive but never walk again. And yet, I would – at least, that was my assumption in that moment.

It was then that an unexpected wave of gratitude swept over me, powerful and overwhelming, undoubtedly intensified by the haze of medication, but no less real for it. I had never felt anything quite like it.

Despite the severity of my injuries, I was alive. I *would* walk out of that hospital in a matter of weeks. And although my recovery, treatments and the series of surgeries that awaited me would stretch on for a year or more, I would heal. I would most likely return to a life that, in time, would feel normal again.

That moment marked my first actual encounter with profound gratitude. It taught me, unmistakably, that life is shaped by perspective and by our willingness to reach out to those who are less fortunate or who need support. Gratitude, I discovered, is the antidote to almost everything. That single shift in perspective has served me faithfully through the many moments of misfortune and despair that have punctuated my life since. Even now, I remain convinced that I am, in many ways, remarkably fortunate.

## THE FOUNDATION OF A HAPPY LIFE

Gratitude is, without question, the single most significant contributor to lasting happiness and the cultivation of a positive, resilient mindset. It can become the very foundation upon which belief is built – the belief that you can rise above any obstacle and achieve whatever you set your sights on. Two decades ago, during a period marked by mild depression, I began refining my approach to gratitude until it evolved into a deliberate, daily practice. Without a doubt, this practice – paired with steady, unwavering effort – did more than help me withstand immense challenges; it enabled me to thrive through them.

Surviving adversity and thriving through adversity are worlds apart. Thriving transforms your mindset in a way that endures, strengthening your resilience and deepening your confidence each time hardship reappears. Initially, my goal was to feel grateful once a day. In time, that grew into moments of gratitude scattered throughout the day, often arising spontaneously. A mindset anchored in gratitude carries extraordinary power. Once you experience its impact, once gratitude becomes the lens through which you view the world, you feel compelled to create positive change, to grow and, ultimately, to uncover your greatness.

## THE PERSPECTIVE THAT CHANGES EVERYTHING

Martin Luther King Jr. lived with gratitude even in the shadow of injustice. He gave thanks not for comfort, but for cause, for the chance to serve, to stand and to love in a world that desperately needed more of it. He understood that gratitude and faith are intertwined. One feeds the other. Gratitude allows faith to endure when evidence falters. Faith allows gratitude to survive when pain persists.

He once said, 'I have decided to stick with love. Hate is too great a burden to bear.' That's gratitude in action, the recognition that love itself is a gift and that giving it keeps you free.

Nelson Mandela's gratitude was shaped by suffering. After 27 years of imprisonment, he emerged not with bitterness, but with appreciation – for the light on his face, for the laughter of others, for the smallest freedoms most take for granted.

He often spoke of how he cherished the first sunrise he saw as a free man, not as a political symbol, but as a personal awakening. Gratitude, for him, was not sentiment; it was strength. It allowed him to see that life's worth is not measured in length, but in how deeply one can appreciate even the ordinary moments.

Burt Munro found gratitude in creation. He didn't chase glory; he cherished craft. He treated every tool, every setback and every slight improvement as blessings. He didn't lament his lack of resources. He gave thanks for what he had and used it to its fullest. Gratitude gave him resilience. It transformed limitation into liberation. His world was small – a workshop, a machine, a dream – but within that smallness was infinity. Gratitude made it vast.

Diana Nyad's gratitude was oceanic. After her final crossing, when she finally stood on the Florida shore, her victory speech wasn't boastful – it was thankful. She thanked her team, the sea and even the hardships that had shaped her. She spoke not like a conqueror, but like a pilgrim – someone who had journeyed through suffering and returned home with reverence.

That's what gratitude does: it turns victory into humility and pain into wisdom.

The Stoics considered gratitude a moral obligation. Seneca wrote, 'No man is more unhappy than he who never faces adversity. For he is not permitted to prove himself.' To them, gratitude was not merely for what was pleasant, but for what was difficult – because difficulty refines virtue.

Marcus Aurelius thanked the gods for the teachers, friends and even adversaries who shaped his strength. Epictetus taught that gratitude is the recognition that every challenge is a lesson and every loss a reminder of what remains.

For the Stoics, gratitude was a discipline of perception – choosing to see abundance instead of lack, opportunity instead of misfortune and gifts instead of burdens. It was a practice that nurtured resilience, contentment and moral clarity.

To the Stoics, ingratitude was blindness, the refusal to see the abundance that exists even in limitation.

I've come to see gratitude in the same way. There was a time I believed gratitude was something you expressed *after* achieving something – after success or after joy. But now I know it's something you practise throughout life, especially when it hurts.

During long races, when the body aches and the mind begins to unravel, I've learned to turn to gratitude, not as comfort, but as power. Gratitude transforms suffering by reminding you that to feel pain is to be alive, that to struggle is to be capable, and that to endure is to be blessed with strength.

It's gratitude that turns exhaustion into reverence, effort into privilege and survival into celebration.

Every finish line I've crossed has been a moment of thanks, not just for the victory, but for the challenge itself. Gratitude rewrites pain's story. It makes every scar a reminder, not of what broke you, but of what built you.

King was grateful for purpose. Mandela was thankful for peace. Munro was grateful for the process. Nyad was grateful for perseverance. The Stoics were thankful for life itself.

## THE SCALES OF GRATITUDE

That fateful day in July 1981, the day that almost claimed my life, was the genesis of my lifelong gratitude. From that moment on, I recognised every breath as both a gift and an opportunity to practise mastery over my mind. Gratitude was no longer an occasional feeling; it became a discipline that, with time, transformed into instinct.

One of the most powerful techniques I've cultivated to nurture this state of mind is what I call 'the Scales of Gratitude'. I imagine an old-fashioned set of brass scales like the kind once used to measure precious commodities. On one side, I place whatever burden is troubling me: a worry, a loss, a frustration that clouds my peace. Then, slowly and deliberately, I begin placing blessings on the other side – one by one – until the balance shifts.

At first, I list the fundamentals: health, safety, a roof over my head and the simple privilege of waking to another day. These may seem ordinary, yet they are treasures denied to so many. Each acknowledgement adds weight to the grateful side, until the scale tips completely, pressing down with such abundance that no negative thought can lift it again.

Every morning, I begin my day by piling gratitude upon gratitude, until the side of blessing becomes so heavy it rests firmly on the table of life. And throughout the day, no matter what challenges arise, they are never enough to disturb that equilibrium. Even when hardship strikes, I recall the countless positives that anchor me, such as family, friendships, health, freedom and purpose, and the scale remains steady.

The goal is simple yet transformative: to feel gratitude multiple times a day, not merely think it, and to live within a constant awareness of the blessings that surround you. That is true happiness – a peace that inspires action, compassion and the quiet pursuit of greatness.

This practice has been my greatest superpower. It has shielded me through difficulty and reminded me that I am already rich beyond measure. For those who find it difficult at first, I recommend a simple start: draw a set of scales on a piece of paper. On one side, write your worries, and on the other, your blessings. Add to it daily. Over time, you'll notice the weight shifting – as it always does – towards gratitude.

With consistent practice, this exercise evolves from a deliberate act into a natural state. For me, it no longer requires conscious effort. Gratitude has, alongside each of the other steps to greatness, become instinct – a permanent orientation of the heart. My scales, once carefully balanced by thought, now rest effortlessly in peace.

For context, and to illustrate my philosophy, I often wonder how many people in Australia truly feel blessed to have a roof over their heads every night, or a meal to eat. The United Nations has estimated that around 1.6 billion people worldwide live in inadequate housing – lacking secure shelter, basic sanitation, or reliable access to clean water and essential services. This staggering number serves as a stark reminder of how fortunate many of us truly are, even in the darkest moments.

I firmly believe that during times of distress, when everything appears to be falling apart, you can find solace and gratitude by comparing your circumstances to those of billions of less fortunate individuals around the world. This approach has consistently worked for me, inducing instant shame for my selfish and ungrateful state of mind. Sometimes, all it takes is changing the lens through which you view your life and circumstances. Furthermore, it is a constant reminder that we all need to show empathy for others and reach out without hesitation to offer our help and support.

This change in perspective not only alters your outlook but also fosters humility and empathy towards others. It empowers and inspires you to extend help to those less fortunate than you.

My affinity for helping others began when I was just 13. During the harshest weeks of winter, I volunteered at the local aged-care home, shovelling salt across frozen paths before sunrise so the residents could walk safely. Afterwards, I would knock on doors and offer to run errands for anyone who needed a hand. At 16, driven by the same instinct to serve, I organised a charity event at my school, Monk's Walk, where 30 classmates and I played six-a-side football for 24 hours straight to raise funds for a local cause.

Decades later, I feel deeply privileged to have supported and uplifted countless people through various fundraising initiatives. Yet the most profound experiences have come from my direct involvement with my two favourite charities: St Vincent de Paul and The Salvation Army. My participation has ranged from speaking at high-end fundraising events for philanthropists to mentoring young people through the Youth Homeless Program and sleeping on a piece of cardboard in the freezing winter night during the annual CEO Sleepout – four times. I even undertook a 333-kilometre challenge across the Himalayas and three of the highest drivable roads in the world, all in the name of raising awareness and support.

Each of these moments has shaped me. They deepened my understanding of the invisible struggles countless people endure each day, and they strengthened my conviction that compassion is not an obligation – it is a privilege.

In recent years, my focus has centred on helping anyone with the desire to become better – anyone with a spark, however faint, to uncover their own greatness. My reward is not financial, nor based on recognition or reciprocation. It is the immeasurable satisfaction of knowing I have helped someone live a richer, more meaningful life. That is, and always will be, enough.

As you master this technique, whether through mental visualisation or a physical representation, such as a piece of paper with a line drawn down the middle or an image of scales, your positive, gratitude-filled state will begin to evolve and outweigh the negative one. When I first started using this powerful method, I made it a daily practice to allow only positive thoughts into my mind as I woke each day. I filled my mind with the numerous things I had to be genuinely grateful for, essentially cramming it with positivity. Over time, this practice evolved into a powerful tool that shaped my mindset and enabled me to find happiness daily, despite numerous challenges – some truly devastating.

You can create your own written inventory of gratitude and continuously build upon the positive elements. You might even consider starting your gratitude stocktake and making copies so that you can revisit and add new positive aspects as you identify them. I guarantee that, eventually, your positive side will consistently outweigh any troubling aspects of a given day. With practice, you'll develop the ability to recall these positive aspects in your mind instantly.

## YOU ONLY EVER GET TODAY, SO MAKE IT COUNT

'Live for today' is a common mantra that makes good sense, but its true power lies in the intent that underpins it. For some, it becomes a justification for indulging in temporary pleasures or instant gratification, as I did, like an emotional sugar rush that offers short-lived endorphins and quick fixes, creating a cycle of fleeting highs. While occasional self-reward is essential, habitual short-term gratification will become your identity if you allow this practice to continue.

For me, this mantra serves as a daily motivation to engage in activities that enrich my life, rather than seeking shortcuts or fleeting pleasures. It means not postponing challenging tasks, because tomorrow never truly arrives; we only ever have today to make a difference. Delaying what you don't want to do will become a habit, leading to regret that consumes happiness, positivity and legacy.

Harnessing the power of recognising that today is all you have by spending a few minutes each evening reflecting on the positive impact you've made during the day can be uplifting and motivating. It can also serve as a process of self-accountability. If you don't subscribe to the valuable practice of daily journalling, I urge you to acquire a suitable journal and address your thoughts each day. This daily discipline holds you accountable for actions from your to-do list or your 90-Day High-Performance Plan that you didn't accomplish that day and serves as motivation to avoid regrets and ensure progress.

This daily discipline should also motivate you to change before your next review the following evening, eventually becoming a learned habit. Consider this exercise a significant self-investment that will help you continue your pathway to greatness. The choice is yours: take the easier road or the more challenging road. One will likely lead you to the same place you are at now, while the other offers the potential for meaningful transformation.

Another significant benefit of this practice and mindset is the ability to be fully present in the moment. There have been times in my life when I failed to be fully present, or was perhaps even absent, wasting opportunities to make the most of the day. As you age, your self-awareness should make you increasingly uncomfortable if you don't make each day count.

There is no greater example in modern life today of a 'presence' thief than the destructive force of technology. Constant communication and access to everything has become addictive and pervasive. It often consumes our daily lives, distracting us from the world around us and robbing us of precious moments that should make us feel grateful, as can be observed at a resort when families go on vacation together. Holidays are valuable opportunities for families to interact and enjoy each other's company. However, it's disheartening to see many families spending too much time glued to their phones, missing out on precious moments of togetherness. It feels the same to observe people sitting around a pool in a beautiful location, oblivious to their surroundings and fixated on their phone screens. Or a family of four that goes out to dinner while on vacation, yet all four individuals are immersed in their phones, failing to communicate with one another or appreciate the beautiful, unique surroundings. This is a tragic waste of precious moments.

Or there is the insidious societal practice many people adopt of dreading Mondays as the start of the workweek, rather than celebrating Fridays as the gateway to the weekend. Having worked in large Australian corporations, I can confidently say that the vibe in an organisation is dramatically different on a Monday than on a Friday. But why does this happen on regular days with the same number of hours? While it's natural to look forward to the weekend, making Monday feel like a waste can cause you to miss out on life.

Practising this daily will help you develop the skill of creating perspective. I also recommend replicating this exercise whenever you feel mentally affected by an issue, as it's even better if you write it down in your gratitude inventory, which will change your perspective on

Mondays, at least. As you become more proficient with this technique, you'll be able to use it instantly and efficiently in your mind.

## HACKS FOR FOSTERING GRATITUDE

Here are some simple, practical tips for improving your sense of gratitude:

- **Keep a gratitude journal.** Write down three to five things each day you're grateful for, no matter how small. Over time, this rewires your mind to focus on the positives.
- **Practise 'mental replays'.** At the end of the day, replay moments you're thankful for – conversations, kindnesses, or simple joys.
- **Express thanks directly.** Tell people you appreciate them – whether it's a friend, a colleague, or even a stranger who smiled at you.
- **Shift focus to 'what's there' instead of 'what's missing'.** When you notice yourself focusing on lack, gently reframe by asking, 'what do i already have that matters?'
- **Create gratitude rituals.** Build a habit of gratitude. For example, think of one thing you're grateful for before meals, or every morning when you wake up.
- **Appreciate the ordinary.** Notice small comforts – clean water, a safe home, or a favourite song. Gratitude grows when we stop overlooking the everyday.
- **Reframe challenges.** Look at things differently and ask, 'what lesson or strength did this difficulty give me?' Even struggles can hold seeds of gratitude.
- **Limit comparison.** Instead of comparing upward (to those who seem to have more), compare yourself today with your past self – or those less fortunate – to foster perspective.
- **Use visual reminders.** Post a note, photo, or symbol in your space that reminds you to pause and appreciate.

- **Practise mindfulness.** Slowing down and being fully present makes it easier to notice and appreciate small blessings in real time.

As for me, I'm grateful for the chance to keep going, to fall and rise, to fail and learn, to move and breathe and try again.

## THE QUIET LIGHT THAT CHANGES EVERYTHING

In the end, gratitude is not simply a feeling; it is a discipline, a lens, a way of being in the world that transforms how you carry your pain, interpret your past and walk into your future. It softens what is hard, steadies what is trembling and illuminates what is overlooked. Gratitude is the quiet light that allows us to see the extraordinary in the ordinary and the possible within the difficult.

Gratitude does not deny suffering – it reframes it. It does not erase hardship – it redeems it. It does not pretend the world is perfect; it reminds us that small mercies still exist in even the most imperfect days. Gratitude is not naïve – it is courageous.

Martin Luther King Jr. knew that gratitude was not the luxury of the comfortable but the strength of the committed. Mandela knew that gratitude could survive even within stone walls. Munro knew that gratitude makes scarcity irrelevant. Nyad knew that gratitude is the anchor that steadies you when the sea is too wide. The Stoics knew that gratitude is the antidote to entitlement and the birthplace of clarity.

And you, like me, will come to know this: gratitude is not occasional – it is a practice. A muscle. A daily decision to tip your inner scales towards perspective, compassion and meaning.

Because the truth is this: without gratitude, ambition becomes hunger, achievement becomes emptiness, and even success loses its flavour. Gratitude is what makes greatness humane. It is what gives depth to victory and dignity to struggle. It is what keeps achievement from becoming ego and growth from becoming greed. Gratitude protects the soul while the rest of the world measures outcomes.

My own gratitude began in a hospital bed, wrapped in bandages, staring at a future I could not recognise. It started in pain, in confusion, in survival, yet also in an awakening. That day, I learned that gratitude is possible even when life is unfair, even when the world is unrecognisable, even when you are broken. Especially then.

And it has followed me ever since. Into races. Into business. Into heartbreak. Into healing. Into purpose. It is the steadying rhythm beneath the chaos, the reminder that life does not owe us anything – and yet, every morning, it gives us everything: breath, opportunity, choice, and another chance to try again.

Gratitude transforms the way you move through the world. It makes you more present, more empathetic and more aware of the fragility and beauty that coexist in every moment. It makes you a better leader, a deeper lover, a kinder human. It makes you more resilient because you recognise that even in loss, something remains.

And this is the great paradox: gratitude is not a reaction to greatness; it is one of the things that creates greatness.

Gratitude fuels purpose.

It clarifies sacrifice.

It strengthens resilience.

It humbles courage.

It anchors belief.

It enriches the connection.

It expands joy.

In gratitude, we stop chasing more and start becoming enough.

# REFLECTION, ACTION AND GROWTH

## NOTICE WHAT'S ALREADY PRESENT

**Reflection:** Where in your life are you overlooking the blessings that are already present?

**Action:** Create a two-column 'Gratitude Scale' on paper:

- In the left column, list every frustration, fear, or burden currently weighing on you.
- In the right column, list every blessing (e.g. health, safety, relationships, opportunities, freedoms, experiences).

Keep adding to the right column until the scale tips. Repeat this every morning for seven days and observe how your emotional baseline shifts.

## EXPAND YOUR PERSPECTIVE TOWARDS ABUNDANCE

**Reflection:** How often do you allow your perspective to narrow towards what's missing instead of expanding towards what's abundant?

**Action:** Set three 'Gratitude Interruptions' throughout your day – morning, midday and evening. When the reminder appears, pause for 20 seconds and identify one thing right in front of you that you typically take for granted (e.g. mobility, breath, sunlight, water, or connection). This trains your mind to practise real-time gratitude instead of retrospective gratitude.

## REFRAME HARDSHIP AS WISDOM

**Reflection:** How are you using your hardships – as wounds to relive or as wisdom to be grateful for?

**Action:** Choose a challenging experience from your past – an accident, failure, heartbreak, humiliation, or loss. Write a one-page reflection answering:

- What strength did this give you?
- Who did it help you become?
- What do you now appreciate that you didn't before?

Allow this exercise to transform adversity into insight and a source of power, reinforcing the Stoic principle of gratitude through difficulty.

## EXPRESS GRATITUDE DELIBERATELY

**Reflection:** Who in your life has shaped or supported you in ways you have never fully acknowledged?

**Action:** For the next five days, write and send one gratitude message each day. It could be a text, a phone call, or a handwritten note. Thank someone specifically for their impact on your life. This shifts gratitude from an internal feeling to an external force, deepening connection, humility and presence.

SS GREAT
ATNESS G
SS GREAT
ATNESS G
SS GREAT
ATNESS G
SS GREAT
ATNESS G

# CHAPTER 14
# NUTRITION

**'THOSE WHO THINK THEY HAVE NO TIME FOR HEALTHY EATING WILL SOONER OR LATER HAVE TO FIND TIME FOR ILLNESS.'** – EDWARD STANLEY

Nutrition is not vanity; it is vitality. It is how the body honours the mind's mission. Food is more than fuel; it is the partnership between purpose and endurance, the unseen energy that enables courage, resilience and creation in the physical world.

Most people think of nutrition as a matter of appearance, but it is a matter of capacity – the ability to sustain the pursuit of what matters most. Poor nourishment clouds thought, dulls spirit and weakens resolve. Good nutrition sharpens clarity, stabilises emotion and feeds the strength required to turn vision into reality.

While a diet rich in quality nutrition may not be an essential step on the pathway to greatness, much like movement, I have no doubt it makes a significant difference to all endeavours. And what point is there in achieving greatness without good health? The worst-case scenario is that your vitality, energy levels, mood and overall happiness will likely improve dramatically. Oh, and there's a good chance it may also increase longevity.

Great nutrition is essential for optimal brain and physical function. The food we eat provides the energy and raw materials needed for all cellular processes, including those in the brain, muscles, heart and immune system. Poor nutrition can lead to fatigue, cognitive decline, mood imbalances and physical underperformance, while great nutrition enhances mental clarity, emotional balance, energy levels, strength and resilience.

So, how does excellent nutrition improve brain function, which is essential in almost all endeavours?

Neurotransmitters – including serotonin, dopamine and acetylcholine – are produced from key nutrients such as amino acids (for example, tryptophan supports serotonin production), B vitamins (especially B6, B12 and folate) and minerals such as magnesium, zinc and iron. Glucose from low-GI carbohydrates is the brain's primary energy source, and stable glucose levels help maintain concentration and memory, boosting cognitive performance. Omega-3 fatty acids (especially DHA) are also critical for brain cell membranes and communication. Antioxidants, including vitamins C and E and polyphenols, further protect brain tissue from oxidative stress.

Nutrition also plays a central role in mood and mental health. Research has linked deficiencies in nutrients such as B12, folate and omega-3 fatty acids to higher rates of depression and anxiety. Gut health, influenced by fibre intake and fermented foods, directly affects the gut–brain axis and emotional wellbeing. This connection is often overlooked, despite growing evidence that a healthy gut contributes to clearer thinking, more stable moods and improved resilience to stress.

Most people focus on caloric intake, which, although beneficial, is not a panacea for wellness. Your gut health is the foundation of all health, wellness and even fitness, because it is the engine room of your mind and body. Those who have researched gut wellness extensively are likely to describe your gut as your second brain.

A diet rich in anti-inflammatory compounds can help reduce the risk of cognitive decline and neurodegenerative diseases such as Alzheimer's. In some developed countries, dementia-related illnesses are now among the leading causes of death, highlighting the growing importance of a diet rich in anti-inflammatory compounds. Caloric control and nutrient density also support mitochondrial function and help reduce oxidative stress in neurons.

## IMPORTANCE OF NUTRITION ON PHYSICAL FUNCTION

Nutrition underpins how the body moves, recovers and performs each day. The following table outlines the key ways nutrition supports physical function, brain health and long-term wellbeing.

| AREA | HOW NUTRITION SUPPORTS THE BODY |
|---|---|
| MUSCLE GROWTH AND REPAIR | Protein - especially complete proteins from animal or plant combinations - is essential for muscle maintenance and recovery. Leucine, a branched-chain amino acid, directly stimulates muscle protein synthesis. |
| ENERGY PRODUCTION | Carbohydrates replenish muscle glycogen for energy during workouts, while fats serve as a significant fuel for low- to moderate-intensity activity. Micronutrients such as B vitamins, magnesium and iron are essential for ATP production. |
| HYDRATION AND ELECTROLYTE BALANCE | Water regulates body temperature and joint lubrication, and is complemented by essential minerals such as sodium, potassium, magnesium and calcium, which help maintain fluid balance and prevent muscle cramps. |
| BONE AND JOINT HEALTH | Calcium and vitamin D are crucial for bone density, while collagen-rich foods, vitamin C and anti-inflammatory fats support joint health. |
| IMMUNE SYSTEM SUPPORT | Nutrients like vitamins A, C, D and E, as well as zinc and selenium, strengthen immune defences, which are critical for recovery and for preventing illness. |
| WHOLE FOODS-BASED DIET | Minimally processed, nutrient-dense foods, such as vegetables and fruits, are high in antioxidants, vitamins and fibre. Leafy greens (spinach, kale) and berries (blueberries, strawberries) are especially beneficial. Whole grains, such as brown rice, quinoa and oats, provide fibre and B vitamins. |

| AREA | HOW NUTRITION SUPPORTS THE BODY |
|---|---|
| HEALTHY FATS: OMEGA-3S | Include fatty fish (salmon, sardines), flaxseeds and chia seeds in your diet. |
| MONOUN-SATURATED FATS | Sources include olive oil, avocados and nuts. |
| PROTEIN SOURCES | Choose protein sources such as lean meats (chicken, turkey), fish, eggs, legumes, tofu, tempeh and Greek yoghurt. |
| FERMENTED FOODS | Foods such as yoghurt, kefir, kimchi and sauerkraut support gut health. |
| NUTS AND SEEDS | Almonds, walnuts and sunflower seeds are rich in vitamin E and healthy fats. |
| HYDRATION | Aim for 2–3 litres (8–12 cups) of water daily and add electrolytes during intense physical activity. |
| BALANCED MACRONUTRIENT RATIOS | Carbohydrates should make up 40–60% of intake, preferably from complex carbs. Protein should account for 15–25%, adjusted for activity level. Fats should comprise 20–35%, with an emphasis on unsaturated fats. |
| TIME-RESTRICTED EATING/ INTERMITTENT FASTING (OPTIONAL) | Emerging evidence suggests that time-restricted eating and intermittent fasting may support metabolic efficiency, brain health and cellular repair. However, individual responses vary, and factors such as metabolism, activity levels and overall health should be considered before adopting this approach. |
| WHAT TO AVOID | Ultra-processed foods, which are often loaded with additives, sugar and unhealthy fats, should be limited. Refined sugar and high-fructose corn syrup have been linked to cognitive decline and inflammation. Trans fats and excessive saturated fats can impair brain function and cardiovascular health. Excess alcohol is neurotoxic and can deplete essential nutrients. Chronic caloric excess is associated with metabolic syndrome and decreased brain plasticity. |

Great nutrition isn't about rigid diets or trends; it's about consistency, variety and nutrient quality. Eating in a way that fuels both your body and brain lays the foundation for lifelong vitality, mental clarity, physical strength and disease prevention.

Martin Luther King Jr. understood that greatness demands endurance – not just of spirit, but of body. His life was spent on the road, in meetings, in marches and under constant threat. Though he rarely spoke of food, his ability to withstand exhaustion, stress and pressure was inseparable from his care for the vessel that carried his cause. The body, to him, was not an object of indulgence but an instrument of service – something to be maintained so the mission could endure.

Nelson Mandela proved that nourishment can be an act of resistance. On Robben Island, food was weaponised – sparse, spoiled and intended to strip prisoners of dignity. But Mandela fought for better meals, knowing that nutrition meant survival, and survival meant defiance. Even in deprivation, he built discipline around his health, exercising, studying and preserving strength. When freedom finally came, he emerged unbroken – his body lean, his spirit unyielding. To him, caring for the body was caring for the cause.

Burt Munro's approach to nutrition was simpler but no less meaningful. He lived modestly, eating plainly, viewing food as fuel for the work he loved. His body was his machine as much as his motorcycle was, and he treated both with respect. A steady diet and simple habits sustained his strength long past the age when most men surrender to decline. His greatness was proof that consistency – not excess – sustains endurance.

Diana Nyad knew nutrition as a lifeline. For her, it was survival measured in minutes, sips and calories. Swimming across the ocean for 53 unbroken hours, she relied on liquid nourishment delivered every 45 minutes – a rhythm of fuel and faith. Without it, her body would have failed. Nutrition became her invisible teammate, keeping her strong when the sea and the mind turned against her. Every carefully planned intake was a declaration: I am still in this.

The Stoics, too, recognised that food shapes not just the body but the mind. They ate, knowing indulgence enslaves. Seneca warned that luxury weakens character. Marcus Aurelius wrote that heavy meals dull clarity. Epictetus taught that moderation builds freedom. To them, nourishment was a discipline of virtue, eating not for pleasure, but for purpose.

I've learned the same truth through endurance. Training, along with every aspect of daily life, demands energy measured not just in willpower, but in what you put into your body. Every long run, every race, every recovery depends on what fuels you. When nutrition is clean, the mind sharpens; when it's careless, everything falters. Food becomes philosophy, a way of saying: I respect the vessel that carries my purpose.

Nutrition is not about perfection; it's about presence. It's the quiet decision to give your body what it needs so your spirit can do what it's meant to. It's fuel for faith, energy for endurance, and clarity for calling.

King nourished his strength for justice. Mandela nourished his dignity in captivity. Munro nourished his craft through simplicity. Nyad nourished her endurance through precision. The Stoics nourished their virtue through restraint.

Greatness requires energy, not the fleeting kind born of emotion, but the steady kind built through care. Nutrition is that care made tangible. It's the daily act of feeding the body so the dream can stay alive. Feed your purpose well, and it will carry you farther than you ever imagined.

## CHANGING NUTRITION CHANGED EVERYTHING

Firstly, please understand that I am not here to judge. Still, I intend to preach and simply share what has worked for me, while recognising that it may not work for everyone. I believe that healthy changes to a balanced diet can transform your life.

About 20 years ago, I made a conscious and deliberate decision to become a vegetarian. That choice was grounded in two convictions. The first was my opposition to the abhorrent treatment of most animals that are bred for human consumption. The second was my belief that a plant-based diet would benefit my health and physical performance as I pursued my purpose to discover my physical and mental limits.

Within a few years, buoyed by the dramatic benefits that my newfound diet had delivered, I enthusiastically converted to a vegan diet, which I attribute to my athletic achievements in my late 40s and well into my 50s. There is no doubt in my mind that these pivotal, life-changing choices have significantly improved my health and fitness and, consequently, I enjoy the physical and mental wellbeing that I experience at age 62. The other choice that I made 27 years ago was to change my often-excessive alcohol consumption to zero alcoholic consumption, until a few years ago, when I reintroduced a moderate alcohol intake. This significant decision was made before my nutritional switch, although it was for the same health and performance-related benefits. All these moves have been life-changing for me.

Consuming healthy food, though, is first a matter of choice. Your choice. The motivation, discipline and sacrifice required to make a life-changing choice, especially if your diet is unhealthy and convenience-driven, must be grounded in a purpose that drives positive change. Without a burning purpose to guide you, your brain craves the foods you've chosen to feed it.

I respect that you may already follow an exceptional, balanced diet – one that has required some effort, discipline and sacrifice. Over time, however, healthy eating becomes less of a conscious choice and more of a habit, bolstered by the benefits it delivers.

Once you achieve this state of wellness – and often increased fitness, as healthy change tends to inspire exercise – your old mindset, your old brain and your redundant identity will concede – overruled by the new one that loves the way you feel now.

## HACKS TO IMPROVE YOUR NUTRITION

Here are some simple, realistic tips for adopting a healthier diet to get you going without feeling overwhelmed:

- **Start small, not perfect.** Don't try to overhaul everything at once. Pick one habit (like drinking more water or eating an extra serving of vegetables) and build from there.

- **Add before you subtract.** Instead of cutting out all 'unhealthy' foods, focus on adding more nourishing ones first (fruits, veggies, whole grains, lean proteins). Over time, the good naturally crowds out the less healthy.
- **Plan ahead.** Prep simple snacks (like chopped veggies, fruit, or nuts), so you're not stuck grabbing fast food when hungry. Having healthy options readily available makes it easier to make better choices.
- **Eat more colours.** Aim to fill half your plate with colourful fruits and vegetables. Different colours usually mean different nutrients.
- **Watch liquid calories.** Sugary drinks, sodas and even some juices can contain a significant amount of empty calories. Try water, sparkling water, or herbal teas instead.
- **Portion mindfully.** Use smaller plates, eat slowly and check in with your hunger cues before going for seconds.
- **Balance, don't ban.** Allow yourself treats occasionally without guilt. It's easier to sustain a balanced approach than a restrictive one.
- **Cook at home more often.** Even simple meals, such as stir-fries, salads, or grilled proteins, are often healthier than takeout. You control the ingredients, salt and oils.
- **Make protein and fibre your friends.** Protein and fibre keep you fuller longer and stabilise energy levels. Think beans, lentils, eggs, chicken, fish, nuts and whole grains.
- **Stay hydrated.** Sometimes thirst feels like hunger. Drinking enough water can help regulate energy, mood and appetite.

## NUTRITION THAT WORKS

There are many excellent books on nutrition, but it's hard to go past Jamie Oliver's *Eat Yourself Healthy*. I found it to be a practical, optimistic guide to improving health through everyday food choices without dieting, deprivation or complexity. The book's central idea is simple and empowering: small, consistent changes in what you eat can dramatically improve energy, mood, immunity and long-term health.

Rather than promoting rigid rules, Jamie focuses on nutrient density – foods that deliver the greatest health benefit per calorie. He reframes healthy eating as a form of self-respect and long-term investment, not punishment.

Jamie argues that many modern health issues, such as fatigue, inflammation, poor digestion and weight gain, stem from nutritional gaps, not a lack of willpower. His solution is not restriction, but addition: adding more vegetables, fibre, healthy fats and whole foods to your plate.

My key takeaways from the book that I encourage you to explore are as follows:

- **Nutrition as prevention.** Food plays a powerful role in reducing the risk of chronic disease, including heart disease, type 2 diabetes and obesity. Jamie explains nutritional science in plain language, showing how everyday ingredients support gut health, brain function and immune resilience.
- **Balance over extremes.** No food group is demonised. Carbohydrates, fats and proteins all have a place when chosen wisely, and sustainable habits are valued over short-term fads.
- **Fibre is king.** A strong focus is placed on fibre for digestion, blood sugar control and gut health, with whole grains, legumes, vegetables and seeds featuring prominently throughout the recipes.
- **Healthy fats matter.** Olive oil, nuts, seeds, avocado and oily fish are highlighted as essential for heart health, hormone balance and satiety.
- **Everyday accessibility.** The recipes are simple, family-friendly, affordable, supermarket-accessible and built around familiar flavours – health food that still feels like comfort food.
- **Practical recipe structure.** The book offers breakfasts that stabilise energy, wholesome lunches and dinners, smart snacks and nutrient-dense desserts that reduce sugar while increasing real ingredients.

- **Progress over perfection.** The overall message is encouraging and realistic – health is built through small, consistent choices rather than dramatic overhauls.
- **A performance mindset.** Nutrition is framed as a way to support energy, resilience and long-term vitality, aligning food choices with the capacity to live and perform at your best.

## FEED YOUR GREATNESS

If you are unsure where to start with your nutrition, I recommend you spend some time considering your health and wellbeing purpose. Once you have established your purpose – what a healthier you will feel like, and what this will mean to your daily life – then plan what small changes you can implement to begin or accelerate your nutritional improvement. This might involve something as simple as adding vegetables to each meal, cutting out processed foods, reducing your sugar intake, or incorporating a vegetable-and-fruit smoothie into your daily routine. At the very least, that one morning change will boost your fibre intake, improving your gut health. It will also increase your nutritional intake, providing a wealth of healthy vitamins, minerals and powerful antioxidants. I can't see a downside to making that one small change.

In the end, nutrition is not merely about food; it is about honour. It is how we honour the life we have been given. It is how we honour the mind that dreams, the body that carries those dreams and the purpose that demands strength, clarity and endurance. Every choice you make about what you consume is a quiet vote for the life you want, the energy you need and the future you intend to build.

The truth is simple, but profound: you cannot pursue greatness on an empty foundation. You cannot think sharply, feel deeply, move powerfully, or endure meaningfully when your body is starved of the ingredients that make you whole. Greatness requires fuel – clean, intentional fuel that steadies the mind and strengthens the spirit.

Martin Luther King Jr. understood that his body was a vessel for his cause. Mandela understood that nourishment was survival. Munro proved that consistency sustains endurance. Nyad showed the world that fuel is faith in physical form. And the Stoics reminded us that food is a mirror – an invitation to choose virtue over impulse, clarity over comfort, and purpose over pleasure.

Your nutritional choices may seem small, but they shape everything: your energy, your mood, your clarity, your resilience, your longevity, your capacity, your joy. Over time, these choices become your identity – an identity capable of more than you once believed possible.

My own journey into plant-based living was never about perfection. It was about alignment. It was about creating the conditions that allowed me to discover what I was truly capable of at an age when most people begin to slow down. Some of the changes were instant, undeniable – more energy, more lightness, more clarity, more life. Nutrition didn't just strengthen my body – it expanded my world.

Yours can, too.

Greatness doesn't require strict diets, deprivation, or obsession. It simply asks you to care enough about your purpose that you nourish the vessel entrusted with delivering it. It asks you to make one better choice today than you did yesterday. To build habits that make you feel alive. To give your body what it needs so your spirit can do what it's meant to.

Start small. Begin anywhere. Add before you subtract. Drink water. Eat colour. Honour your second brain. Seek food that restores rather than steals. Let consistency – not perfection – be your guide.

Because in the grand story of your life, nutrition is not the headline.

It is the ink.

It colours everything you create, everything you attempt and everything you become.

Feed your purpose well.

Feed your future well.

Feed your greatness well.

Doing so will carry you farther than you ever imagined.

## REFLECTION, ACTION AND GROWTH

### ALIGN NUTRITION WITH WHAT MATTERS MOST

**Reflection:** How is your current nutrition supporting – or sabotaging – your ability to pursue what matters most?

**Action:** Write down your health purpose and top three goals. Next to each one, note whether your current eating habits make that pursuit easier or harder. Then choose one nutritional change that directly supports one of those goals. Implement it for seven consecutive days.

### REWRITE THE STORIES YOU TELL ABOUT FOOD

**Reflection:** What stories do you tell yourself about food that limit your energy, clarity, or health?

**Action:** Identify the beliefs shaping your choices:

- List three unhelpful beliefs you hold around eating (e.g. 'I don't have time', 'healthy food is boring', 'I'll start next week').
- Rewrite each belief into a new identity-based statement (e.g. 'I fuel my purpose', 'I prioritise energy over convenience', 'I eat to strengthen my body and mind').
- Read your new statements aloud each morning for a week.

### NOURISH THE BODY THAT CARRIES YOUR PURPOSE

**Reflection:** If your body is the vessel that carries your purpose, what does it need more of – and what does it require less of?

**Action:** Complete a simple two-column exercise:

- Column 1 – foods and habits to increase (water, fibre, colours, omega-3s, whole foods)
- Column 2 – foods and habits to reduce (ultra-processed items, excess sugar, alcohol, overeating).

Choose one item from each column to act on for the next three days. Evaluate how you feel at the end of the third day.

## EAT WITH INTENTION, NOT CONVENIENCE

**Reflection:** What would your life look and feel like if you nourished yourself with intention instead of convenience?

**Action:** Commit to eating with awareness for the next 48 hours:

- Prepare or choose three intentional meals chosen for their nutrition rather than speed or habit.
- Before each meal, pause for 10 seconds and ask, 'will this help me think clearly, feel stronger, and live longer?'
- After two days, journal how your energy, mood and clarity changed.

SS GREAT
EATNESS
SS GREAT
EATNESS
SS GREAT
EATNESS
SS GREAT
EATNESS

# CHAPTER 15
# VULNERABILITY

***'VULNERABILITY IS THE BIRTHPLACE OF INNOVATION, CREATIVITY AND CHANGE.'* - BRENÉ BROWN**

We are taught to hide the parts of ourselves that hurt, to armour up, to hold back, to appear unshakable. But real strength begins where the armour ends. Vulnerability is not the opposite of courage; it is courage refined to its purest form.

To be vulnerable is to be open to truth, to be seen, known and touched by life. It's the decision to risk heartbreak for authenticity, to choose honesty over image, and to live without the false safety of perfection.

Of the 14 steps to greatness, vulnerability has been the preeminent instigator of growth across my three life seasons. In fact, being vulnerable has heralded my finest season yet – my summer! So, if you are still of the view that you can't teach an old dog new tricks, think again!

As we age, we accumulate experiences that impact us in various ways, depending on how we choose to process and apply them to our daily lives. Wisdom, though, is the process in which we capitalise on our expertise by translating our learnings into something positive and meaningful. And by 'meaningful', I mean beneficial to our friends, family, coworkers and the broader community. There's a famous saying you may know, which goes, 'You can't teach an old dog new tricks.' This phrase highlights the common human tendency to slow down learning, wisdom and behaviour as we age – a counterintuitive phenomenon but all too real.

When you open yourself to vulnerability, you also open the door to deeper wisdom. Without it, your ability to recognise and accept your own limitations can be stifled, slowing your growth and progress towards greatness.

At 62 years of age, many childhood memories elude me, but I have an overwhelming sense that my childhood fostered the need to project an aura of self-control and strength, and never to show weakness. The manifestation of this was to block out any feelings of vulnerability and, most certainly, not share them externally. I inherited this from my parents. Consequently, for most of my life, I have not shown vulnerability or even allowed myself to feel vulnerable. Don't get me wrong, this has served me well on many occasions and enabled me not only to survive through extremely tough times, but also to thrive.

However, perhaps I might have achieved more had I been predisposed to vulnerability. Who knows. This shortfall has influenced both my personal and professional life. Although my awareness has grown in recent years, I did not fully understand its significance for a long time, as it remained hidden behind the façade I had erected. My stoic aura shaped how friends and family perceived me, and only recently have I begun to realise how significant this has been for others.

Recently, a very dear friend of mine, John Rojas – a man I hold in the highest regard and trust implicitly – shared an insight that caught me entirely off guard. By chance, we were both in Florence, Italy, for the same four days, a coincidence we only discovered a couple of weeks beforehand. Over nearly 15 years of friendship, we have weathered both triumph and turbulence side by side, and I say without hesitation that John is one of the few people I would trust with my life.

That evening in Florence, over dinner with his partner and with Lisa beside me, John began recounting stories from our shared past, partly for their benefit, as it was the first time the two women had met. Within moments, I had a sense of where he might head – after all, we had endured a lot together. But his first revelation struck me with surprising force. He began speaking not about our shared battles, but about me – how profoundly he felt I had changed. Although I had sensed certain shifts in myself over the past couple of years, I had not grasped the magnitude of that transformation. As I squirmed quietly in my chair, Lisa listened with a growing smile as each anecdote unfolded.

John shared that, for most of the years he had known me, he saw me as serious, relentlessly driven and perpetually in pursuit of whatever mission lay before me. What I did not expect was the clarity of his observation about who I had become. He spoke of a deeper connection between us, one he said was only made possible by my willingness to be vulnerable. I did not see that coming. His words felt like an epiphany dropped gently, yet unmistakably, upon the table between us.

As he described this new version of me, I realised something important. Throughout our 15-year relationship, including a decade of working side by side, I had always believed we were deeply connected. What I had not recognised was that the missing piece had been my vulnerability. Hearing him unravel our story through this new lens was both enlightening and disarming. For a moment, I wasn't sure how to react, primarily as his interpretation of my identity differed from the one I had built in my own mind. But the newer version of me – the one I have been learning to embrace – responded with laughter, humility and gratitude. And I acknowledged, without hesitation, that Lisa had been the catalyst for this change.

So, indulge me for a moment as I credit and thank Lisa, my love, my partner, my one, with helping shape the best version of me. The version that accepts and welcomes vulnerability. The version that recognises my own imperfections. The version that no longer needs to be right, invincible, or impenetrable. The version that listens and cares without expectation. The version that finally understands that vulnerability does not weaken you – instead, it reveals your humanity and invites others to show theirs.

Entering my third life season, vulnerability has been the most profound change that has set me free above all others. If it weren't for Lisa nurturing my vulnerability, I would never have written my first book, *UNLIMITED*, or this book. Had I not found the courage to let my old identity go – the version I misguidedly interpreted as Stoic – it is highly likely that my second life season would have continued until a third, uninvited season took hold. I feel forever grateful and blessed that summer has finally arrived!

## DARING GREATLY

Of all the books about vulnerability that I've had the pleasure of reading, Brené Brown's *Daring Greatly* is my favourite.

The book explores how vulnerability is not weakness, but rather the courage to show up and be seen even when the outcome is uncertain. Brown argues that embracing vulnerability is the path to authenticity, creativity, connection, love and meaningful leadership.

Here are some key insights from this brilliant book:

- **The myth of vulnerability as weakness.** Society often equates vulnerability with fragility, but in truth, it's the birthplace of courage and strength.
- **Shame and fear.** Shame is the biggest obstacle to vulnerability. By confronting shame and fear of judgment, people can live with more openness and resilience.
- **Wholehearted living.** To live fully, one must embrace imperfection, practise self-compassion and engage in life with courage.
- **Leadership and culture.** In workplaces, vulnerability fosters innovation and trust. Leaders who admit uncertainty and model openness create stronger, more creative teams.

- **Relationships and connection.** True intimacy and trust require vulnerability, allowing oneself to be seen as one truly is.

The title *Daring Greatly* emanates from Theodore Roosevelt's famous 'Man in the Arena' speech, which praises those who step into the arena and risk failure rather than standing back safely. Brown uses this metaphor to illustrate that choosing vulnerability is, in fact, choosing courage.

## MAKE VULNERABILITY YOUR STRENGTH

As I have learned much later in life, allowing yourself to be vulnerable can be a powerful catalyst for personal and professional growth. Though often seen as a weakness, vulnerability requires courage and self-awareness. Making a deliberate decision to learn and grow from our experiences and self-reflection is essential, rather than simply going through our busy lives. So, here's how your vulnerability can nurture and propagate your growth.

### BUILD AUTHENTIC CONNECTIONS

As an executive leader and CEO, I juggled numerous significant responsibilities, including leading leaders and people across various businesses. As my career progressed, I gained valuable experience in leading people and managing companies, often under immense pressure to perform. I believed that to instil confidence in my people, I had to project a person who embodied confidence, with an almost bulletproof façade. I could count on one hand the number of times I allowed myself to be vulnerable over the course of 40 years.

Looking back, with hindsight and through the eyes of the vulnerable-friendly version of me, I would go back and change my acceptance of my vulnerability, because authentic vulnerability builds connection and trust. But of course, you can't go back and change. This, however, drives my desire to change and become who I should be. What matters most is that you find a way to be true to yourself today.

When you're vulnerable, you open up honestly about your fears, mistakes and needs, which makes you human, just like the people around you. Feeling fear or making mistakes does not make you a lesser leader, as I once believed. Quite the opposite, in fact. Sharing vulnerability and admitting to faults fosters trust and deeper relationships, whether with friends, family, colleagues, or partners. Genuine connections create a support system that helps you grow in the following ways.

## ENHANCE SELF-AWARENESS

Acknowledging your insecurities and emotions forces you to confront who you really are. This type of self-reflection is crucial for understanding your triggers, patterns and desires, making it easier to change and improve. When you achieve that level of self-awareness, it is helpful to keep a journal to reflect on and record actions you will take to evolve your identity.

## FUEL CREATIVITY AND INNOVATION

Creativity thrives in uncertainty and risk. When you're vulnerable, you're more willing to take creative risks and put your ideas out there, even if they might fail. Many breakthroughs come from moments of uncertainty and openness.

Breakthroughs made through creativity often require vulnerability. Creativity is about bringing something new into the world, such as an idea, a perspective, a piece of art – and that means exposing part of yourself.

Vulnerability allows creators to tap into raw emotions, inner conflicts and real-life struggles. Some of the most powerful art, music, writing, or design comes from someone daring to say what others won't. Honesty connects deeply with audiences and sparks meaningful change.

Letting go of 'looking good' will change you. When you're vulnerable, you stop creating to impress. Instead, you choose to explore, connect, or heal. This shift often leads to more authentic, original work and unexpected breakthroughs.

For me, letting go of the pursuit of looking good has enabled exponential growth at a stage of life that I could not have imagined, and this action has brought another level of peace within me. An example that resonated with me recently is the ever-increasing cohort of stand-up comedians (like Hannah Gadsby in *Nanette*) who have shifted from pure comedy to deeply vulnerable storytelling, which resonates even more powerfully.

Allowing vulnerability allows people to transform personal pain into universal meaning. This often leads to breakthroughs in storytelling, poetry, music and visual art. There is something cathartic about saying, 'What the hell, I am going to do this anyway!' A prime example is Frida Kahlo's deeply personal and painful self-portraits, which have become symbols of resilience, identity and emotional truth.

Taking on new creative risks requires innovation, which is so often stifled by the fear of failure. Vulnerability is what allows someone to take that leap – to submit the screenplay, pitch the idea, or share the prototype before it's 'perfect'. In my case, it's writing my life story and releasing it to the world, bravely exposing myself to public opinion and the potential for crushing failure.

Inviting collaboration was not a strength of mine for much of my career, which I chalk up to my ego. Accountability, though, is strangely freeing. Accepting that you operated over an extended period in a manner not conducive to growth and productivity is equally liberating. There is something very special about sharing your faults or shortfalls with others around you, then dedicating yourself to self-improvement.

I have found that by confronting my shortfalls and sharing them, I've created a stronger bond with those in my world who have experienced similar shortcomings, and who have experienced my weaknesses. Remarkably, such action is typically an elevated, deeper relationship. Sharing incomplete ideas or asking for feedback requires vulnerability. Positively, though, such openness to critique often leads to refining a concept beyond what one person could create alone.

Vulnerability isn't just part of the creative process – it *is* the creative process. When you risk being seen and heard for who you truly are, the result isn't just better art or ideas but more meaningful, human work that breaks through walls and touches people.

## BUILD RESILIENCE AND PERSONAL GROWTH

For most of my life, I believed that vulnerability equalled weakness. My lived experience, however, has shown me the opposite: vulnerability builds resilience in a surprisingly effective way. It means facing the possibility of rejection or failure and choosing to show up anyway. The more you practise this, the more emotionally resilient you become. You begin to understand that failure is survivable – and often necessary for growth.

Vulnerability also promotes learning and feedback, both of which are vital to personal growth. Admitting you don't know something or acknowledging that you've made a mistake creates space for learning. It becomes easier to ask for help, accept constructive criticism and grow from it without defensiveness.

This shift began for me while facilitating conferences and growth workshops. For decades, my default behaviour had been to 'fake it until I make it'. But as I began hosting more of my own development programs, I realised that openness and honesty were far more effective in building trust and meaningful connections.

Counterintuitively, the attendees often sat in one of two camps. The first group contributed only when they felt informed and comfortable, remaining silent for most of the sessions out of concern that revealing their gaps or shortfalls would expose them. The second, smaller group had adopted and owned a growth mindset. Unlike the majority, who were trying to appear interested, these individuals were genuinely interested. They were inquisitive, asked a wide variety of questions and showed a clear willingness to learn. Their curiosity inspired my belief that their intent was not to impress but to grow.

## STRENGTHEN LEADERSHIP AND CONNECTION

Vulnerability also breaks perfectionism. Letting go of the need to be perfect allows you to grow more freely. Vulnerability helps you embrace imperfection as part of being human, reducing anxiety and increasing self-compassion. Another benefit is the impetus it creates for more effective leadership and empathy.

Leaders who openly discuss their struggles and uncertainties are often more respected and relatable. Vulnerability shows humility and empathy, creating psychologically safe environments where others feel seen and supported. The openness also signals to others that it is okay to acknowledge their own challenges. When people feel safe enough to be vulnerable, they are more likely to seek help and embrace growth opportunities rather than hiding their shortcomings.

My understanding of vulnerability's role in human connection deepened when I began posting in various Facebook fitness groups a couple of years ago. While there were individuals with ulterior motives or ego-driven promotion, I found that most people desperately wanted help and were prepared to be extremely humble and vulnerable. One pattern stood out clearly: those who showed vulnerability received stronger support and a deeper connection from other group members. People love to share their experiences to help others, and a uniquely powerful bond forms through vulnerability.

In short, vulnerability isn't about exposing yourself recklessly; it's about showing up with honesty and courage. Growth happens in those raw, uncertain spaces between fear and authenticity.

## THE STRENGTH OF BEING SEEN

Martin Luther King Jr.'s vulnerability wasn't only in his speeches; it lived in his heart. Every time he stepped onto a stage, he risked not only his safety but his spirit. He revealed his fears, his exhaustion and his doubts, yet he stood anyway.

That is vulnerability: the willingness to act in full awareness of your fragility. It's not the absence of fear, but the decision that fear will not define you. King's power came from that openness. His followers saw not a flawless hero, but a human being – tired, burdened, faithful. His transparency permitted others to be brave, too.

Vulnerability, when embraced, becomes contagious.

Nelson Mandela understood this, too. He could have emerged from prison hardened, untouchable. Instead, he chose softness. He met his former captors with grace. He cried in public. He spoke not as a saint, but as a man who had been broken and rebuilt by love. That's the brilliance of Mandela's strength, that he didn't pretend to be invulnerable. His humanity was his message. He knew that the world doesn't need more masks; it needs more mirrors. By revealing the cracks, he let the light through.

Burt Munro's vulnerability was quieter, expressed through his willingness to fail in front of the world. He didn't hide his mistakes, his mishaps, or his lack of resources. He shared them. He invited others to see the process, the trial, the tinkering, the tenacity. He wasn't afraid of being seen as imperfect. He feared not trying. That's what made him relatable, not his record, but his realism. To show up while still unfinished is one of the most extraordinary acts of courage.

Diana Nyad embodied vulnerability in motion. She swam through fear, pain and self-doubt – all while the world watched. She cried, screamed, faltered and began again. She didn't hide the struggle; she let it be seen. Her vulnerability didn't weaken her – it deepened her. It made her victory not just about distance, but about humanity. When she finally reached shore, her tears said more than any speech ever could.

That's the paradox of vulnerability: the more open you are, the stronger you become.

The Stoics, though often imagined as stoic in the modern sense – unemotional, detached – were, in truth, profoundly vulnerable. Their writings are journals of honesty. Marcus Aurelius wrote to himself about his insecurities, his failures, his weariness. He didn't hide his weakness; he studied it.

Seneca confessed his flaws in letters to friends, not to seek pity but to seek growth. Epictetus, once enslaved and injured, spoke openly about pain, not as shame, but as a teacher. Their vulnerability was intellectual and spiritual; a willingness to confront themselves. That's the essence of Stoicism: not suppression of emotion, but mastery through understanding.

For the Stoics, vulnerability was not something to be denied or feared. It was a reality of human existence – physical, emotional and social. What mattered was distinguishing between what is truly ours – our reason, virtue, choices – and what lies beyond our control. Accepting vulnerability in the external world became a source of inner strength and resilience.

For me, vulnerability has always been the hardest lesson. Endurance teaches toughness, but vulnerability teaches truth. You can train your body to withstand pain, but to open your heart – to admit fear, doubt, or longing – that's another kind of endurance entirely. There have been races where I've cried, not from exhaustion, but from release – the breaking of the walls I built to appear strong. Out there, stripped of pretence, you meet yourself. You realise that strength isn't about resistance; it's about honesty. Vulnerability connects us to everything that matters – to people, to purpose, to meaning. Without it, achievement becomes performance. With it, every effort becomes alive.

King's vulnerability humanised his movement. Mandela's healed a nation. Munro's inspired generations. Nyad's empowered millions. The Stoics' vulnerability still teaches us today.

## HACKS FOR FINDING VULNERABILITY

Vulnerability often begins with awareness, presence and gratitude. Here are some simple, practical ways to cultivate that mindset:

- **Keep a gratitude journal.** Each night, write down three things you're thankful for, no matter how small. Over time, this trains your brain to focus on positives rather than negatives.
- **Pause and appreciate the ordinary.** When drinking water, eating a meal, or feeling the sun, pause for a few seconds and recognise it as a gift. The small daily moments build a deeper baseline of gratitude.
- **Express thanks out loud.** Tell people directly when you appreciate them – family, coworkers, even strangers. Spoken gratitude deepens relationships and makes the feeling more real.

- **Practise 'gratitude reframes'.** When faced with challenges, ask, 'What can this teach me?' or, 'Is there any hidden blessing here?' This helps you identify growth opportunities rather than just problems.
- **Create gratitude triggers.** Tie gratitude to habits you already do, like brushing your teeth or making coffee. For example, *While brushing my teeth, I'll think of one thing I'm grateful for today.*
- **Visualise the absence.** Imagine life without something you take for granted – your phone, your home, your health. This mental exercise makes you appreciate what you already have more deeply.
- **Slow down.** Rushing makes it harder to notice good things. Build in brief pauses during the day to breathe and reflect.

Through these small practices, vulnerability becomes a path to letting go of control and releasing yourself from the burden of perfection, from the fear of being seen.

## THE DOORWAY TO YOUR DEEPEST STRENGTH

In the end, vulnerability is not about confessing weakness. It is about claiming truth. It is the quiet courage to stand without armour, to stop performing, to let the world see you not as a constructed ideal but as a human being – imperfect, evolving, honest, alive.

Vulnerability is the birthplace of connection, the engine of growth, the pulse beneath courage. It is what allows us to be moved, to be shaped, to be known. It takes far more strength to say, 'Here I am, as I am' than to hide behind certainty or control.

Martin Luther King Jr. understood that vulnerability is what keeps courage human. Mandela knew it was what kept power humble. Munro showed that vulnerability is what keeps failure from becoming final. Nyad proved that vulnerability is what keeps persistence tender instead of brittle. The Stoics taught that vulnerability is the truth of being alive, that control is limited, but choice is infinite.

And you, like me, will discover that vulnerability is not something you practise once; it is something you live. It is a continual softening, a continual opening, a continual willingness to grow. It is the quiet voice inside that says:

- *I don't have to be perfect to be powerful.*
- *I don't have to be certain to be committed.*
- *I don't have to be invincible to be worthy.*

For me, vulnerability has been the most profound transformation of my third season. It has deepened my relationships, softened my edges, widened my perspective, and brought me more peace than any achievement ever has. It is the reason I have written these books. It is the reason I am still growing. It is the reason my summer arrived.

This is the paradox: the moment you stop trying to look invulnerable is the moment you finally become strong.

When you let yourself be seen – truly seen – you invite others to step towards you instead of around you. You turn hierarchy into humanity. You turn performance into presence. You turn fear into fuel. Vulnerability frees you from the exhausting burden of pretending and replaces it with the liberating power of being.

So let yourself be real.

Let yourself be uncertain.

Let yourself be unfinished.

Let yourself be human.

Because vulnerability is not the crack in your armour – it is the doorway to your greatness. It is how love enters. It is how courage expands. It is how truth takes root. It is how purpose becomes personal. And it is how your best season – your summer – begins.

If there is one lesson that I hope you carry from this chapter, it is this:

Strength built on fear collapses.

Strength built on vulnerability endures.

So, take the risk.

Open the gate.

Step into the arena of your own becoming – even if your knees shake, even if your voice trembles, even if the outcome is unknown.

Because the moment you dare to be vulnerable, you are no longer hiding from your life – you are finally, courageously, living it.

# REFLECTION, ACTION AND GROWTH

## NOTICE WHERE YOU'RE WEARING ARMOUR

**Reflection:** Where are you still wearing armour, and what is it costing you?

**Action:** Take a blank page and draw three columns titled:

1. Where I wear armour (e.g. at work, with partner, with friends, with children)
2. What I'm afraid will happen if I take it off (e.g. rejection, judgment, loss of control, 'looking weak')
3. What it's actually costing me (e.g. connection, trust, peace, creativity, love).

Choose one situation from your list. Within the next seven days, take one small risk of honesty – admit a fear, a mistake, or a doubt instead of pretending you're fine. Afterwards, write two lines:

1. What happened?
2. What did I learn about my armour?

## LET SOMEONE SEE THE REAL YOU

**Reflection:** Who in your life only knows the 'strong' version of you? What might change if they met the real one?

**Action:** Identify one person (partner, close friend, colleague, or family member) with whom you've kept your guard up. Within the next week, have a deliberate conversation where you:

- share something you're struggling with right now
- admit a past mistake you've never voiced, or

- express a need you usually hide ('I need support with…', 'I've been more affected by this than I've let on…').

Afterwards, journal for five to 10 minutes:

- How did they respond?
- How did it feel in your body to tell the truth?
- What does this show you about the story you've been telling yourself about 'being strong'?

## SHARE THE PART OF YOUR STORY THAT STILL FEELS RISKY

**Reflection:** What essential part of your story are you still hiding? Who might it help if you shared it?

**Action:** Think of a chapter of your life you rarely talk about (e.g. shame, failure, grief, addiction, burnout, humiliation, or fear). Write a one-page version of that story and focus on:

- what you went through
- what it taught you
- how it changed who you are.

Then choose a safe context to share a small piece of it:

- with one trusted person, or
- in a journal group, coaching setting, or online community where you feel safe.

Notice what happens. Did sharing deepen connection, invite support, or help someone else feel seen? Let that be evidence that your vulnerability is a gift, not a liability.

## CHOOSE GROWTH OVER IMAGE

**Reflection:** Where are you choosing 'looking good' over learning and growth?

**Action:** For the next five days, choose one arena each day (work, relationships, creative projects, training, parenting, leadership). In each arena, do one of the following:

- Ask a direct question you'd generally avoid because you 'should' already know the answer.
- Request honest feedback on something important to you – 'what's one thing I could do better here?'
- Admit 'I don't know' or 'I was wrong' where you would usually defend or deflect.

At the end of each day, answer these three questions in your journal:

1. Where did I choose growth over image today?
2. What discomfort did I feel – and survive?
3. What new clarity, connection, or possibility opened up because I allowed myself to be vulnerable?

SS GREAT
ATNESS G
SS GREAT
ATNESS G
SS GREAT
ATNESS G
SS GREAT
ATNESS G

# YOUR GREATNESS

***'GREATNESS ISN'T RESERVED FOR THE PRIVILEGED OR THE PERFECT. IT DOESN'T CARE WHERE YOU COME FROM, YOUR AGE, WHAT YOU LOOK LIKE, HOW MUCH YOU HAVE, YOUR GENDER, YOUR RELIGION, OR WHAT YOU'VE BEEN THROUGH. WHAT IT DOES ASK OF YOU IS THIS: FIND YOUR PURPOSE – AND CHASE IT WITH EVERYTHING YOU'VE GOT.' – JASON DUNN***

If there is a formula for greatness, it is written not in mathematics but in motion – in the way a person chooses to live when the world stops believing in them. Greatness isn't a single act or achievement. It's a pattern, a rhythm of purpose, courage, belief, discipline and love repeated through time until it becomes identity.

It is less a destination and more a direction. The way light leans towards the horizon, the way a seed turns towards the sun. It is the alignment of who you are with what you can become.

When I began this journey, I thought greatness was something external – a title, a finish line, a moment that would finally silence doubt. But I've learned that greatness is not found out there. It begins in here, in the quiet space between effort and intention, between fear and faith.

Martin Luther King Jr. lived that truth every day. His greatness was not his fame or his words, but his unwavering integrity – the way his values never bent, even under immense pressure. His formula was faith plus discipline multiplied by love.

Nelson Mandela's greatness was the same formula, expressed through endurance. His courage was patient, his forgiveness radical, his faith relentless. He lived the equation of resilience over resentment, compassion over control.

Burt Munro's greatness was the formula of devotion and the willingness to give decades of life to a dream no one else could see. His belief was not loud; it was methodical – purpose plus persistence, multiplied by precision.

Diana Nyad's greatness was belief in motion. She lived the formula of courage multiplied by consistency, divided by fear. Each stroke of her hand through the dark water was a calculation – effort turned into faith; faith turned into freedom.

The Stoics wrote their formula in thought. Virtue plus wisdom plus discipline equals peace. They believed that greatness is not in what happens to us, but in how we respond. That the formula for mastery begins and ends with the self.

And me, my formula has been built one step at a time. Purpose gave me direction. Courage kept me moving. Discipline gave my life structure. Stillness gave it clarity. Gratitude gave it peace. Belief gave it fuel. Resilience gave it longevity. Sacrifice gave it meaning.

Each element alone is incomplete. Together, they form something whole. That's the truth of every great life: greatness is not a single quality but a composition – a symphony of virtues played in harmony.

If I could write it as an equation, it might look like this: **(Purpose + Courage + Belief + Discipline + Stillness + Gratitude +**

**Resilience + Sacrifice + Vulnerability + Movement) × Time = Greatness.**

But even that doesn't capture it. Because greatness is not a formula to be solved, it's a relationship to be lived.

Every day offers a new variable: fatigue, doubt, failure, fear. And the answer changes with each one. The formula only works when applied with faith.

That's what Martin, Nelson, Burt, Diana and the Stoics all understood – that greatness is not perfection but participation. It's showing up again, giving your whole self to the process. And the beauty of it is that this formula is available to everyone. Greatness doesn't care about your past, your background, or your mistakes. It only cares about your effort, honesty, and persistence. We each carry the same potential – a raw, limitless capacity waiting to be called forth by commitment.

I've learned that greatness doesn't come from chasing the extraordinary. It comes from doing the ordinary with exceptional devotion – from how you live to how you speak, how you love and how you endure. Greatness is purpose with direction, courage with action, belief with endurance and gratitude with awareness. It's the willingness to fail and begin again, to forgive, to serve, to grow, to give.

It's what remains when ego fades, when the noise quiets, when you've given everything you have, and there is still something in you left to give. Maybe that's the real formula: to keep becoming. Because greatness doesn't care about applause; it doesn't care about how fast you arrive or how long it takes.

It only asks that you live honestly, love deeply and rise again. If there is a secret to greatness, it is this: it was never waiting for you somewhere out there – it was waiting for you to realise it has always been within you.

Greatness doesn't care who you are. It doesn't care where you came from, what you've lost, or how many times you've fallen. It doesn't care about talent, privilege, or luck. It only cares that you try. That you rise. That you keep showing up when it would be easier not to. Because greatness, in the end, is not about being the best. It's about becoming your best, again, in every season of life.

When I began this journey, I thought greatness was something I had to chase. A summit somewhere out there waiting to be conquered. I thought if I worked hard enough, trained long enough, achieved enough, I'd finally arrive.

But the truth I've learned – through races run and dreams tested, through exhaustion, failure and faith – is that greatness isn't a place you reach but the way you walk. It's the honesty in your effort, the integrity in your struggle and the love behind your persistence. It's not the record that defines you, but the rhythm of showing up, moving forwards and living with purpose, even when no one is watching.

If you have journeyed with me to this point in my story, allow me to thank you, sincerely, deeply and without reservation. Your time, your attention and your willingness to walk beside me through these pages mean more than I can express.

I could never have imagined standing where I stand today – writing these words, sharing this second book and offering my heart and experience to you – even with the greatness in myself I have discovered. The fact that you are here, reading or listening to this, is something I do not take lightly.

If nothing else, I hope my story serves as living proof that when purpose settles into both your head and your heart, absolutely anything becomes possible. Purpose reshapes identity, rewrites limitations and reveals pathways that once seemed unimaginable.

If you choose – truly choose – to walk the 14 steps to greatness or commit yourself wholeheartedly to the ones you have not yet mastered, then I do not doubt that you, too, will discover your own greatness. Not the world's version, not anyone else's expectation – *yours*. The greatness that has always lived within you, waiting for the moment you were ready to claim it.

Despite what most of the world tells us, greatness is not comparison, because comparison is the thief of joy. And without joy and meaning, what is the value of greatness? Framed another way, it is only possible to achieve your limitless potential – your true greatness – if you find joy and meaning along the way. Therefore, to derive meaning, you *must* discover your purpose! That must be your priority, whether you've yet defined it or are living your purpose.

Your pathway will be littered with struggle and adversity. But you must never forget that struggle is the parent of greatness. Without struggle, there will be no greatness. So, learn to recognise struggle as inevitable, even essential. Nurture your mind to process struggle in a way that flips your human instinct on its head.

And what of fear? Well, fear is a liar of the most cunning order. Fear gathers up all your life experiences, then selects the occasions when you've lived in its domain. It selects the times when you have failed and any negative experiences it can identify. To this cohort of neurological captors, it extracts and adds our brain's hard wiring to prehistoric man, who existed in a world dominated by two daily options: fight or flight. Then fear whispers in your ear, regurgitating everything it has acquired to substantiate its case, to convince you that you will fail if you give greatness a go. That you will humiliate yourself. That the wisest course of action is to bury your dreams and conform to whatever it is that you think is expected of you to live a comfortable, safe life.

But I say, 'Fuck that!' You are more – so much more. I urge you to look that liar in the eyes, fix your stare and find the courage to squash it. Banish it from your mind, because there is no room for that liar on your road to greatness.

In the end, greatness is not a gift given to the fortunate, the talented, or the blessed. It is a choice – a fiercely personal decision to live your life awake, engaged and responsible for the one thing that has always been yours: your next step. Greatness is not a mystery reserved for legends; it is the natural consequence of a human being willing to live with intention, courage and love.

If there is a secret to greatness, it is this: you do not wait for it. You create it, not in grand gestures, but in the daily honesty of how you move through the world. Not in the applause of others, but in the quiet courage of showing up when it would be easier not to. Not in perfection, but in persistence.

By now, you've walked through the blueprint – purpose, courage, belief, discipline, stillness, resilience, gratitude, sacrifice, presence, planning, movement, nutrition, vulnerability and the architecture of your mind. These 14 steps are not promises or shortcuts but invitations to participate fully in your own becoming.

Greatness has never belonged to the untouchable few; it belongs to the ones who try, who rise and who keep rising.

If my journey proves anything, it is that the boundaries you feel pressing against you – fear, doubt, circumstance, history – are not walls, but invitations to test what exists on the other side of your perceived limits. At age 59, I could never have imagined writing a second book. I could never have imagined the chapters of life that followed the ones I thought were my last. But purpose, once found, is a compass that refuses to stay silent. And belief, once practised, refuses to let you shrink.

And now the moment arrives – your moment, the one this entire journey has been building towards. I do not write the final chapter of this book; you will.

You have agency. You have a choice. You have time – perhaps more than you believe, certainly more than you have been using. And no matter what season of life you stand in now – spring in its beginning, summer in its vigour, autumn in its wisdom, or winter in its quiet – a new season is available to you the moment you decide to live differently.

Greatness is yours the moment you stop waiting for permission and start taking responsibility for the direction of your life.

It will not be easy. That voice – the one that has rehearsed your failures, magnified your insecurities and collected your worst memories like ammunition – will try to keep you small. It will tell you that comfort is safer, that effort is foolish, that dreams belong to other people.

Look that liar in the eye.

Call it what it is.

And walk past it.

You are more capable than your history, more potent than your obstacles and more extraordinary than you have ever allowed yourself to believe. The blueprint is in your hands now. The path is under your feet. The next season of your life is waiting for its author – you.

So, go.

Chase your purpose with everything you have.

Honour the struggle.

Defy the fear.

Rebuild belief daily.

Show up when no one claps.

Rise after the fall.

Live with intention, with courage, with integrity and with heart.

Because greatness doesn't care who you've been.

It cares about who you're willing to become.

# ABOUT THE AUTHOR

Jason Dunn is an elite ultra-endurance athlete, having completed more than 14 IRONMAN competitions, multiple ultramarathons, and placing 2nd overall at the Athletics Australia 100k National Road Running Championships.

As well as his sporting achievements, Jason had a successful career in finance and wealth management. He is a leader, founder, CEO, high-performance mindset coach, keynote speaker, author and entrepreneur.

Jason now pursues his interests as an author. His first book, *UNLIMITED*, self-published in late 2023, ranked number one in the Sports Health & Safety category on Amazon.

## CONNECT WITH JASON

greatnessdoesntcare.com
greatnessdoesntcare@gmail.com
f unlimited.862
in jason-dunn-72650227

SS GREAT
ATNESS G
SS GREAT
ATNESS G
SS GREAT
ATNESS G
SS GREAT
ATNESS G

# REFERENCES


## Chapter 2

Alimujiang, A, Wiensch, A, Boss, J et al. 'Association Between Life Purpose and Mortality Among US Adults Older Than 50 Years', *JAMA Network Open*, 2019, https://doi.org/10.1001/jamanetworkopen.2019.4270

Boyle, P, Buchman, A, Barnes, L and Bennett D, 'Effect of a Purpose in Life on Risk of Incident Alzheimer Disease and Mild Cognitive Impairment in Community-Dwelling Older Persons', *Archives of General Psychiatry*, 2010, https://doi.org/10.1001/archgenpsychiatry.2009.208

Buettner, D, *The Blue Zones: Lessons for Living Longer from the People Who've Lived the Longest*, National Geographic, 2008

Frankl, V, *Man's Search for Meaning*, Beacon Press, 2006

Hill, P and Turiano, N, 'Purpose in Life as a Predictor of Mortality Across Adulthood', *Psychological Science*, 2014

Lieberman, D and Long, M, *The Molecule of More: How a Single Chemical in Your Brain Drives Love, Sex, and Creativity–and Will Determine the Fate of the Human Race*, BenBella Books, 2018

Netflix. *Live to 100: Secrets of the Blue Zones*, documentary series, 2023

## Chapter 4

American Psychological Association, 'Manage Your Stress with Social Support', *APA.org*, accessed 2026, https://www.apa.org/topics/stress/manage-social-support

Bolbol-Haghighi, N, Masoumi, S and Kazemi, F, 'Effect of Massage Therapy on Duration of Labour', *Journal of Clinical and Diagnostic Research*, 2016, https://doi.org/10.7860/JCDR/2016/17447.7688

Dweck, C, *Mindset: The New Psychology of Success*, Ballantine Books, 2008

Field, T, Hernandez-Reif, M, Diego, M, Schanberg, S and Kuhn, C, 'Cortisol Decreases and Serotonin and Dopamine Increase Following Massage Therapy', *International Journal of Neuroscience*, 2005, https://doi.org/10.1080/00207450590956459

Holiday, R, *The Obstacle Is the Way: The Timeless Art of Turning Trials Into Triumph*, Portfolio, 2014

Healthline Editorial Team, 'Everything You Need to Know about Stress', *Healthline*, 2020, https://www.healthline.com/health/stress

Uvnäs-Moberg, K, Handlin, L and Petersson, M, 'Self-Soothing Behaviors with Particular Reference to Oxytocin Release', *Frontiers in Psychology*, 2015, https://doi.org/10.3389/fpsyg.2014.01529

Weinstein, D, Launay, J, Pearce, E, Dunbar, R and Stewart, L, 'Singing and Social Bonding', *Evolution and Human Behavior*, 2016, https://doi.org/10.1016/j.evolhumbehav.2015.10.002

## Chapter 5

Clear, J, *Atomic Habits*, Avery, 2018

## Chapter 6

Arjuna, M, *Those Who Live Without Discipline, Die Without Honor*, 2025

Goggins, D, *Can't Hurt Me: Master Your Mind and Defy the Odds*, Lioncrest Publishing, 2018

Greene, R. *Mastery*, Penguin, 2012

## Chapter 7

Becker, J, *The More of Less: Finding the Life You Want Under Everything You Own*, Random House US, 2018

## Chapter 8

Archbold, T, *Self-Belief Is Your Superpower*, Mango Media Inc, 2023

Carney, DR, Cuddy, AJ, Yap, AJ, 'Power posing: brief nonverbal displays affect neuroendocrine levels and risk tolerance', *Psychol Sci.* 2010 Oct;21(10):1363-8. https://pubmed.ncbi.nlm.nih.gov/20855902/.

Karnazes, D, *Ultramarathon Man: Confessions of an All-Night Runner*, Allen & Unwin, 2023

## Chapter 9

Baumeister, R, and Tierney, J, *Willpower: Rediscovering the Greatest Human Strength*, Penguin, 2011

Hill, N, *Think and Grow Rich*, Napoleon Hill Foundation, 1937

## Chapter 10

Aurelius, M, *Meditations*, Modern Library, 2002

Holiday, R, *Stillness Is the Key*, Portfolio, 2019

## Chapter 11

Howden, E, Sarma, S, Lawley, J et al. 'Reversing the Cardiac Effects of Sedentary Aging', *Circulation*, 2018, https://doi.org/10.1161/CIRCULATIONAHA.117.030617

Levine, B, 'Can Intensive Exercise Reverse the Effects of a Sedentary Lifestyle?', *Circulation*, 2018, https://doi.org/10.1161/CIRCULATIONAHA.118.034480
McDougall, C, *Born to Run*, Alfred A. Knopf, 2009

## Chapter 12

Lally, P, van Jaarsveld, C, Potts, H and Wardle, J, 'How Are Habits Formed: Modelling Habit Formation in the Real World.' *European Journal of Social Psychology* 40 (6): 998–1009, 2010, https://doi.org/10.1002/ejsp.674.
Maltz, M, *Psycho-Cybernetics*, Prentice Hall, 1960

## Chapter 13

King, M, *Where Do We Go from Here: Chaos or Community?*, Beacon Press, 1967
Lyubomirsky, S, *The How of Happiness*, Penguin Press, 2007
United Nations Human Settlements Programme. 'Adequate Housing', *UN-Habitat*, 2023, https://unhabitat.org/topic/adequate-housing

## Chapter 14

Oliver, J, *Eat Yourself Healthy*, Penguin, 2024

## Chapter 15

Brown, B, *Daring Greatly: How the Courage to Be Vulnerable Transforms the Way We Live, Love, Parent, and Lead*, Avery, 2015
Gadsby, H, *Nanette*, Netflix, 2018
Kahlo, F, *Self-Portrait with Thorn Necklace and Hummingbird*, artwork, 1940
Roosevelt, T, 'Citizenship in a Republic (Man in the Arena Speech)', speech delivered 1910